CONGRESS AND NUCLEAR WEAPONS

Congress

and Nuclear

Weapons ≫ ≪

James M. Lindsay

The Johns Hopkins University Press
Baltimore and London

The Johns Hopkins University Press
701 West 40th Street
Baltimore, Maryland 21211
The Johns Hopkins Press Ltd., London

The paper used in this book meets the minimum requirements
of American National Standard for Information Sciences—Permanence
of Paper for Printed Library Materials, ANSI Z39.48-1984.

Library of Congress Cataloging-in-Publication Data

Lindsay, James M., 1959–
  Congress and nuclear weapons / James M. Lindsay.
    p.   cm.
  Includes bibliographical references and index.
  ISBN 0-8018-4141-0
  1. United States—Military policy.   2. Nuclear warfare.   3. United
States. Congress.   I. Title.
UA23.L5765   1991
355.8′25119′0973—dc20   90-49522

To My Parents

Contents

Tables and Figures

Tables

Figures

Preface

FOR THE FIRST three decades after World War II Congress was a silent partner in U.S. nuclear weapons policy making. Despite its substantial constitutional powers and despite the awesome destructive power of nuclear weapons, Congress seldom challenged administration policy, and virtually all members of Congress were content to fund whatever programs the administration requested. That congressional deference collapsed in the wake of the Vietnam War. In the 1970s and 1980s nuclear weapons policy moved to the forefront of the legislative agenda on Capitol Hill. Congress clashed with the president over an array of weapons programs, including the B-1 bomber, counterforce weapons, the MX missile, antisatellite weapons, and the Strategic Defense Initiative. Commentators dispute whether Congress's activism helps or hinders the national interest. What is clear is that today Congress is playing a significant role in U.S. nuclear weapons policy making.

Far less clear is what drives congressional behavior on nuclear weapons policy. Political scientists seldom study how Congress handles national security issues; most of the classic works on Congress and defense are more than two decades old and badly out of date. With scholarly interest absent, anecdotes substitute for systematic knowledge. But anecdotes are dangerous things. Psychologists repeatedly remind us that human beings process information selectively. We vividly remember stories that confirm our biases; we discount events that contradict our deep-seated beliefs. Such selective perception encourages anecdotes to take on a truth independent of the facts.

The story of Sen. Alan Cranston and the B-1 bomber illustrates the danger of relying on anecdotes for our understanding of politics. In the 1970s Senator Cranston supported production of the B-1 despite his general dovishness on defense issues. Political self-interest appeared to motivate Cranston's support for the B-1: his home state of California was the biggest beneficiary of the program. Whatever effect Cranston's support for the B-1 had on his electoral prospects, it made him a staple in the writings on Congress and defense. Over the past decade Cranston's support for the B-1 has been regularly offered in popular and scholarly writings as evidence that parochialism drives congressional decision making on defense policy.

The story of Senator Cranston and the B-1 is told and retold because it appeals to our intuitive sense about the way politics works; the legislator as porkbarreler is part of American political folklore. But the anecdote tells us only about the behavior of one individual; it is a shaky foundation for making claims about the behavior of Congress as an institution. The history of the battle over the B-1 could be told very differently, with very different normative implications. Several senators voted to cancel the B-1 even though their states benefited substantially from the program. Their political courage is seldom mentioned in discussions about Congress and defense. Systematic research in fact suggests that Cranston's behavior was atypical; statistical studies repeatedly find that state economic benefit does not predict how individual senators voted on the B-1. And to further confound the pork-barreling story line, Senator Cranston helped lead the legislative efforts to derail the Strategic Defense Initiative and the B-2 bomber. California benefited handsomely from both programs. The lesson here is simple: even intuitively appealing anecdotes can grossly distort the complexities of congressional decision making.

This book seeks to move the discussion of Congress and nuclear weapons policy, and defense policy more generally, beyond anecdotes. It does so by systematically evaluating three different perspectives on congressional behavior. The general argument made here is that congressional deference and parochialism play a subsidiary role in Congress's deliberations on nuclear weapons. What best explains congressional decision making are the personal policy preferences of individual members. Simply put, no theory that ignores the policy beliefs of legislators will work well in explaining congressional behavior. And recognizing the importance of personal policy preferences does not require any heroic assumptions about what motivates members of Congress. Legislators are not angels; for most the overriding goal is to be reelected. But contrary to conventional wisdom, reelection provides members of Congress with powerful incentives to address the substance of public policy and to vote their individual policy views. That is the genius of the American political system.

In the course of writing this book I incurred numerous debts. David Mayhew and Bruce Russett read numerous drafts carefully and without complaint. Much of what is good about the book (and none of what is bad) owes to them. Joseph White generously shared with me his insights into the workings of the House and Senate as well as his interviews with members of Congress. Edward A. Kolodziej made several helpful suggestions for improving the manuscript. Theodore Marmor asked a question at a Yale University Faculty Seminar on Arms Control that led me to write the book. Ivo Daalder, Elisa Harris, Robert Higgs, Dwight Lee, Ken Mayer, Larry Smith, and Chris Wlezien all offered useful advice. Joel Barkan, John Conybeare, Timothy Hagle, Douglas Madsen, Art Miller, Peverill Squire, and Karen Stewart made it a pleasure to go to the office. Patrick Anderson, F. Gregory Gause III, David Menefee-Libey, Eve Sandberg, Frank Shemanski, and Stephen Silvia provided friendship and encouragement along the way.

The people at the Johns Hopkins University Press deserve thanks for smoothly translating a raw manuscript into a finished book. Henry Y. K. Tom, my editor, merits especially high praise for being both efficient and encouraging. And Sharon Ritenour Stevens took great care in copyediting a manuscript that wasn't as finished as I had thought.

Numerous members of Congress, congressional staff, Department of Defense officials, and members of the arms control community graciously consented to be interviewed. The ground rules for the interviews prevent me from mentioning people by name, but the ground rules do not prevent me from being grateful. To everyone I spoke with, thank you. I profited enormously from our conversations.

The Social Science Research Council provided financial assistance in the form of a MacArthur Foundation Fellowship in International Security. The Center for International Affairs at Harvard University, the Center for Science and International Affairs at Harvard University, the Government Studies Program at the Brookings Institution, and the Political Science Department at the University of Iowa all offered comfortable places to research, think, and write. The University of Iowa provided an Old Gold Summer Fellowship that enabled me to finish the manuscript.

Finally, I owe much to my family. Phoebe and Zooey provided many diversions from the trials of writing. My wife and best friend, Marci, helped me in more ways than I can count. May I someday return the favor. Finally, I wish to thank my parents, who always understood. They have my gratitude and my love.

Abbreviations and Acronyms

ABM	antiballistic missile
ACDA	Arms Control and Disarmament Agency
ACIS	arms control impact statement
AFB	air force base
ALCM	air-launched cruise missile
AMSA	Advanced Manned Strategic Aircraft
ASAT	antisatellite program
ASMS	Advanced Strategic Missile System
ASW	antisubmarine warfare
ATACMS	Army Tactical Missile System
CR	continuing resolution
DIVAD	Division Air Defense gun
DoD	Department of Defense
ELF	extremely low frequency communications system
FY	fiscal year
GLCM	ground-launched cruise missile
HADS	House Appropriations Defense Subcommittee
HASC	House Armed Services Committee
HSTC	House Science and Technology Committee
ICBM	intercontinental ballistic missile
INF	intermediate-range nuclear forces
JCAE	Joint Committee on Atomic Energy
JCS	Joint Chiefs of Staff
MHV	Miniature Homing Vehicle
MIRV	multiple independently targetable reentry vehicle
MPS	Multiple Protective Shelter basing system
NSI	National Security Index (American Security Council)
O&M	operations and maintenance
OSD	Office of the Secretary of Defense

RDT&E	research, development, testing, and evaluation
SADS	Senate Appropriations Defense Subcommittee
SALT	Strategic Arms Limitation Talks
SASC	Senate Armed Services Committee
SDI	Strategic Defense Initiative
SICBM	small intercontinental ballistic missile
SLCM	sea-launched cruise missile
SLBM	submarine-launched ballistic missile
SRAM	Short-Range Attack Missile
SSBN	ballistic missile submarine
START	Strategic Arms Reduction Talks
ULMS	Undersea Long-Range Missile System (Trident)

CONGRESS AND NUCLEAR WEAPONS

Introduction

WHY DID THE MX missile program trigger acrimonious debate in Congress while the Trident I missile program did not? Was the resistance on Capitol Hill to President Carter's decision to cancel the B-1 bomber rooted in pork-barrel politics or a different conception of America's security needs? Are members of Congress competent to judge nuclear weapons programs, or would the national interest be better served if these decisions were made solely by the executive branch? Answers to these questions are in short supply. Although writings on nuclear weapons abound—the subject is now a cottage industry—few studies discuss the weapons acquisition process. Even fewer studies discuss how Congress makes so-called hardware decisions, despite increased congressional activism on defense and foreign policy in the 1980s.

The scant attention paid to Congress's role in nuclear weapons policy reflects biases in both the congressional and national security literatures. Defense policy lies outside the mainstream of congressional studies. Most scholars prefer to study congressional behavior in general rather than to study how Congress acts in a specific policy area. When scholars do analyze specific policy domains, they focus overwhelmingly on domestic issues. Disciplinary boundaries explain the tilt. Defense issues straddle the worlds of domestic *and* international politics, so many congressional scholars find that defense policy raises substantive issues outside their own area of expertise.

For its part the national security literature favors discussions of policy proposals over discussions of how policy is made. Even a cursory review of the leading national security journals reveals that most articles address technical topics such as the utility of strategic defense, the merits of counterforce targeting, and problems in command and control. Far less attention is paid to the process by which the United States (or any other country) develops weapons. When national security analysts do turn their sights to process questions, they generally look to the executive branch. Congress is treated perfunctorily, if at all. Although the bias made sense in the 1960s when Congress regularly deferred to the executive branch on defense issues, it no longer does.

An analysis, then, of Congress's role in nuclear weapons policy addresses gaps in both the congressional and national security literatures. It offers to increase our understanding of how Congress makes decisions and why weapons develop as they do. Equally important, it addresses the question of how groups and individuals outside the executive branch influence nuclear weapons policy. The weapons acquisition literature long ago discredited the notion that weapons develop by virtue of some objective, nonpolitical process; intra- and interservice rivalries often shape acquisition decisions. Can and does Congress bring alternative views and values to bear on the subject of nuclear weapons?

This is not mere scholastic wondering. The historic political changes now sweeping Europe portend dramatic changes in U.S. nuclear weapons policy in the 1990s. But substantial differences exist within the defense community and the broader public over the future of U.S. policy. National security analysts argue that different force postures entail different consequences for deterrence and the likelihood of war. Most writings on U.S. nuclear weapons policy conclude with a discussion of how the United States should restructure its forces. The more ticklish question of how to translate such proposals into policy, or whether they can be given existing political forces, is almost always left unanswered. Yet the mere act of offering a remedy, no matter how intelligent or sincere the proponent, will not translate a policy preference into a policy outcome. This holds true even for presidents, as President Reagan discovered with the Strategic Defense Initiative (SDI). The ability to influence acquisition policy depends on an understanding of the policy-making process.

The same may be said of arms control policy. What a nation needs to control depends not only on its adversary's arsenal but also on what it has or is planning to build. The United States has discovered on several occasions that its technological prowess hindered arms control talks. At the first Strategic Arms Limitation Talks (SALT), for example, the Soviet Union failed to pursue a U.S. proposal to ban multiple independently targetable reentry vehicles (MIRVs). The United States had a clear lead in MIRV technology, and the Soviets did not want to be frozen into a disadvantageous strategic position. Weapons programs in research and development today also threaten to restrict the room for verifiable arms control in the future. The development of small, concealable, multipurpose weapons like the sea-launched cruise missile (SLCM) raises verification nightmares and threatens to impede arms control efforts. So arms control analysts need to know what kinds of weapons systems the acquisition process is likely to produce. But "arms control analysts have persistently and systematically neglected the processes by which nations develop and procure weapons."[1]

The study of Congress can answer questions about only one phase of the acquisition process. Studying Congress may not even answer the most pertinent process questions. Given the executive branch's dominance of nuclear weapons policy, a focus on Congress in many respects represents "a Ptolemaic view of a Copernican universe."[2] Yet the observation that the executive branch is the most influential actor in policy making does not warrant the conclusion that Congress is irrelevant. Moreover, a study of Congress and nuclear weapons raises the fundamental question of how well elected representatives handle an issue that almost everyone agrees is of supreme importance to the nation. For a country that takes great pride in its democratic heritage, the answer to that question is important.

Does Congress Matter?

Observers often note that Congress never cancels major nuclear weapons programs and that the executive branch, not Congress, sets the policy agenda. The conclusion many draw from this is straightforward: "Congress does not participate in the process of military force design."[3] The pessimist's conclusion raises an inevitable question: Does Congress even matter?

Five reasons suggest that Congress matters more than pessimists allow. First, the idea that Congress must cancel weapons systems to be judged influential is policy-biased: it ignores the possibility that Congress may impose a weapon on the Department of Defense (DoD). In 1983, for example, Congress directed the Pentagon to develop Midgetman, a small intercontinental ballistic missile (SICBM). Midgetman is not an isolated incident. In 1977 President Carter canceled the B-1 bomber. Congress, however, insisted on keeping the B-1 production line "warm," and in 1980 it added $300 million to the defense budget to develop a new strategic bomber. Congress's actions encouraged President Reagan to revive the B-1 program.

Second, the cancellation of a weapons system is an exceptionally high threshold for ascribing congressional influence. Congress can undertake a variety of actions between canceling a program and approving it. Congress did not cancel the MX missile program, for instance, but it barred research on several different MX basing modes, and it eventually funded only one-fourth the number of missiles initially requested. In the 1980s Congress regularly funded the antisatellite (ASAT) weapon, but it restricted ASAT testing against targets in space. The test moratorium effectively blocked development of an operational ASAT capability, and in 1988 the air force canceled the program.

Third, the mere fact that Congress participates in policy making may influence acquisition decisions. The White House often initiates or modifies programs in anticipation of the mood in Congress. Lyndon Johnson, for instance, chose to procure the Sentinel antiballistic missile (ABM) system partly because of pressure from Capitol Hill. Increasing the scope of the decision-making arena may also dramatically affect the ultimate decision.[4] This happened with the neutron bomb. So long as only a few defense officials knew about the weapon, development work went forward. When the neutron bomb became the target of attacks in Congress, however, the Carter administration discovered it had a problem. Congress eventually voted to fund the neutron bomb, but the furor led President Carter to postpone production.

Fourth, most discussions of congressional influence focus on procurement decisions. Yet Congress also influences programs during research and development. In 1976, for example, Congress barred DoD from conducting research on fixed silo basing for the MX. The prohibition launched a protracted search for a mobile basing system. Congress also intervened in the research and development process in the mid-1970s to force the air force to develop an armed cruise missile. The air force had opposed the cruise missile because it competed with the B-1 bomber program.

Finally, pessimists overemphasize the importance of initiative. No one can doubt that the executive branch dominates agenda setting, but agenda setting is only one aspect of policy making.[5] Equally important is process: What does Congress do with administration requests? Some may argue that Congress operates on the margins of policy. This need not be the case; Congress is free to alter programs as it sees fit. But even if Congress does operate on the margins, it still should not be dismissed as irrelevant. As Alton Frye writes, "the margins are frequently the vital edges, and Congress' ability to shape them is of real importance."[6]

Organization of the Study

The chapters that follow explore congressional decision making on nuclear weapons acquisition policy. The related but distinct topic of Congress's influence on arms control policy, though, is not at issue here. The Senate's treaty powers, the consultative role members of Congress sometimes play in arms control talks, and congressional attempts to use the power of the purse to force changes in arms control policy are all matters of great importance. But because the Constitution grants Congress the power to appropriate and not the power to conduct foreign policy, Congress's role in arms control differs in key respects from its role in weapons acquisition. The congressional role in arms control has also received attention elsewhere.[7] For both reasons the chapters that follow discuss arms control talks and treaties only insofar as they affect Congress's deliberations on hardware matters.

To understand Congress's role in nuclear weapons policy three sets of questions need to be answered. First, what is the nature of congressional activity on nuclear weapons acquisition issues? Who are the actors in Congress on these issues? What do they do? Second, why does Congress approve, modify, or disallow the administration's requests? What motivates senators and representatives to support or oppose requests for new weapons programs? Third, does Congress influence nuclear weapons policy?

Chapter 1 begins to answer these questions by reviewing what we know about how Congress decides policy issues. The chapter reviews three perspectives on congressional decision making that yield three different sets of expectations about legislative behavior. Chapter 2 examines the defense committees—the armed services committees and the defense appropriations subcommittees in each chamber—and traces their evolution toward a more aggressive posture on weapons requests. Chapter 3 maps how growing floor interest in nuclear weapons policy (and defense policy more generally) changed congressional decision making from an "inside" to an "outside game." Chapter 4 examines how Congress handled administration requests to develop the MX missile, the Trident submarine, the Pershing II missile, and the ASAT program. The four case studies illustrate how congressional decisions affect the evolution of individual weapons programs.

Chapters 5, 6, and 7 explore the whys of congressional decision making. Chapter 5 addresses the issue of why some weapons programs become controversial while others sail through Congress. The differing characteristics of controversial and noncontroversial weapons systems are discussed in depth. Chapter 6 analyzes the determinants of congressional voting on nuclear weapons. Particular attention is paid to the conventional wisdom that members of Congress vote parochially. Chapter 7 compares Congress's involvement in nuclear weapons policy with several other areas of defense policy. The chapter explores the reasons for the great diversity in legislative behavior in different parts of the defense budget.

Chapters 8 and 9 address the question of influence. Chapter 8 assesses Congress's influence on nuclear weapons policy and explores the constraints that Congress faces. The potential for increasing Congress's influence over weapons acquisition is also addressed. Chapter 9 concludes the study by discussing the pros and cons of congressional activism on nuclear weapons policy. The chapter assesses the claim that the common good would be better served if Congress deferred to the executive branch.

To explain Congress's role in nuclear weapons policy, the study reviews congressional decision making on *all* nuclear weapons. These include strategic offensive forces, strategic defensive forces, nonstrategic nuclear forces, and associated command and control systems. The study begins in 1968 because until that year Congress generally did not intervene in nuclear weapons policy, a passivity that extended to Congress's consideration of defense policy more generally.[8] In 1968, Congress began to shift to a more aggressive review of defense policy with the floor debate on the Sentinel ABM system. Although the Sentinel debate was brief (extensive debate on ABM would not occur until 1969 and then only in the Senate), it opened an era in which Congress would begin to take an interest in nuclear weapons policy.

Finally, a word about sources. The study draws mostly from the public record. Classified defense programs do not pose a major problem because most of Congress's actions take place in public and because until the mid-1980s "black" programs constituted a minuscule portion of DoD's requests (see table 8-1). To supplement the public record, I conducted more than seventy-five interviews with members of Congress, congressional staff, members of the arms control community, and DoD officials. To ensure frankness, all interviews proceeded on a not-for-attribution basis. Where interviews provided specific information, I did not use the information unless it was substantiated by the written record. As it turns out, the public record is surprisingly thorough.

1 ≫ ≪

Explanations

NO AGREED-UPON theory of congressional decision making exists. What the scholarly and popular writings on Congress and defense policy provide instead are three distinct "conceptual lenses" through which to view congressional decision making.[1] The *deferential* lens holds that members of Congress defer to the executive branch on weapons acquisition issues. Members generally decline to question the substantive issues at stake; hence, Congress does not influence nuclear weapons policy. The *parochial* lens contends that members evaluate weapons systems in terms of how programs affect the local economic and social concerns of constituents; members do not worry about whether weapons programs advance the national interest. Parochial pressures lead Congress to promote weapons systems that are not needed. The *policy* lens argues that members care about the substantive issues surrounding weapons programs. Legislators probe the merits of DoD requests, which in turn gives Congress substantial influence over nuclear weapons policy.

The deferential, parochial, and policy lenses all recognize that the "electoral connection" shapes what happens on Capitol Hill. Each lens acknowledges that members of Congress first and foremost want to be reelected. All three lenses also agree that norms—that is, notions about what constitutes proper legislative behavior—shape congressional decision making as well. But the three lenses make different predictions about how legislators react to electoral incentives, and each lens has different expectations about the norms that legislators observe. Bringing all three lenses to bear on Congress's deliberations on nuclear weapons policy makes it possible to move toward a true theory of congressional decision making.

Deference

One perspective on the role Congress plays in nuclear weapons policy (and defense policy more generally) emphasizes congressional deference to executive branch, and especially military, judgment on force design issues. One reason why members of Congress defer to DoD is because they believe they should;

that is, deference is a norm. Many members believe the military possess superior expertise; hence, congressional intervention only injects extraneous political factors into defense planning. Rep. L. Mendel Rivers (D-S.C.), chair of the House Armed Services Committee (HASC) from 1966 to 1970, put the deferential view bluntly: "Congressmen don't understand these military things. My members rely on me, and I know who to rely on. I'd rather have one general who knows this business than a hundred senators who don't."[2]

The flip side of the coin is that many members believe they are not qualified to judge DoD's requests. One representative, bewildered by the intricacies of military programs, complained: "You have to be a nuclear physicist or a Ph.D. or something to even understand what's involved. A common member of Congress can't make an independent judgment on it no matter how hard he tries."[3] The disparity of information resources between Congress and DoD reinforces congressional passivity. Legislators may turn to the civilian defense community for advice, but civilian defense analysts often are not privy to the alternatives that DoD has examined. Without knowing the merits of other options, many members believe they cannot intelligently assess DoD's requests.

Deference as a norm may also stem from respect for executive branch authority. Many legislators take the lesson of the 1930s to be that Congress should place few constraints on presidential action in foreign affairs. The belief in the need for strong presidential leadership affects acquisition decisions because weapons are seen to have value as bargaining chips at arms control talks. Even when members doubt the utility of a weapons system, they may believe that intervening in the acquisition process will restrict the president's negotiating flexibility and harm the national interest. As Rep. Jack Kemp (R-N.Y.) argued about the MX missile: "I would suggest that if we simply said no to a new generation ICBM [intercontinental ballistic missile] . . . that would doom our negotiations at Geneva to defeat; and we might as well just tell our negotiators to come home."[4]

The other impetus for congressional deference stems from the desire to win reelection. To start with, members may find that deference is a position-taking stance that offers electoral benefits.[5] Some legislators choose to develop reputations as superpatriots who support a strong military because such stands are popular among constituents. These legislators eagerly herald each new weapon proposal that emerges from DoD as necessary to "keep America strong." Flag-waving no doubt helps members who represent conservative constituencies or constituencies that host large numbers of military personnel. Yet the superpatriotic legislator accrues electoral benefits by being *seen* supporting the military and not by questioning the substance of defense policy.

Reelection may also discourage members from addressing policy issues. Attempts to review the substance of defense programs pose opportunity costs. Many legislators find the time needed to oversee DoD too large given the likelihood their efforts will succeed. The Pentagon often resists congressional directives, which dissuades many legislators from trying.[6] Members can use the time that would be devoted to defense oversight to more electorally profitable activities such as constituency service or to legislative work in policy areas where their efforts are more likely to have an impact.

Attempts at oversight pose direct costs as well. In evaluating DoD requests legislators face an "approve/deny" dilemma. DoD virtually always culls a single weapon from a variety of proposals and then presents legislators with the task of deciding whether to fund the program. There is "the politician's reasonable fear that if he is responsible for denying a military request, and the national security is then impaired—or believed to be impaired—he will be blamed."[7] Future electoral opponents may use a "no" vote as evidence that a member of Congress is "soft" on national defense. Legislators also fear that the administration will punish aggressive oversight by manipulating defense spending in the constituency or by refusing to cooperate with the member on other issues. Finally, members worry that criticism of DoD will expose them to political embarrassment. "There always lurks the fear that some classified information, selectively declassified or leaked, may sabotage [their] case."[8]

Both norms and the desire to win reelection, then, encourage members to defer to DoD. Of course, some legislators may want to challenge the Pentagon; but because their colleagues are reluctant to do so, even potentially activist legislators decline to take up defense issues. As Sen. J. W. Fulbright (D-Ark.) said during his tenure in the Senate: "I must confess that I have not really exerted myself as I might have in an effort to control the military. . . . Actually, I have been under the feeling that it was useless and utterly futile, that nothing could be done, for example, to cut an appropriation for the Department of Defense no matter what I did."[9]

Predictions

The deferential lens sees the defense committees as the main forum for congressional activity on nuclear weapons policy. The committees attract legislators who are more pro-defense than the average member of Congress. Hawkish legislators seek defense committee seats either because they support a strong military (hence they do not object to executive branch dominance of the agenda), or because the defense committees offer the best vantage point for position taking. Whichever the motive, committee members see their primary task as promoting the interests of the services. As Representative Rivers explained the role of HASC: "You must remember this is the most important committee in this Congress. This is the only voice, official voice, the military has in the House of Representatives."[10] Dovish members generally do not seek a defense committee assignment because they have less interest in flag-waving and because oversight is too costly.

The defense committees focus predominantly on fiscal and management oversight rather than policy oversight.[11] The defense committees have the primary congressional responsibility for bringing the president's defense budget into accord with the Congress's desired level of defense spending. Whether fiscal oversight leads to increases or decreases in individual programs depends on whether the president's requested spending is higher or lower than that Congress prefers. The defense committees also devote substantial energies to overseeing the management of programs. The desire for a strong defense encourages the committees to worry about whether programs can be produced on schedule and can meet their design specifications. The defense committees, however, do not favor aggressive policy oversight. Committee members do not claim to match the expertise of the military on substantive issues; on these matters the military "knows best." Defense committees' recommendations almost always win on the floor because nonmembers generally decline to challenge the committees.

The deferential lens expects a high level of congressional activity in only two instances. The first arises when the executive branch is divided over the merits of a weapons system. The losing side in executive branch battles usually seeks to export the debate to Capitol Hill in the hope that Congress will reverse the decision. Congressional activity will be especially intense if the divisions within the executive branch pit the uniformed military against civilians. Legislators, especially those on the defense committees, distrust civilian strategists because bureaucrats "know the price of the defense systems they evaluate, but little about their military value."[12] Most legislators believe only the services possess the expertise necessary to evaluate weapons systems.

The second set of circumstances that produces intense congressional activity involves weapons systems that suffer cost overruns. Legislators feel comfortable investigating charges of cost overruns because the military does not possess a claim to specialized knowledge on management issues. The defense committees especially dislike cost overruns because stories about Pentagon waste and abuse weaken support for high levels of defense spending. Members also find investigations into cost overruns to be politically attractive because voters typically applaud efforts to curb government mismanagement.

Even when Congress does become active, the deferential lens predicts that legislators will not change the substance of DoD policy. When the executive branch is divided over the merits of a program, Congress generally refrains from overruling the president. Legislators much prefer that the president revise the program than for Congress to modify it; congressional intervention may restrict the president's negotiating leverage with the Soviet Union. When cost overruns occur, Congress may order management changes or delay production. But members will not use cost overruns as a reason to cancel or scale down a weapons program. Because Congress refuses to change DoD requests, it has no influence on nuclear weapons policy.

Plausibility

Anecdotal evidence supports the notion of congressional deference. Members often charge that Congress fails to debate the fundamental issues in defense policy. Rep. Les Aspin (D-Wis.), who became chair of HASC in 1985, complains: "Our problem is that everybody just goes through the budget trying not to question the policy, but just going and looking for ways to save some money by re-estimating, by stretching out, looking at the usual places you might save . . . without ever questioning policy."[13] Rep. Thomas J. Downey (D-N.Y.) says that after his amendment to kill the Trident II missile lost by a three to one margin, a HASC staff member told him: "Tom, why are you wasting your time with that destabilizing crap? If you wanted to win your amendment, you should have talked about cost."[14] The experiences of the 1970s and 1980s also bear out the basic prediction of the deferential lens: Congress refused to cancel any nuclear weapons system. Congress even approved deployment of the MX missile, the most hotly contested weapon in the annals of U.S. defense policy.

Additional support for the deferential lens comes from the disparity between the information resources that Congress and DoD possess. While chair of the research and development subcommittee of the Senate Armed Services Committee (SASC), Sen. Thomas McIntyre (D-N.H.) admitted: "We spend an awful lot of time, but we are lucky if we can take a look or have a briefing or hearing on, say, 15 percent of those projects."[15] Despite adding staff in the 1970s, Congress still operates at a disadvantage. DoD presses its advantage by making it difficult for members to obtain information about defense programs. J. Ronald Fox, a former assistant secretary of defense, writes that when pressed for damaging information the services know "We can drag our feet and delay the submission of the data, or we can present the Congressman with so much detail that he will never figure out what is happening."[16]

The deferential lens gains additional credence from the political science literature. The deferential lens once dominated scholarly discussions of Congress and defense; most of the works written in the 1950s and 1960s emphasized Congress's unwillingness to intervene in defense policy.[17] The lack of attention today to Congress's role in nuclear weapons policy suggests that the deferential view still dominates the discipline.

The primary counterevidence to the deferential lens comes from the marked increase in congressional activity on nuclear weapons issues in the 1980s. The increase in congressional activity has three possible implications for the deferential lens. First, congressional deference may still operate but the "noise" in Congress has increased. Some individual legislators may be more willing to challenge DoD, but Congress as a whole may still defer to the executive branch. Second, the explanatory relevance of the deferential lens may have shrunk.

Members may still defer to the executive branch on some types of weapons but not on others. Third, deference may no longer explain how Congress acts on nuclear force issues. Congressional decision making may have changed, and explaining legislative behavior may require another analytical framework. Only further analysis can determine which explanation is correct. What remains is that the deferential lens was the major explanation for congressional decision making before 1968, that members of Congress give testimony on its behalf, and that its most basic prediction remains correct.

Parochialism

A second perspective on congressional decision making on nuclear weapons policy argues that members of Congress evaluate weapons programs parochially. The most common form of parochialism is *pork barreling,* where members review a weapons system in terms of how it affects the job prospects of constituents. If a program employs their constituents, legislators can be counted on to support it. A less common form of parochialism involves *bile barreling*.[18] On occasion, and particularly with basing modes for nuclear weapons, the economic benefits of a program may be outweighed by the costs it inflicts on a constituency in terms of (among other things) environmental damage, the loss of public land, or an influx of outsiders. In such cases, members from the affected constituencies will oppose the program even though it provides jobs.

As with deference, parochial behavior results from norms and the desire to be reelected. In terms of norms, some members believe they *should* "bring home the bacon" and spare constituents from the costs of government activity. Yet most legislators probably obey the *parochial imperative* as part of a calculated strategy to enhance their electoral prospects.[19] Constituents often notice a new defense contract for a local company (especially if they work for the firm), and they are likely to credit their legislators for securing it (something members invariably will do their best to broadcast). Legislators also know that if they fail (or are seen to have failed) to fight for the interests of the constituency or against an unwanted program, then voters may punish them at the polls. So members have good reason to act parochially.

Legislators who obey the parochial imperative may adopt one of two distinct roles.[20] The first is to act as an entrepreneur. Here members push DoD to continue existing programs or to initiate new ones in the hope that a local firm will win a contract. Members may also lobby the Pentagon to modify proposals that impose significant costs on constituents. Entrepreneurial behavior, however, characterizes only a few legislators. DoD dominates the policy agenda, and DoD officials are not likely to initiate, modify, or extend programs simply to please individual members of Congress. Lobbying DoD also takes time away from other electorally useful activities. So instead of acting as entrepreneurs, most legislators act as local agents. Here they simply endorse and vote for (or in the case of bile barrels, oppose) programs important to constituents.

Parochialism also discourages legislators from questioning the substance of policy. For members motivated by norms, policy issues are irrelevant; what matters is where a weapon will be built and where it will be based. Representative Downey once confessed, "When the A-6 Intruder [airplane] was going to be killed, I'm the congressman from that district and I'm on the Armed Services Committee. It's my job, *whether I think the A-6 is good or not*, to support it."[21] Members motivated by electoral incentives find the substance of policy equally unappealing. Policy oversight takes time away from more electorally valuable activities. Former Rep. Charles A. Vanik (D-Ohio) observes: "Now under the unique American process, the legislator can be deliberate and thoughtful, but these are *privileges* which must be compressed out of the legislator's time. This *privilege* comes after and in the time that remains after . . . [a legislator's] essential functions," which Vanik lists as (among others things) constituent service, press conferences, and visits to the district.[22] To make matters worse, constituents usually do not notice policy oversight, and they are unlikely to credit their elected representative even if they did. "Most constituents do have some vague notion that their congressman is only one of hundreds and their senator one of an even hundred. Even committee chairmen may have a difficult time claiming credit for a piece of major legislation, let alone a rank-and-file congressman."[23]

Detailed legislative work may attract the attention of the attentive public. Even here, however, attention to the substance of nuclear weapons policy offers at best a mix of benefits and costs. On the one hand, a legislator might win allies among like-minded people. On the other hand, a legislator may alienate people who hold different views. And if one policy stand makes some enemies, several policy stands will make many enemies. Most legislators cannot afford to create ill will, so they refrain from questioning the substance of nuclear weapons policy.

The end result is that Congress avoids the substance of policy issues. Morris Fiorina puts the point most forcefully: "Public policy emerges from the system almost as an afterthought. The shape of policy is a by-product of the way the system operates, rather than a consciously directed effort to deal with social and economic problems. . . . In order to purchase a steady flow of [federal projects and individual favors for constituents] congressmen trade away less valuable currency—their views on public policy."[24] The parochial imperative generally overrides any qualms legislators might have on the military or political merits of specific weapons programs. Reelection matters more than policy.

Predictions

The parochial lens makes several predictions about congressional decision making. For one it suggests the defense committees will attract legislators who represent constituencies that are more dependent on defense spending than those of nonmembers. The defense committees attract these legislators because the committees mark up the defense budget, giving committee members the best chance to influence program funding. The defense committees also write reports, which are useful in directing DoD to pursue desired actions. Like the deferential lens, the parochial lens anticipates that members of the defense committees will seek to maximize defense spending. Again, whether this leads to efforts to increase or decrease DoD requests depends on the level of defense spending the parent chambers are willing to support. But the defense committees will focus on fiscal and management oversight, not policy oversight.

Unlike the deferential lens, the parochial lens expects that some legislators will seek to change DoD requests. Challenges occur because legislators want to add funds to nuclear weapons programs that employ their constituents. Although some challenges will be conducted on the floor, they occur more often in the defense committees because the committees possess superior information and bargaining resources. Nevertheless, the entrepreneurial legislator faces constraints. Defense spending is not infinite and large requests threaten to "bust" the budget. Arms control agreements limit the size and composition of the nuclear arsenal so some programs cannot be expanded. Budgetary and arms control constraints push entrepreneurial activity toward attempts to make small additions to existing programs not constrained by arms agreements. Efforts to add-on to existing line items are likely to succeed, provided the add-ons are not prohibitively expensive.

The parochial lens further anticipates that major conflict will arise in Congress over nuclear weapons in two situations. One is when DoD decides to cancel or curtail a program. Unlike the deferential lens, the parochial lens expects that members will not defer to executive branch judgment when that judgment means constituents will lose jobs. Congressional opposition will increase as the size of the program increases; hence, Congress is most likely to override the president on big ticket items. The other situation in which congressional conflict is likely involves bile barrels. Whether such challenges will succeed depends on the number of constituencies hurt by the program relative to the number of constituencies that stand to benefit from it. In general, if a program inflicts costs on a few constituencies but provides tangible benefits to many, then DoD's proposal should prevail. Because Congress occasionally changes DoD's requests, the parochial lens credits Congress with some influence over nuclear weapons policy.

Plausibility

Anecdotes about the parochial imperative abound. Legislators often mention it. Representative Aspin writes: "Because of the nature of the information a congressman gets, the Armed Services Committee is typically less concerned about the question of how much we are buying in defense than the question of where we are buying it."[25] Rep. Tommy Robinson (D-Ark.) said after he voted for the MX missile in 1985: "I'm always asking [the White House] for something. They didn't have to trade with me because I was committed to the MX. But be honest. One has to look out for one's self and one's district. That's just the way the game is played."[26] The popularity of the parochial lens extends even to the other side of the Atlantic. In dismissing the claim that British firms would win SDI research contracts, one London newspaper wrote: "SDI may become the biggest procurement pork-barrel in history, but congressional leaders will make sure that the snouts in the trough will be those of their constituents."[27]

The parochial imperative has drawn the attention of a wide variety of scholars. One popular approach tests the proposition that the constituencies represented on the defense committees benefit disproportionately relative to other constituencies.[28] Studies generally find that defense committee members tend to come from constituencies with greater levels of DoD civilian and military employment than nonmembers. Yet virtually all studies fail to find evidence that committee members use their positions to benefit their constituents, regardless of whether the observed variable is gross DoD spending, military employment, or prime military contracts. Does this mean that defense committee members do not use their committee assignment to benefit constituents? Not necessarily. Scholars appear to have tested the proposition incorrectly.[29] Even if better tests produced the same results, it may be that *all* members seek defense-related benefits for constituents and a seat on the defense committees does not give a legislator additional influence.

A second line of quantitative research tests the proposition that defense spending influences how legislators vote on defense and foreign policy.[30] Most voting studies find no evidence that constituency benefits influence how members vote, a surprising result given the intuitive appeal of the parochial lens. Studies generally conclude instead that a legislator's ideology and party affiliation provide better predictors of voting behavior. As with analyses of the influence of members of the defense committees, however, these findings do not disprove the parochial lens; methodological and theoretical flaws plague many voting studies.[31] In light of these complaints and the intuitive appeal of parochialism, the parochial lens remains a compelling if unsubstantiated explanation of legislative behavior.

Policy

A third perspective on congressional decision making contends that members of Congress use the legislative process to advance their conceptions of good public policy. Again, norms provide one incentive. People run for Congress because they want to shape public policy and further what they see as the common good. Contrary to the claims of critics, members are not content merely to provide casework services. Members have a deeper human need to contribute, to matter. "Men and women want to count for something. . . . The need for meaning prods legislators to be something more than freeloading hypocrites."[32] For some members, defense policy is the area in which they want to make their mark.

To suggest that members try to advance their conceptions of good public policy does not deny that they also want to be reelected. Reelection is a necessary goal for all legislators; if they fail to win reelection they cannot pursue their policy objectives. Still, the two goals are not mutually exclusive, and members do not believe they should be. The advice of Rep. Carl Vinson (D-Ga.), a longtime chair of HASC, to a state legislator considering a race for Congress underscores the relationship between the reelection and policy goals: "The State legislator . . . asked Mr. Vinson whether a Congressman should represent the interests of his district or of the country as a whole? Mr. Vinson without hesitation shot back—'If you don't represent the Nation as a whole and have your horizons beyond the limits of your Congressional district, we don't need you in Congress.' He then quickly added—'By the same token, if you're not representing your district you won't be in Congress long enough to make a difference.' "[33]

But electoral incentives do not simply constrain legislative behavior; they also encourage members to address policy issues. "Substantive actions appear 'responsible' and 'statesmanlike' to constituents; this is good electoral politics."[34] Although skeptics may dismiss this claim as a bromide, members have an incentive to do legislative work "when there is credit to be gained for legislative maneuvers."[35] Some constituents care deeply about defense issues. For example, a dovish constituency may place great stock in restraining the arms race while a hawkish constituency may reward members who fight for a strong military.

Members may also address defense policy because it offers a chance to build a reputation as a "player" in Congress. Sen. Sam Nunn (D-Ga.), for example, used his expertise on defense matters to become a major figure in the Senate. Becoming a player in Congress offers several benefits. A legislative player by definition exercises more influence *within* Congress, influence that can be used to benefit constituents. Establishing a reputation as a player attracts the attention of interest groups that can provide the contributions in cash and kind needed to run a congressional reelection campaign. And being recognized as a congressional powerbroker helps gain media attention back home, thereby providing free advertising for the next campaign.

Finally, legislators may see substantive work as a means for gaining higher office. Take the advocacy of Rep. Albert Gore, Jr. (D-Tenn.), on behalf of the Midgetman missile program. "It is difficult for a young House member to get much notice, but Gore chose one of the surer routes; he picked a few good issues, worked hard at them, and methodically made a name for himself. The single-warhead missile was one of his issues. He made speeches about it, wrote articles about it, made contact with journalists about it, and eventually, as the idea came into fashion, he more than anybody else in public life was identified with it."[36] Gore's visibility on Midgetman helped him win a seat in the Senate. Nor was Gore's strategy unique. Several senators who launched presidential bids, including John Glenn (D-Ohio), Gary Hart (D-Colo.), and Henry Jackson (D-Wash.), made military issues a focal point of their work in the Senate.

In seeking to shape nuclear weapons policy, members fall into three distinct ideological camps. Doves generally oppose nuclear weapons. These members typically prefer the strategic doctrine of minimum deterrence, the belief that deterrence requires a secure, second-strike capability. Hawks generally support new weapons systems. These members tend to favor the strategic doctrine of counterforce, the view that deterrence requires the ability to destroy Soviet missile silos and command and control centers. For all their ideological differences, however, doves and hawks both have fixed preferences. They generally know in advance how they will vote on any issue, and therefore they use information to justify their positions rather than to reach decisions. Between the dovish and hawkish poles lie the moderates. Moderates see merit in both minimum deterrence and counterforce targeting without being convinced that either doctrine is totally right; hence, they will support some weapons systems and not others. Because moderates have flexible preferences, they constitute the swing bloc that determines outcomes in Congress.

Members also differ in their knowledge of and interest in nuclear weapons issues. Most members have only surface knowledge of nuclear doctrine; their expertise and passions lie in other policy domains. These legislators essentially are followers who help determine the decisions Congress makes—they vote—but they do not shape the debate on Capitol Hill. Other legislators, however, have considerable knowledge of and interest in nuclear weapons issues. These members constitute the leaders in Congress; they attempt to push issues onto the agenda and to shape the decisions of other members. Many leaders have developed their expertise by virtue of a defense committee assignment. These leaders make their influence felt both in committee and on the floor. Other leaders, though, come to their knowledge through their tenure on congressional committees with related jurisdictions, such as Foreign Affairs and Foreign Relations, or through idiosyncratic interests. These leaders generally make their presence felt during the floor debates.

Taken together, moderates and leaders constitute the engine that drives policy oversight in Congress; moderates because they are open to arguments on the merits of programs and leaders because they seek to provide information that supports their case. To argue that leaders continually try to persuade moderate followers does not mean, however, that legislators "pass judgment in Jovian calm."[37] At times, persuasion may be done politely and calmly through private discussions or eloquent floor speeches. Yet congressional decision making frequently produces heated exchanges. Many members believe deeply in their views, and, as a result, expound their arguments and castigate opposing views with vigor. Members also are not altruists; they exploit parliamentary maneuvers and party loyalty to their benefit. Nonetheless, impassioned debates and parliamentary machinations do not prevent oversight. In large part they are how policy oversight is done.[38]

Finally, to suggest that representatives seek to advance their conceptions of good public policy does not mean that congressional decision making produces the common good. It takes omniscience (not to mention arrogance) to know which nuclear policies and programs best serve U.S. interests, assuming these interests could even be identified. Even if an objective truth existed, the individual pursuit of good policy does not guarantee that the collective product will be "good" policy. Legislators may fail to perceive problems, take too long to reach decisions, or make bad choices. This is especially true with nuclear weapons policy because tremendous uncertainty surrounds concepts as basic as how deterrence works.

Predictions

The policy lens agrees that the defense committees are the main arenas of congressional activity on nuclear weapons policy. The defense committees have the primary jurisdiction over defense policy and can delve deeper into nuclear weapons issues than other committees or members on the floor. Unlike the deferential and parochial lenses, however, the policy lens does not expect the defense committees to be biased. Since members from across the ideological spectrum should want to influence defense policy, the defense committees should mirror the distribution of views found in the full House and Senate.

The policy lens predicts the defense committees will focus heavily on fiscal and management oversight. After all, the defense committees have to shepherd the defense bill through Congress, and legislators want to curtail wasteful expenditures. The defense committees also evaluate the merits of DoD's plans. Legislators do not necessarily approach the task of policy oversight in the spirit of open-minded objectivity (although this may be true of some). Much of the scrutiny of DoD's programs is the result of efforts by members to find information that supports their views and discredits opposing ones. The defense committees also can expect to face challenges from the floor. Floor challenges arise because members who lost in committee seek to have the decision overturned, or because nonmembers question the recommendations of the defense committees.

The policy lens does not predict which programs will attract scrutiny. Which programs appear on the agenda depends on the merits of DoD requests and the mix of attitudes in Congress. The policy lens also does not predict the outcome of any particular congressional debate. The decisions Congress makes depend on what legislators see as being wrong with the program in question and what is needed to redress the problem. Still, the policy lens expects that Congress will modify some DoD requests, including those that become controversial on policy grounds. Because Congress challenges the substance of DoD's weapons plans, the policy lens contends that Congress exercises considerable influence over nuclear weapons policy.

Plausibility

Some anecdotal evidence supports the policy lens. At times, administration officials testify to the need to argue the merits of their proposals. Donald C. Latham, a former assistant secretary of defense, comments: "It turns out that, even with guys like Rep. Joseph Addabbo and others who are not at all that much in love with defense at times, I have succeeded in convincing them of the merits of our programs."[39] Members of Congress also allude to the need to argue the merits of policy issues. Sen. Phil Gramm (D-Tex.) once commented: "When I came to Congress, one of the things I was interested in was whether vested interests or ideas dominate. As an outsider, that is an open question. But I can tell you as a result of my . . . experience here that I am more convinced than ever that Keynes was right when he said it is ideas, not vested interests, which are important for good or evil."[40] At the height of the MX debate, Rep. Thomas S. Foley (D-Wash.), the House Majority Whip, said about efforts to cancel the missile: "We're in a rowboat looking down 16-inch [battleship] guns if you're talking about promises. We have to appeal to the judgment of members, not goods and services."[41] Similarly, Alton Frye, a former Senate staff member, writes "that policy concerns are far more important to members' judgments on defense issues than the often-cited pork-barrel considerations."[42]

Some congressional scholars attest to the importance of policy motives in Congress. John Kingdon writes: "It's hard to account for the observed voting structure [in Congress] without invoking some version of legislators' ideology or conception of good public policy as a major part of the explanation."[43] Arthur Maass argues that congressional decision making should be understood in terms of a discussion model in which Congress articulates views in the body politic and responds to issues facing the community. "Government conducts a process of deliberation and discussion that results in decisions that are based on broader community interests."[44] In a similar vein, Joseph Bessette argues that "a full explanation of the structure and functioning of Congress must be sensitive to both deliberative and 'political' forces."[45] Bernard Asbell also highlights the importance of deliberation: "To the outsider . . . it may come as a surprise that more than ninety-nine percent of lobbying effort is spent not on parties, weekend hosting, and passing plain white envelopes, but trying to persuade minds through facts and reason."[46]

The policy lens finds support as well in several of the studies done in the 1960s on Congress and defense policy. A minority of scholars writing then concluded that the defense committees paid much more attention to the substance of defense policy than the dominant deferential perspective recognized. Bernard Gordon argued that the appropriations subcommittees reviewed Pentagon requests in detail, and had become "respected as much for their concern and familiarity with major policy as for their interest in dollar efficiency."[47] Raymond Dawson found that the traditional practice of line-item authorization of military construction projects had had the unintended effect of involving the armed services committees in detailed consideration of continental air defense. In reviewing plans to construct air defense bases, legislators gained greater knowledge of the actual weapons systems, knowledge that enabled the armed services committees to uncover major problems with DoD's plans. Dawson expected that the 1959 decision to require line-item authorizations for major weapons systems would open the door to "effective searching debate of strategic issues and choices."[48] Edward Kolodziej found that the defense appropriations subcommittees became increasingly interested in defense policy as the 1950s wore on. The actions of the subcommittees in turn "inspired a number of specific, yet beneficial, changes in the nation's defense establishment."[49]

Some systematic evidence supports the policy lens. If Congress evaluates defense requests in fiscal, dollar-saving terms and not policy terms, then it should focus on items that have an immediate impact on federal expenditures. This would lead budget cutters to concentrate on operations and maintenance (O&M) and personnel accounts, since most of these funds are spent in the year they are appropriated, while the research, development, testing, and evaluation (RDT&E) and procurement accounts typically are "spent out" over several years. Studies show, however, that Congress cuts most heavily from RDT&E and procurement.[50] Although these results lend credence to the policy lens, they are not definitive. Decisions to stretch out the development of weapons over several years for fiscal reasons or to delay a program because of test failures may also account for the observed budgetary behavior.[51] Only the analysis of individual programs can determine whether Congress changes RDT&E and procurement programs because of policy concerns. So far no one has undertaken the task.

Evidence for the policy lens also comes from the previously mentioned studies that examine the link between military procurement contracts and congressional voting on defense and foreign policy. To repeat, these studies find that ideology and not constituency benefit provides the best predictor of how members vote. Like studies of congressional budgetary behavior, voting studies are suggestive but not definitive. Most voting studies examine a mix of defense and foreign policy votes; votes on nuclear weapons may or may not reflect the same determinants. Voting studies also say nothing about the number, distribution, or content of the votes on nuclear weapons. Congress may consider few votes on nuclear weapons, those that are cast may have consistently lopsided outcomes, and they may revolve around management rather than policy issues. If this turned out to be the case, then the finding that ideology was the best predictor of congressional voting would support the deferential lens.

Some evidence, then, supports the policy lens. Overall, though, political scientists give the policy lens short shrift. Neglect of the policy lens stems partly from a scholarly bias toward quantitative research; the policy lens does not lend itself to statistical analysis. As the studies of congressional voting on defense policy illustrate, statistical analyses can lend support to the policy lens but they cannot substantiate it. The same statistical results may be compatible with divergent views of congressional behavior. Neglect of the policy lens also reflects the dominance of the electoral connection in congressional studies. Proponents of electoral connection models recognize that reelection can promote legislative work in Congress.[52] Nevertheless, most studies focus on how reelection discourages policy oversight and encourages behaviors like parochialism. Because so many studies look for evidence of parochialism, it is not surprising that they find no evidence of policy considerations. As the philosopher George Berkeley wrote: "To exist is one thing, and to be perceived is another."[53]

Conclusion

The chapters that follow test the explanatory power of the deferential, parochial, and policy lenses. What does each lens reveal about how Congress decides nuclear weapons issues? What does each lens miss? Do we need one lens to explain committee behavior and another to explain floor behavior? Does one lens explain agenda setting while another explains decision making? In evaluating the deferential, parochial, and policy lenses in this fashion the goal is not to advance one of the lenses as *the* explanation of congressional decision making. Too much evidence exists already on behalf of each lens to suppose that two of the three lenses could ever be dismissed as irrelevant to explaining congressional behavior. Rather the goal is to use the insights gleaned from examining each lens to construct a general theory of congressional decision making. Chapter 7 attempts just such a synthesis.

2 ≫ ≪

The Defense Committees

MUCH OF THE work of Congress is done in committee, and nuclear weapons policy is no exception. The committees that exercise the most influence over nuclear weapons policy are the defense committees of the House and Senate. The power of the defense committees stems from their jurisdiction over the defense budget. Other committees occasionally try to invade the turf of the defense committees and to stake a claim to some aspect of nuclear weapons policy, but such challenges inevitably falter. In defense policy, perhaps more so than any other policy domain, "dollars are policy," and the nondefense committees have no say over DoD's program requests.[1]

In the 1960s most discussions of the defense committees portrayed the committees as staunchly pro-military. Autocratic chairs presided over committees composed overwhelmingly of hawks. Committee members saw their job as advocating the military's interests on Capitol Hill rather than overseeing DoD's programs. On substantive issues, including nuclear weapons policy, the defense committees almost always deferred to military expertise. Most legislators shared the belief of longtime HASC chair Rep. Carl Vinson (D-Ga.) that "military men should make military decisions."[2]

In the 1980s parts of the traditional description of the defense committees continued to be true. Even though several doves joined the defense committees and some doves even won important committee positions, the defense committees remained more hawkish than the full House and Senate. But the structure and operations of the defense committees looked very different. The reform movement that swept Capitol Hill in the 1970s decentralized committee decision making. Junior committee members gained more power, and the armed services committees each developed a subcommittee system. The dispersion of committee power combined with rising floor pressure to push the defense committees into more active oversight. Although the defense committees did not become antimilitary, the automatic deference to military expertise that Vinson and his colleagues knew so well disappeared.

Membership

Rep. Otis Pike (D-N.Y.) once complained: "Congress is representative of the American people, but none of the committees is representative of Congress."[3] Many agree.[4] Perhaps the most common proposition about the defense committees is that they attract members who are significantly more hawkish than nonmembers. This is what the deferential lens predicts. To repeat that argument briefly, hawks find a defense committee assignment rewarding either because they share the same goals as the military or because the committee helps them engage in position taking. Doves usually do not want a defense committee seat because they have less interest in flag-waving, and, given DoD's historical resistance to external pressure, they cannot influence policy.

Table 2-1 sheds light on the proposition that defense committee members are more hawkish than nonmembers. Using the American Security Council's National Security Index (NSI) of legislators' support for defense (where 0 is most dovish and 100 is most hawkish), the table compares the average hawkishness of defense committee members with that of nonmembers.[5] But first a warning. Because the votes used to compile the ratings change from year to year and differ from chamber to chamber, table 2-1 cannot be used to determine whether the House is more hawkish than the Senate, or whether Congress became more hawkish over time. The only legitimate comparisons are those confined to a single term and a single chamber.

Caveats aside, table 2-1 shows that for the Ninety-first through Hundredth Congresses (1969–88), three of the four defense committees averaged significantly higher mean NSI scores than nonmembers. HASC and SASC remained much more hawkish than their parent chambers even though several longtime critics of DoD—most notably Reps. Les Aspin (D-Wis.) and Ron Dellums (D-Calif.)—assumed committee leadership positions in the 1980s. The House Appropriations Defense Subcommittee (HADS) was always more hawkish than the full House, though the difference was slight during the Ninety-sixth Congress (1979–80). HADS remained more hawkish than the House as a whole even in the 1980s when the dovish Joseph Addabbo (D-N.Y.) chaired the subcommittee.

The average hawkishness of the Senate Appropriations Defense Subcommittee (SADS) differs from the other three committees. In the Ninety-fourth through Ninety-eighth Congresses (1975–84), SADS registered mean NSI ratings fairly close to those of nonmembers. The Legislative Reorganization Act of 1970 accounts for the difference in SADS's orientation. The law limited future senators to only one seat on the Senate's top four committees—Appropriations, Armed Services, Finance, and Foreign Relations. Over several years the reform broke the grip that a small group of conservative (and hawkish) senators held on major committee assignments. Doves interested in defense policy apparently found SADS to be a more hospitable committee assignment than SASC, perhaps because the Appropriations Committee also oversees other policy domains.

Table 2-1 also shows how the ideological gap between the defense committees and their parent chambers changed over time. Of the four committees, only HASC grew more hawkish relative to its parent chamber; whereas the ideological gap between HASC and the House averaged 129 for the Ninety-first through Ninety-sixth Congresses (1969–80), it averaged 151 for the Ninety-seventh through Hundredth Congresses (1981–88).[6] In the case of SASC and HADS, although some fluctuations occurred, the gap between these committees and their parent chambers did not follow any long-term trend either up or down. Finally, the gap between SADS and the full Senate narrowed, reflecting the impact of the Legislative Reorganization Act.

A second common proposition about the defense committees holds that their members represent constituencies that benefit more from military expenditures than do those represented by nonmembers. This, of course, is a basic prediction of the parochial lens. To review that argument, members may seek a defense committee assignment because their constituencies already have a large stake in defense spending and they want to protect that interest. Members may also seek defense committee seats because these committees provide the best vantage point from which to steer defense dollars to local firms.

Considerable effort has been devoted to testing this proposition, especially with regard to the House.[7] Studies of HASC generally conclude that its members represent districts receiving higher levels of defense expenditures than the districts of nonmembers. Yet the presence of military installations accounts for this result; no studies have found a significant correlation between membership on HASC and private defense plant employment or contracts. Moreover, a model of House committee requests that used both military base *and* private defense employment as indicators of district interest did poorly in explaining requests for assignments to HASC.[8] Conversely, every study has found that members of HADS represent districts roughly representative of the House as a whole, regardless of the measure of constituency interest.

Two possible explanations exist for the findings about membership on HADS. The first is that the Appropriations Committee discourages its members from seeking a seat on a subcommittee that oversees a policy area where their districts have a large interest at stake.[9] A second and by no means contradictory explanation is that members representing districts with a high stake in defense spending may prefer a seat on HASC to a seat on HADS. Several legislators explained that although HADS provides a better vantage point from which to protect local interests—largely because it goes last in the budget cycle—many constituents believe only HASC deals with military affairs. So when these members first sought office they campaigned on a pledge to win a seat on HASC.[10]

The interview data in table 2-2 provide an additional window on why mem-

Table 2-1.
Hawkishness of the Defense Committees Compared with Their Parent
Chambers, 91st–100th Congresses

Armed Services Committees

		Mean Hawkishness Rating*						
Congress	HASC	Non-Members	Gap†	T-Stat‡	SASC	Non-Members	Gap†	T-Stat‡
91st	86.4	74.0	117	.02	68.7	53.6	128	.16
92d	82.7	67.0	123	.02	74.0	54.2	137	.06
93d	80.4	62.3	129	.00	76.4	47.9	160	.01
94th	75.6	58.5	129	.01	70.3	48.7	144	.05
95th	78.5	58.8	133	.00	62.2	43.3	144	.04
96th	74.3	52.5	141	.00	65.5	50.7	129	.11
97th	88.3	63.3	139	.00	80.7	61.0	132	.03
98th	76.6	49.9	153	.00	67.0	55.0	122	.23
99th	78.0	47.1	166	.00	73.1	57.1	128	.11
100th	73.0	50.6	144	.00	75.8	50.1	151	.01

Defense Appropriations Subcommittees

		Mean Hawkishness Rating*						
Congress	HASC	Non-Members	Gap†	T-Stat‡	SADS	Non-Members	Gap†	T-Stat‡
91st	91.1	74.7	122	.11	74.9	53.0	141	.06
92d	91.8	67.8	135	.04	69.6	55.2	126	.19
93d	74.0	63.9	116	.29	65.3	49.7	131	.16
94th	79.9	59.5	134	.05	60.6	50.3	120	.32
95th	75.8	60.2	126	.12	43.2	47.0	97	.71
96th	57.4	54.5	105	.82	55.7	52.7	106	.74
97th	84.4	65.4	129	.09	72.0	62.8	115	.32
98th	71.5	52.0	138	.10	59.8	56.5	106	.75
99th	65.5	49.9	131	.23	71.4	57.6	124	.18
100th	72.7	52.7	138	.13	66.6	52.8	126	.21

Abbreviations: HADS, House Appropriations Defense Subcommittee; HASC, House Armed Services Committee; SADS, Senate Appropriations Defense Subcommittee; SASC, Senate Armed Services Committee

*Percentage of the time each member voted "correctly" on selected national security issues, as determined by the American Security Council.

†The mean score of defense committee members expressed as a percentage of the mean score of nonmembers. The higher this figure the greater the ideological gap between the committee and the parent chamber.

‡Although these are means for populations (and hence probability statistics are not applicable) t-statistics are provided for heuristic purposes.

Table 2-2.
Defense Committee Preference Motivation Frequencies, Selected Congresses

Committee	Congress	N	Constituency	Policy	Prestige
HASC	92d	n.a.	5	3	1
	97th	n.a.	11	7	0
	100th	19	13	8	1
HADS	100th	3	2	2	3
SASC	92d	n.a.	4	4	0
	97th	n.a.	4	6	0

Note: The interviews for the Ninety-second Congress (1971–72) and Ninety-seventh Congress (1981–82) were with first-term members who had sought seats or their staff. The figures for the Hundredth Congress are based on interviews with members of HASC. Reading across the numbers sum to greater than N because respondents often gave more than one answer. See table 2-1 for abbreviations.

Source: The figures for the Ninety-second Congress are from Charles Bullock III, "Motivations for U.S. Congressional Committee Preferences: Freshmen of the 92d Congress," *Legislative Studies Quarterly* 1 (May 1976): 201–12. The figures for the Ninety-seventh Congress are taken from Steven S. Smith and Christopher J. Deering, *Committees in Congress* (Washington, D.C.: CQ Press, 1984), p. 90. The interview data for the Hundredth Congress are described in chapter 1.

bers join the defense committees. Representatives seek seats on HASC and HADS for both constituency and policy reasons. This departs somewhat from conventional wisdom—policy concerns are seldom noted as motives for defense committee membership. Still, constituency concerns are mentioned more frequently. Of course, claims of policy concerns may be mere political posturing designed to obscure a member's parochialism. Yet members of other committees do not feel compelled to cloak their committee preference motives under a guise of highmindedness.[11] Members of the defense committees probably are no less candid.

Disaggregating the House data also corroborates a key finding of statistical studies, namely, that representatives show more interest in military bases than in defense contracts. "Eight of the 97th Congress's freshmen said that their primary interest in Armed Services rested on the committee's jurisdiction over military installations in their districts. Three others mentioned the importance of defense contracts with industries in their districts."[12] Likewise in the Hundredth Congress; of the thirteen members of HASC who mentioned parochial motives, ten mentioned only military bases. This finding is especially notable since these members were interviewed because they sat on either the procurement, seapower, or research and development subcommittees; only four of the thirteen also sat on the military installations subcommittee, which has the greatest influence over defense facilities. In the case of HADS, of the two members who listed constituency motives, one mentioned military installations in his district and the other mentioned both bases and defense contracts. And most relevant to nuclear weapons policy, only one member or representative mentioned a district interest in the manufacture of nuclear weapons.

The motives for committee membership in the Senate are less well understood than those in the House. No statistical analyses have been done on the relationship between membership on the Senate defense committees and state defense benefits, and interview data are available only for SASC. The figures suggest that members of SASC, like their counterparts in the House, seek their seats for a mix of constituency and policy motives. And SASC seems to have become more of a policy committee over time. An analysis of committee requests made by Democratic senators between 1953 and 1971 found that none of the senators seeking assignment to SASC mentioned policy motives.[13]

Do members of the defense committees have a disproportionate stake in expenditures on nuclear weapons program? None of the statistical studies speaks to this point. DoD does not publish data on the geographical allocation of nuclear weapons contracts, so it is impossible to answer the question definitively. But the interview data do not suggest that nuclear weapons contracts provide a motive for seeking a seat on one of the defense committees. The evidence indicates instead that military bases provide the single biggest incentive for seeking a defense committee assignment. Since military bases tend to be in rural areas while weapons manufacturers tend to locate in urban areas, the defense committees probably do not overrepresent constituencies dependent on nuclear weapons programs.

Structure

Which members sit on the defense committees explains only part of committee decision making. Equally important is how committee decision making is structured. During the 1960s senior members, and especially the chairs, dominated decision making within the defense committees. By virtue of congressional rules the chairs had the power to create subcommittees, set committee agendas, choose committee staff, and manage defense bills on the floor. The norms of behavior on Capitol Hill buttressed the formal rules; it was routinely expected that junior committee members would see their tenure as an apprenticeship and defer to committee leaders.

Given their formal and informal powers, the chairs of HASC and SASC—Reps. Carl Vinson (D-Ga.) and L. Mendel Rivers (D-S.C.) and Sens. Richard Russell (D-Ga.) and John Stennis (D-Miss.)—ran the committees as their personal baronies. In both committees, hearings and markups were done in full committee, where the chairs dominated deliberations. Neither HASC nor SASC had standing subcommittees with formal jurisdiction over any element of the authorization bill or any major aspect of defense policy. In HASC's case the standing subcommittees lacked even names; they were simply numbered one through four. The armed services committees instead relied on temporary subcommittees, which seldom addressed nuclear weapons policy. The chair of HASC also relied on advice from an informal policy panel composed of senior committee members. The chair chose the members of the panel and he usually did not inform the full committee, let alone the broader public, of his choices.[14]

Within the armed services committees, junior members were expected "to be seen but not heard." Members of HASC had to serve lengthy apprenticeships, sometimes as long as ten years, before they were allowed to play a major role in committee business. In 1969 Rep. Robert Leggett (D-Calif.) complained that junior members had no say in committee decisions:

> But we have another thing on our committee. It is called the policy committee. . . . I do not know what it is. I have been on the [Armed Services] committee only 4½ years. I do not know who the members of the policy committee are. . . . I have never seen a scratch of a pen before our committee authorizing what the policy committee does. I know on the day of our committee markup, it was reported to us that the policy committee had recommended such and such with respect to all of these various systems, but I have never heard one member of the policy committee . . . relate what was happening, relate an argument, or relate some of the democracy that has taken place on that very important committee.[15]

Members of HASC disliked Leggett's frequent criticisms, and at one point Chairman Rivers "took to the floor to threaten revenge on Leggett."[16] Rivers was not reprimanded for breaching House etiquette, implicit testimony to his power. Junior senators fared no better than their House counterparts. Senator Russell not only dominated SASC, he was widely regarded as the "president" of the Senate's "inner club."[17] According to Sen. Thomas McIntyre (D-N.H.), who joined SASC in 1964: "Russell and the senior members would sit way down at one end of the table and the junior members would sit at the other end. I'm partially deaf in my right ear and I couldn't even hear what the hell was going on. Finally one day I spoke up and asked Russell if he would mind talking louder so we could hear what decisions were being made!"[18]

The defense appropriations subcommittees differed slightly from the armed services committees. As subcommittees themselves, HADS and SADS had no subcommittees of their own. Still, the most senior members dominated the subcommittees' business. Senator Russell chaired SADS, and he ran it as he ran SASC. Like Russell, Rep. George Mahon (D-Tex.) was one of the most powerful men on Capitol Hill; Mahon either chaired or was the ranking minority member on HADS and its predecessor every year from 1949 to 1978. Both HADS and SADS attracted senior legislators and experienced little turnover. Of the seven Democrats on HADS in 1968, five joined the subcommittee before 1957. All fifteen members of SADS in 1968 had served at least two full terms in the Senate.

Centralized committee decision making came under attack in the 1970s.[19] The challenge to the defense committees, part of a broader trend in Congress, reflected both internal and external pressures. Many legislators, especially those in the House, chafed against the tremendous power of the chairs. Some sought to increase the potential for gaining political credit with constituents through committee work.[20] Others hoped to increase their say in policy making. Senator McIntyre, for example, agreed to stay on SASC only after Senator Stennis promised to establish a subcommittee on research and development for McIntyre to chair.[21] The reformists' cause was aided by the arrival in the late 1960s and early 1970s of more individualist legislators who refused to enter into an apprenticeship while more senior members managed the business of Congress.

The House instituted several reforms in the 1970s that affected HASC. The most important came in 1973 when the House Democratic Caucus adopted the Subcommittee Bill of Rights. The new rules stripped committee chairs of the power to make subcommittee assignments and mandated that subcommittees have formal jurisdictions, authority to hold hearings, and a staff selected by the subcommittee chair. F. Edward Hebert (D-La.), who became chair of HASC in 1971, resisted the caucus reforms, however, and opposed House Democrats on several key issues. Faced with this intransigence the caucus removed Hebert as chair in January 1975, and it named Melvin Price (D-Ill.), the next ranking committee member, the new chair.

Price accepted the will of the caucus and moved to decentralize HASC. The most important step he took was to assign the subcommittees fixed jurisdictions over aspects of the defense budget. Responsibility for nuclear weapons initially was shared among the Subcommittee on Research and Development, the Subcommittee on Seapower and Strategic and Critical Minerals, and the full committee (which oversaw requests for the procurement of weapons). In 1979 the Subcommittee on Procurement and Military Nuclear Systems was established, and it was given jurisdiction over nuclear weapons procurement. Price also was less involved in the work of the subcommittees than his predecessors. He remained the single most powerful member of HASC, although "as a group the [subcommittee] chairmen equalled the Committee head in power."[22]

The Senate adopted several rules changes in the 1970s that encouraged decentralization within SASC. Informal changes, however, played a bigger role. Senator Stennis, who became committee chair in 1969, was a "conservative innovator" who was more willing than Senator Russell to allow other senators to participate in committee business.[23] In 1969 Stennis created *ad hoc* subcommittees on tactical air power and research and development, and he elevated them to full subcommittee status in 1973. The research and development subcommittee subsequently played a major role in the Senate's deliberations on several nuclear weapons programs. In 1977 Stennis also created a subcommittee on general procurement matters. The increased aggressiveness of junior senators reinforced Stennis's willingness to give other committee members more responsibility.

The growth of the subcommittee system was greater within HASC than within SASC. By 1979 HASC's subcommittees marked up the entire annual defense authorization bill, and they had the right to schedule hearings on virtually any subject they chose. SASC, however, continued to mark up procurement requests, except those for tactical aircraft, in full committee. The chair of SASC also retained the power to schedule hearings and meetings, and the committee staff remained more centralized than in the House. Finally, SASC's small size (ranging from fifteen to eighteen members compared with forty to forty-five in HASC) meant that most of its subcommittees included nearly half of SASC's members.

The congressional reforms of the 1970s had a less dramatic impact on the operations of the defense appropriations subcommittees. The Legislative Reorganization Act of 1970 broke the interlocking directorate that governed both SASC and SADS; by 1979 only Senator Stennis continued to sit on both committees. In 1977 SADS ended the tradition of having three senior members of SASC sit as ex officio members with voting rights during the subcommittee's deliberations. The only major change in HADS was that the Subcommittee Bill of Rights required that the chairs of appropriations subcommittees be elected through the same caucus mechanism that selected full committee chairs. This change ratified the fact that the appropriations subcommittees operated as the equivalent of full committees.

The reforms of the 1970s were institutionalized in the 1980s. HASC's subcommittee structure remained unchanged. When the Republicans gained control of the Senate in 1981, the new chair, Sen. John Tower (D-Tex.), reorganized SASC's subcommittees along mission lines. This consolidated Senate oversight of nuclear programs under the Subcommittee on Strategic and Theater Nuclear Forces. But SASC continued to rely on subcommittees as an integral part of its decision-making process.

The defense committees also increased their staff resources in the 1980s. In 1968 the professional (i.e., nonclerical) staff of the four defense committees totalled less than 30, and as late as 1979 it stood at less than 60. In 1988 the professional staff exceeded 110. The figures do not include personal staff assigned to individual members, which also grew in the 1970s and 1980s.[24] Besides adding staff, the Senate defense committees reorganized the staff structure. When the Republicans gained control of the Senate in 1981, SASC and SADS finally followed the lead of most other Senate committees and established a majority/minority staff. The House defense committees, however, continued to maintain a nonpartisan staff. The reluctance of the House to establish a majority/minority staff owed to two factors. One was that the traditional norm that the business of the defense committees should be bipartisan continued to have appeal. The other reason stemmed from the dominance of Democrats in the House: Republican members feared that creating a majority staff would further diminish their influence over defense policy.[25]

Activities

The interest of the defense committees in nuclear weapons policy increased dramatically in the 1970s and 1980s. One indicator of increased defense committee activity can be found in the annual hearings on the defense budget. Between 1965 and 1969 HASC's hearings on the annual defense authorization bill averaged fewer than seventeen hundred pages. In the 1980s the figure stood at nearly six thousand pages. More and longer hearings gave the defense committees opportunities for more intensive and extensive program reviews, including reviews of less prominent programs. In 1968, for example, SADS held its first review of Sentinel ABM, a program with a projected price tag of $5 billion (with almost $1 billion requested in 1968 alone) and the potential to reshape the strategic balance. The ABM hearing filled only thirty-four pages.[26] In 1985 SADS reviewed a $356 million request for the E-6A strategic communications aircraft, a relatively noncontroversial plane designed to communicate with ballistic missile submarines. The E-6A hearing filled thirty-five pages.[27]

Dramatic changes also occurred in the character of defense committee hearings. In the 1960s hearings were often *pro forma*. "Few committee members attend[ed] defense budget hearings. Few, if any, prepare[d] for the hearings. Few regard[ed] the hearings as a crucial part of the legislative process."[28] Until the early 1970s the defense committees took virtually all their testimony from DoD officials. The tradition of soliciting advice only from the uniformed military was so strong that interested civilians did not even bother to ask to testify.[29] Defense committee members also usually failed to challenge service assessments. As late as 1969 the services commonly supplied committee members with questions to ask at the hearings. The practice fell into disuse only after one committee member read both the supplied question and answer.[30]

The laissez-faire attitude of the defense committees disappeared in the 1970s. All the committees began to call on civilian witnesses, and officials of major arms control groups, such as the Arms Control Association and the Federation of Atomic Scientists, regularly testified at hearings in the 1980s.[31] Not surprisingly, the defense committees continued to solicit most of their testimony from military officials. Still, the collapse of the taboo on nonmilitary testimony meant that the defense committees were less sheltered from opinions and advice that contradicted prevailing DoD policy.

Members of the defense committees also became more willing to challenge DoD witnesses.[32] During a hearing held by SASC in 1986, for instance, Sen. Pete Wilson (R-Calif.) repeatedly asked an air force general to rank strategic weapons in order of importance. When the general refused to answer, Senator Wilson responded: "That's not good enough. I'm not going to let you get out of that chair until you answer the question."[33] Such an outburst, especially from a hawkish junior senator, would have been remarkable in the 1960s. It was not unusual in the 1980s.

Attendance at committee hearings also continued to be sparse at times. Some members prefer to attend only those hearings that bear on matters of particular interest. Most legislators find it difficult to meet all the demands on their time. Sen. William Cohen (R-Maine), a member of SASC, complained:

> One must keep in mind that membership on the Senate Armed Services Committee, or the parallel Committee of the House, is not an exclusive task; it is just one of a number of assignments. I am also on the Intelligence Committee and I used to be the Chairman of the Indian Affairs Committee. I am, moreover, on the Governmental Affairs Committee; I am on nine subcommittees, all of which tend to meet at the same time. Consequently, I am required, like other members, to come in for one hearing, stay for half an hour, or perhaps a little longer, before leaving to go on to another hearing.[34]

Competing claims on a member's time are especially severe in the Senate. In 1988, for example, members of the Senate defense committees averaged three committee and nine subcommittee assignments apiece. As for the House, HADS remained an exclusive committee, but members of HASC averaged two committee and four subcommittee assignments.

Do more hearings provide the defense committees with better information about nuclear weapons programs? Yes, but not always. Committee hearings are an inefficient means of transferring information. "In the words of an SASC staffer, the 'useful content to verbiage ratio is very low.' "[35] The problem is made far worse by DoD's penchant for always trying to present its programs in the best light. As Rep. William Dickinson (R-Ala.) once complained: "You have to be pretty smart to know what the question is that will get the answer you are seeking. And I don't think for a minute that the Services knock themselves out trying to help you ask the right questions, unless they are anxious to have you ask that question."[36]

The history of the B-1B bomber illustrates Dickinson's complaint. In the early 1980s air force officials raved about the plane. But in the mid-1980s the news media began to report about problems bedeviling the B-1B. In March

1986 the deputy chief of staff of the air force was asked at a hearing before HADS about the reported problems. He responded: "I know of no other problems of significance that have been reported to us."[37] Less than a year later the air force admitted that the plane's avionic systems did not function properly and that it would take at least thirty-two months and an additional $1 to $3 billion to fix the problem. Despite air force assurances that the B-1B was "the best warplane in the world today," even Rep. Samuel S. Stratton (D-N.Y.), one of DoD's staunchest allies, lamented that the B-1B "looks to me like a candidate for a pretty substantial disaster on the part of the Air Force."[38]

Additional evidence of increased defense committee activity lies in the annual committee reports on the defense budget. Whereas defense committee reports in the 1960s seldom exceeded seventy pages, in the 1980s the reports commonly ran several hundred pages.[39] Although these figures do not distinguish among different elements of the defense budget, the defense committees' interest in nuclear weapons probably increased at a rate similar to the growth in the length of their annual reports.

Beyond sheer page length, the defense committees also adopted more critical positions in their reports. In the 1960s the defense committees rarely used report language to issue directives to the services, either on policy or management issues. When the committee reports did discuss a particular weapons system in detail, they typically extolled its virtues and argued that its development was critical to national security. Beginning in the mid-1970s, however, the defense committees began to use report language to prod DoD in one direction or another. (Report language is not binding, but DoD often responds to directives contained in committee reports.) Most directions focused on budgetary and management matters, which reflected widespread dissatisfaction on Capitol Hill with the Pentagon's repeated inability to complete programs on time and under budget. Yet report language also targeted policy concerns. In 1976, for example, the conferees on the defense authorization bill prohibited the air force from obligating funds for fixed silo basing for the MX.

In the mid-1970s the defense committees also became more willing to direct DoD to conduct studies. Between 1968 and 1971 the defense committees requested only *one* Pentagon study on nuclear weapons. In 1986 alone the defense committees requested twenty-five DoD reports. Moreover, the defense committees often requested quite detailed reports. To take one example, SASC requested an air force study in 1985 on alternative configurations for the Short-Range Attack Missile II (SRAM II), a nuclear air-to-surface missile. SASC's request stated: "This 'austere' version shall consist of the current SRAM envelope and rocket propulsion, the existing SRAM warhead (or a minor adaptation of any other in-production nuclear warhead), and inertial guidance based on an existing inertial guidance unit."[40]

Do congressionally mandated reports matter? Some clearly do not. Representative Aspin observes that "There are requests where Congress orders up a report, not to aid Congressional deliberations but as a substitute for deliberations."[41] DoD also occasionally submits reports that fall far short of what even defense committee members consider reasonable. In 1986, for instance, the Pentagon filed a classified report on the Stealth bomber that fulfilled the letter but not the spirit of the original congressional request. Rep. Duncan L. Hunter (R-Calif.), a member of HASC, revealed that the report "was less than a page long, highly classified, lacked any substantial information, and has served only to raise further questions and doubts."[42] But many requests for reports are useful for prodding DoD in one direction or another. Reports also are useful for creating a "paper trail" against which future requests may be judged.

The third and most important area where defense committee activity increased in the 1970s and 1980s was budgetary review. Table 2-3 presents data on the changes the defense committees recommended to the president's initial budget requests for nuclear weapons programs. Before FY 1973 the defense committees recommended only small cuts to DoD's requests; between FY 1969 and 1972 HASC made only one $20 million funding cut. Such restraint was typical throughout the 1960s. Each year when it came time for SASC to mark up the RDT&E account, Senator Russell usually lamented: "It's a shame we haven't been able to look at it completely—why don't we just vote it out?"[43] Things were no different in the House. Rep. Michael Harrington (D-Mass.) complained that HASC's motto was "Once over lightly."[44]

The superficial review of weapons requests ended in the early 1970s. With the exception of HASC, all the defense committees began to recommend sizable reductions in DoD's budget requests in FY 1973. In the authorization cycle, SASC remained more inclined to impose budget cuts than HASC was until FY 1978. In the appropriations cycle, neither HADS nor SADS on average established itself during the 1970s as more sympathetic to the administration on the subject of nuclear weapons. In the 1980s the overall dollar requests for nuclear weapons soared as the result of President Reagan's ambitious strategic modernization program. The percentage reductions the defense committees recommended also increased, and the House defense committees became more willing to cut the president's budget. The (Democratic) House defense committees also consistently recommended larger budget reductions than did the (Republican) Senate defense committees. The role reversal, however, did not herald a change in how the defense committees functioned. Rather, it reflected a basic political reality, namely, the Republicans gained control of the Senate in 1981 and were far more willing to support President Reagan's spending plans.

Of course, the percentage changes the defense committees recommend to the budget reveals nothing about the *extent* of defense committee intervention. Sizable recommended changes to the president's budget request may result from changes in a broad array of programs or in only a single program. For

Table 2-3.
Defense Committee Changes to the President's Nuclear Weapons Budget,
FY 1969–1989

Fiscal Year	Request Initial*	HASC	SASC	HADS	SADS
1969	5,347	0	0	0	−6
1970	4,432	0	−4	−5	−8
1971	4,420	0	−3	−7	−3
1972	4,390	0	−4	−4	−3
1973	5,121	0	−10	−14	−12
1974	5,049	−4	−10	−17	−14
1975	4,806	−1	−4	−4	−7
1976	4,223	−4	−6	−6	−5
1977	6,196	+11	−1	−1	−2
1978‡	5,742	−3	−1	−7	−2
1979	5,137	−23	−22	−21	−28
1980	6,102	−4	−1	−4	−5
1981	7,479	−2	0	−5	0
1982	11,622	−10	−8	−11	−3
1983	18,389	−6	−10	−16	−16
1984	20,992	−10	−8	−15	−10
1985	23,401	−6	−5	−18	−5
1986	23,731	−15	−9	−23	−12
1987	21,322	−28	−13	−19	−17
1988	21,688	−11	−10	−25	−25
1989	13,953	−10	−4	−15	−10
1969–80†		−2	−6	−8	−8
1981–89‡		−11	−7	−16	−11

Note: All values are given as percentages. See table 2-1 for abbreviations

*Measured in millions of current dollars. All figures exclude requests for classified programs and include only requests for strategic research, development, testing, and evaluation, the Strategic Defense Initiative, and nuclear weapons procurement. All changes are measured against the president's initial budget request.

†Excludes funding requested for B-1 bomber and ancillary programs.

‡Figures given are averages.

Source: Data on initial budget requests are taken from two internal Department of Defense documents, *R, D, T, & E (R-1) Programs* and *Procurement Programs (P-1)*. Data on congressional changes are taken from two other internal DoD documents *FAD 726* (for the authorization bill) and *FAD 728* (for the appropriations bill), and committee reports. Information on individual line items is not available before fiscal year 1978.

example, the 11 percent funding increase HASC recommended in FY 1977 resulted almost solely from the decision to recommend accelerated construction of the Trident submarine. Similarly, percentage changes may be low either because the defense committees made few changes, or because they reduced and added funds in roughly equal amounts.

To establish the extent of Congress's intervention in the budget, table 2-4 presents data on the percentage of line-item entries for nuclear weapons that the defense committee recommended be changed. All the defense committees changed a sizable number of line items, and the number of budgetary changes grew over time. Although comparable data are not available for earlier years, none of the defense committees showed a similar zest for recommending changes in line items in the 1960s or early 1970s. In 1968, for example, the defense committees combined to recommend changes to only two nuclear weapons programs. By the mid-1980s many members of HASC and SASC had come to believe that the committees had become too involved in budgetary minutiae, and so both committees sought to limit the number of line items they changed in the defense budget.[45]

Besides subjecting DoD's budget requests to more scrutiny, the defense committees also increased their attempts to add programs to the defense budget. Between 1968 and 1979 none of the defense committees recommended that funds be added to the defense bill to establish a new program. Between 1980

Table 2-4.

Line-Item Changes Recommended by the Defense Committees to the President's Nuclear Weapons Budget, FY 1978–1989

		Percentage of Line Items Changed			
Fiscal Year	Number of Line Items	HASC	SASC	HADS	SADS
1978	90	9	11	24	20
1979	92	15	10	13	20
1980	101	21	8	24	25
1981	92	9	10	17	16
1982	91	13	18	24	25
1983	98	15	10	31	27
1984	102	16	15	24	22
1985	98	28	29	40	28
1986	103	31	19	36	44
1987	102	42	15	47	27
1988	103	17	11	39	37
1989	83	10	5	24	18

Source: See table 2-3.

Note: Values are given as percentages. See table 2-1 for abbreviations.

and 1988, though, the defense committees attempted to add thirty-six different programs to the budget. HASC and SASC were the most active in this regard; both attempted to add sixteen programs. Some add-ons addressed key components of the U.S. force structure. The Midgetman program is an obvious example. Other add-ons were less central. In 1982, for example, SASC recommended a new program to develop safety modifications for the Titan II, a missile DoD was seeking to decommission.

Longer committee hearings, more detailed committee reports, and intensified budget review do not necessarily mean that the defense committees' influence over the development of particular weapons systems actually increased. Congressional hearings may be more theater than substance. The services may ignore or finesse congressional directions. The growth in the percentage changes the defense committees recommended may reflect changes in the amount by which the services pad their requests in anticipation of budget cuts on Capitol Hill. The importance of committee activity is discussed in chapter 8. What remains is that in the 1970s and 1980s the defense committees increasingly intervened in nuclear weapons policy.

Why did the defense committees become more involved in nuclear weapons policy? One reason was the rise of the subcommittee system within the armed services committees. The subcommittee system created more actors with the authority to probe weapons programs. Under the leadership of Senator McIntyre, for example, SASC's Subcommittee on Research and Development combed the RDT&E budget with a zeal unknown in the 1960s. Similarly, HASC demonstrated greater interest in the details of the defense budget after Representative Price implemented the caucus-sponsored reforms. Over time more rigorous reviews of DoD plans became accepted as a norm for committee behavior.

The committees also spurred each other to greater activism.[46] As the armed services committees became more involved in program requests, the defense appropriations subcommittees did likewise out of necessity. If HADS and SADS had left the initiative to the authorizing committees, then the armed services committees would have become the major congressional actors on defense issues. The interest other congressional committees displayed in nuclear weapons also pushed the defense committees to greater activism. If the defense committees had not responded to encroachment on their turf, they would have risked losing their authority.

The third and most important reason for increased defense committee activity was growing floor pressure. At the beginning of the 1970s many in Congress believed that the defense committees rubber-stamped DoD requests. Representative Pike, himself a member of HASC, spoke for many of his colleagues when he said: "The House Armed Services Committee doesn't control the Pentagon; the Pentagon controls the House Armed Services Committee."[47] Faced with unprecedented floor opposition the defense committees had to become more critical of defense programs or lose control over defense policy. "Whatever instincts John Stennis may have had to energize the [Senate Armed Services] committee, they were undoubtedly reinforced by the fact that he inherited the chair at a moment when the committee, no less than the Pentagon itself, was beleaguered by critics."[48] HASC was the only defense committee to resist the floor pressure. It was also the only defense committee to have its chair removed. The chairs of the other defense committees almost certainly drew a lesson from this event.

Other Committees

Although the defense committees oversee DoD's requests for nuclear weapons, they are not the only congressional committees with an interest in nuclear weapons policy. At times, other committees play a role. Some of these committees have a clear jurisdictional interest in nuclear weapons policy. Others, however, interpret their mandates (sometimes quite broadly) to allow them to investigate nuclear weapons programs.

The Joint Committee on Atomic Energy (JCAE) long held responsibility for authorizing funds for nuclear warheads. Yet the committee rarely examined DoD requests. Rep. Chet Holifield (D-Calif.), who joined the committee at its inception in 1947, admitted as much during a committee hearing in 1974: "Over the years of existence of this committee we have not gone into the strategy of the use of weapons. . . . We have been a conduit, in a way, for funds going into a part of the Atomic Energy function which was put in there by law but *which we were not charged with the responsibility of sitting in judgment on*."[49] The JCAE and the armed services committees also did not coordinate their activities, even though several members sat on both committees. To justify its status as a separate standing committee, the JCAE consistently refused to allow members of the armed services committees (other than those who sat on the JCAE), or staff members of the armed services committees, to attend its meetings or hearings.[50] By 1977, however, congressional enthusiasm for the JCAE had waned and the committee was abolished. Jurisdiction over the military applications of nuclear energy was then transferred to the armed services committees.

The Senate Foreign Relations Committee has a strong and long-standing interest in nuclear issues. In 1968 the committee held hearings on the Sentinel ABM system, and committee members John Sherman Cooper (R-Ky.) and Philip Hart (D-Mich.) led the anti-ABM coalition. In the years following the ABM debate the Foreign Relations Committee held hearings on a wide variety of nuclear weapons topics, including MIRVs, counterforce targeting, strategic doctrine, and civil defense. In the 1980s the committee held the first congressional hearings on the arms control implications of ASAT weapons, and its members led the anti-ASAT coalition. Foreign Relations' interest in nuclear weapons owes partly to its responsibility for advising the Senate on the merits of treaties. The committee's interest also owes to its liberal, policy-oriented membership.[51] Senators on Foreign Relations traditionally are willing to uncover new policy issues, even at the risk of antagonizing SASC, as the debates over ABM and ASAT attest.

Before 1981 the House Foreign Affairs Committee showed far less interest in nuclear weapons than did its Senate counterpart. The House has no jurisdiction over treaties, and Rep. Thomas E. "Doc" Morgan (D-Pa.), who chaired Foreign Affairs until 1976, "was not an aggressive advocate of congressional involvement in foreign policy and generally supported the Administration position on the principle of 'bipartisanship.' "[52] In the 1980s, however, Foreign Affairs took greater interest in nuclear weapons issues. The committee's increased activism stemmed partly from changes in committee personnel; Morgan's successors as chair, Reps. Clement Zablocki (D-Wis.) and Dante Fascell (D-Fla.), were both less reticent to challenge the executive branch. At the same time, the transfer of control of the Senate to the Republicans in 1981 meant that the Democratic Party lost Foreign Relations as its most visible platform for advocating arms control. House Foreign Affairs was the obvious alternative. Yet the biggest stimulus to Foreign Affairs' activism was the politicization of nuclear weapons issues in the 1980s. In 1981 the committee held its first hearings on nuclear weapons in more than five years just one month after President Reagan unveiled his strategic force modernization program.

Other congressional committees occasionally hold hearings on nuclear weapons programs. These hearings usually are triggered by the emergence elsewhere of politically salient issues that touch on the jurisdiction of a particular committee. For example, after the release of the original "nuclear winter" study, the House Science and Technology Committee (HSTC) held hearings on the biological effects of nuclear war and the implications for strategic policy. Committees often will go to great lengths to interpret an issue as within their mandate. Sen. William Proxmire (D-Wis.), for example, justified a hearing on the MX missile by the Joint Economic Committee on the grounds that "the MX is a weapons system that could have a profound effect on our economy in many ways."[53]

The nondefense committees contribute to nuclear weapons policy by broadening the range of debate. By relying less on DoD testimony, they provide forums for airing views contrary to those held by officials in the executive branch. The reports the nondefense committees issue and request often view acquisition decisions from a different perspective than is the case in the defense committees. In 1975, for example, the SFRC and the HFAC convinced Congress to require that the executive branch submit an arms control impact statement

(ACIS) for any program with an overall cost of $250 million, an annual cost of $50 million, or technology with potential arms control implications. Although observers dispute the importance of the ACIS process, at a minimum the reporting requirement forced DoD to pay greater attention to arms control issues.[54]

Besides broadening congressional debate, the nondefense committees push the defense committees to review nuclear weapons programs more aggressively. The hawkishness of the defense committees tends to make them less critical of DoD. Yet the defense committees zealously guard their turf, and they are sensitive to charges that they rubber-stamp executive branch requests. When members of a nondefense committee investigate a weapons system, they develop expertise they can use to mount credible challenges to DoD plans. The defense committees usually are forced to respond. Thus, the defense committees initiated hearings on ABM, MIRV, and ASAT after each program became an issue elsewhere in Congress.

But the role of the nondefense committees should not be overstated. In the final analysis, Senate Foreign Relations, House Foreign Affairs, and other congressional committees exercise very limited influence over congressional decisions on nuclear weapons policy. The reason they lack influence is simple: the nondefense committees do not oversee budget requests for individual weapons programs. No matter how much attention they attract, the nondefense committees do not directly affect weapons development. As a former Senate staff member put it, "Sense-of-the-Senate resolutions are not the way to make policy."[55] Thus, when the House Foreign Affairs Committee approved a nuclear freeze resolution in 1983, Chairman Zablocki admitted on the floor that the bill would not prevent the development or production of nuclear weapons.[56] When the nondefense committees want to impose constraints on nuclear weapons programs, they inevitably turn to floor amendments to the annual defense authorization and appropriations bills. Thus while the efforts to block the development of MIRVed missiles and ASAT weapons and to limit nuclear weapons testing all originated outside the defense committees (and engendered several nonbinding House and Senate resolutions), the battles eventually shifted to the floor debates on the defense bills.

Conclusion

Review of the defense committees presents mixed results in terms of the deferential, parochial, and policy lenses. As the deferential lens predicts, members of the defense committees (with the exception of SADS) are more hawkish than nonmembers. A major prediction of the parochial lens, that legislators who represent constituencies with a greater than average stake in defense spending, are more likely to seek seats on the defense committees, holds for HASC but not for HADS, and there is not sufficient information on which to pass judgment on the Senate defense committees. Yet members appear to seek seats on HASC primarily because of the committee's jurisdiction over military bases and not because of its handling of defense contracts. Finally, the increased activism of the defense committees since the early 1960s lends some credence to the policy lens, but it remains to be seen (in chapter 6) what ends the new activism sought to accomplish.

3 ≫ ≪

The Floor

THE DEFENSE committees only recommend funding levels for DoD programs. The power to authorize and appropriate funds rests with the full House and Senate. But floor reviews vary in their thoroughness. In the 1960s legislators rarely challenged the defense committees. When members of Congress did take to the floor to overturn a committee recommendation, their amendments almost always met overwhelming defeat. In the late 1960s and early 1970s, however, events within and outside Congress combined to erode the institutional and normative barriers to floor debates. Legislators increasingly began to challenge the defense committees on nuclear weapons, and on numerous occasions succeeded in "rolling" the committees. By the 1980s protracted floor debates over nuclear weapons were commonplace.

The rise in amending activity changed the style of congressional decision making. In the 1960s Congress operated as an "inside game" on defense issues. The most senior members of the defense committees dominated the deliberations of the committees, and the committees in turn dominated Congress's deliberations. Rank-and-file legislators had virtually no influence over Congress's decisions. In the 1980s, however, an "outside game" emerged on Capitol Hill. Floor challenges became more frequent, and in several notable instances the floor overturned committee decisions. Although the defense committees remained major actors in Congress, the parent chambers had circumscribed their freedom of action.

Amendments

Table 3-1 shows the level of amending activity on nuclear weapons issues over three decades. Before 1968 members of Congress seldom debated nuclear weapons programs on the floor. Starting in 1968 both houses showed more interest in nuclear weapons programs. With some variation, more active floor debate persisted until the late 1970s when it dipped slightly. The decline stemmed from a deliberate decision by arms control advocates, who sponsored most of the amendments offered in the 1970s, not to challenge the defense com-

Table 3-1.
Nuclear Weapons Amendments to the Defense Authorization and
Appropriations Bills, 1961–1988

Year	Authorization Bills		Appropriations Bills	
	House	Senate	House	Senate
1961	1	0	0	1
1962	0	0	0	2
1963	0	1	0	1
1964	1	1	0	1
1965	0	0	0	0
1966	0	0	1	1
1967	0	0	0	0
1968	1	2	1	2
1969	4	5	1	1
1970	4	4	1	0
1971	4	9	0	0
1972	5	1	2	1
1973	3	2	0	4
1974	3	7	2	0
1975	3	7	0	3
1976	2	4	5	0
1977	1	1	1	2
1978	2	2	0	0
1979	6	1	0	3
1980	5	5	1	1
1981	5	5	4	11
1982	10	7	5	1
1983	10	16	3	6
1984	27	21	0	0
1985	34	21	1	0
1986	27	19	0	0
1987	27	28	0	0
1988	27	11	0	1

Note: The figures include all amendments, substitute amendments, and amendments to amendments on the subject of nuclear weapons that were offered and voted on. The figures do not include committee and technical amendments, amendments that were offered for consideration but subsequently withdrawn, or amendments that sought to cut defense spending across-the-board.

mittees during the early years of the Carter administration. Doves wanted to avoid losses on the floor because they feared legislative defeats would convince President Carter to reverse his commitment to restrain nuclear weapons acquisition.[1]

In the 1980s amending activity jumped severalfold. To some extent the increase is exaggerated. House and Senate rules allow members to use second-degree and substitute amendments to defeat or gut amendments.[2] So as amendments to the defense bills became commonplace, members began to use such parliamentary maneuvers to secure political advantages for themselves or to block their opponents. Nevertheless, the level of amending activity increased in the 1980s even after such parliamentary amendments are discounted.

The upward trend in nuclear weapons amendments was part of a broader trend in Congress toward greater amending activity.[3] A whole host of developments encouraged the trend. To begin with, the legislative agenda became more complex as governmental responsibilities, the number of interest groups, and the size of congressional staff all grew. At the same time, the new, more aggressive legislators who arrived on Capitol Hill in the late 1960s and early 1970s were more inclined to offer amendments. These members often found their policy goals blocked in committee and were forced to turn to the floor. Finally, an element of "follow-the-leader" was at work. As some members used amendments to obtain their political goals, others emulated the tactic.

Factors specific to defense policy also spurred floor debate. The Vietnam War encouraged the first spurt of amendment activity in the late 1960s. Congress previously had adopted a relatively passive attitude toward defense issues, largely because most members agreed on the goals of national security.[4] The debacle in southeast Asia shattered the consensus. By the end of the 1960s, many members openly criticized the military, something unthinkable only five years earlier. New candidates rode public disillusionment with the war into office. Moreover, stories of immense cost overruns and program mismanagement, particularly the air force's problems with the C-5A transport plane, grabbed national headlines. The tales of Pentagon ineptitude further damaged the military's claim to expertise on defense issues and strengthened the cause of DoD's critics.

While the Vietnam War encouraged floor amendments in the late 1960s, increased public fears of nuclear war stimulated amending activity in the 1980s. In response to the Gallup question "What do you think is the most important problem facing the nation?" (hereafter MIP), neither nuclear war nor nuclear weapons emerged as an issue with those polled between 1968 and 1981.[5] In March 1982, however, 5 percent of the respondents to the MIP question gave answers that suggested they were concerned about nuclear war. The proportion of the public that feared nuclear war continued to rise throughout 1983 before peaking in late November at 27 percent.[6] Also, the freeze movement, which sought a mutual and verifiable moratorium on the production of nuclear weapons by the two superpowers, mushroomed in the early 1980s.[7] Public fear of nuclear war declined after 1983, but it remained a major issue with some Americans.

The primary reason for increased fear of nuclear war was Ronald Reagan's presidency; the new president broke with his predecessors, both Democrat and Republican, on the need for arms control.

Never before had a modern American president entered office so publicly opposed to arms control, so committed to an arms buildup. Mr. Reagan's anti-Soviet and nuclear war remarks ranged from the inflammatory to the outrageous. On the campaign trail he referred to Russians as "monsters" whose goal was to spread "Godless communism." He flirted with the idea of a preemptive first strike and ventured that nuclear war could be survivable. He promised a "housecleaning" of arms control advocates in the State Department. He pledged to accelerate an arms race to make the United States militarily superior to the Soviet Union and to bring the Russian bear to its knees at the negotiating table.[8]

Reagan's aides were even more bellicose in their talk of "limited" and "protracted" wars; T. K. Jones, a deputy undersecretary of defense, gained national notoriety when he claimed the United States could survive a nuclear war "if there are enough shovels to go around."[9]

Did the upswing in amending activity in the 1980s simply reflect position taking, as legislators sought to take stands on an issue important to constituents?[10] Distinguishing whether legislators offer amendments for position-taking or policy reasons is problematic; every amendment offers the opportunity to take a stand that pleases constituents, and members may offer amendments to accomplish both policy and position-taking ends. Even so, position-taking amendments no doubt became more common in the 1980s as nuclear weapons became politically salient. To take one example, every year from 1982 to 1985, Sen. Arlen Specter (R-Pa.) sponsored an amendment that urged President Reagan to meet with the leader of the Soviet Union to discuss arms control. Each year the Senate overwhelmingly adopted the motion. Many of the senators who supported the Specter amendment probably believed a summit was needed (or at least that it would not hurt U.S. interests) and thought that the motion would increase pressure on the president to meet his Soviet counterpart. Yet the amendment also was a useful vehicle for senators to balance their support for weapons programs with a vote in support of arms reduction.

As the level of amending activity rose after 1968, the House and Senate did not always display the same level of interest in nuclear weapons. Between 1968 and 1975 the Senate debated nearly 50 percent more amendments (forty-eight versus thirty-four) than the House, even though there are more than four times as many representatives as senators. There also were dramatic differences in the length of the defense debates in the two chambers during this period. Between 1968 and 1975 the Senate spent an average of fourteen days each year considering the defense authorization bill, while the House devoted on average only two days to reviewing its version of the bill.[11]

One possible explanation for the different environments the armed services committees faced on the floor during the early 1970s is that the House was more hawkish than the Senate. Yet both HASC and SASC were much more hawkish than their parent chambers. Moreover, both the House and Senate included among their members critics of DoD. Given that there were few constraints on amendment activity in the House—HASC consistently reported the defense authorization bill under an open rule that made virtually any amendment germane—House defense critics did not face greater formal obstacles to offering amendments than did their counterparts in the Senate.

The differences in House and Senate amending activity in the late 1960s and early 1970s instead reflected the differences in their attachments to the norm of committee specialization. By tradition, the Senate accords debate a special status, even though the defense committees disliked floor challenges and often sought to discourage them. Sen. Barry Goldwater (R-Ariz.), for example, complained in 1971 that "what this whole question boils down to has been a succession of amendments that, frankly, have questioned the ability, the sincerity, and sometimes even the honesty of the Committee on Armed Services. I take that personally, and I do not like it."[12] Still, in keeping with tradition, SASC's critics were accommodated; the 1969 ABM debate lasted twenty-nine days, at that time the sixth longest Senate debate in the postwar era.

The norm of committee specialization was stronger in the House. Even though HASC consistently reported its bill under an open rule, until the mid-1970s HASC commanded so much respect it generally could convince rank-and-file members to restrict debate. This occurred even when many members desired otherwise. During debate on the FY 1970 defense authorization bill, for example, "the chamber rang with shouts of 'shame,' 'outrage,' and 'gag rule' as opponents of the military programs and Committee procedures protested the limit on their arguments."[13] As a result of this deference to committee leadership, the 1969 House ABM debate lasted only two days.

House amending activity caught up with the Senate in the late 1970s, and between 1980 and 1988 the House actually debated more amendments (186 versus 153). Two factors explain the change. One was that by the end of the 1970s HASC finally lost its privileged position on the floor. The other was that from 1981 through 1986 control of the Senate rested with the Republicans, who were both more attuned ideologically to the hawkish positions SASC staked out and more inclined to support a Republican president. Because hawks were a clear majority in the Senate during this period they had less need than their counterparts in the House to use second-degree and substitute amendments to defeat challenges to DoD's plans. Whenever senators (usually Democrats) offered floor amendments to cut Pentagon spending, the hawkish majority typically just voted them down.

Differences also exist in the levels of amending activity on the authorization and appropriations bills (see table 3-1). Most amendments are offered during consideration of the defense authorization bill. Several factors explain this. One is that the authorization bill comes first in the legislative process, so if an amendment is attached to the bill, there generally is no need to reintroduce it when the appropriations bill comes to the floor. Conversely, when an amendment to the authorization bill is rejected, members often decline to offer it during the appropriations cycle because the disposition of votes is already known. Moreover, amendments containing legislative language can be ruled out of order when the appropriations bill is under consideration. Finally, the appropriations bill generally comes to the floor at the end of the legislative session when members do not have time for protracted debates.

The lack of debate on the appropriations bill, however, did not mean that HADS and SADS acted independently of their parent chambers. Because the authorization bill limits what funds may be appropriated, authorization debates influenced the appropriations subcommittees. Nor did the lack of amending activity mean that those amendments offered were irrelevant. During consideration of the FY 1983 defense appropriations bill, for instance, the House and the Senate adopted amendments that barred the obligation of funds to initiate full-scale engineering development of a basing mode for the MX missile and prohibited any flight testing until both chambers had agreed in a concurrent resolution. The amendments pushed the Reagan administration to establish the President's Commission on Strategic Forces (the Scowcroft Commission) to review the status of the U.S. ICBM force.

Finally, as table 3-2 shows, most amendments seek either to cut weapons spending or to restrict weapons development. Since the committees generally support DoD's plans, this means floor challenges typically attack the executive branch's nuclear weapons plans. Few amendments seek to increase spending. Such a pattern of amending activity is a natural result of the hawkishness of the defense committees. Administration supporters are unlikely to find much to object to in the bill when it emerges from the defense committees. The negativism of floor activity also is not particular to any administration; amendments to reduce spending far outnumbered amendments to increase spending in both the 1970s and 1980s.

The one area where the nature of amending activity changed dramatically was in report and policy statement amendments. These types of amendments only became common in the 1980s; 91 percent of the report amendments and 96 percent of the policy statement amendments were offered after 1980. The fact that report and policy statement amendments proliferated during a period in which public fear of nuclear war grew suggests that these motions had a high position-taking content. Moreover, the Senate considered more report and policy statement amendments than the House did. This agrees with David Mayhew's argument about position taking: "Senators, with their access to the media, seem to put more emphasis on position taking than House members."[14]

Table 3-2.
Objectives of Nuclear Weapons Amendments to the Defense Authorization and Appropriations Bills, 1968–1988

House

Amendment Objective	Authorization	Appropriations
Reduce Funds	81	23
Add Funds	14	1
Restriction	67	2
Request Report	15	0
Policy Statement	13	0
Miscellaneous	20	1

Senate

Amendment Objective	Authorization	Appropriations
Reduce Funds	44	14
Add Funds	15	5
Restriction	37	7
Request Report	27	2
Policy Statement	37	5
Miscellaneous	18	3

Note: The figures are for amendments Congress voted on. Where amendments had multiple goals, one was judged to be primary after review of the debate. *Reduce Funds* and *Add Funds* are self-explanatory. *Restriction* refers to amendments that would limit work on a weapon. *Request Report* covers amendments that require the executive to file a report with Congress. *Policy Statement* covers amendments that state attitudes on nuclear weapons and arms control. *Miscellaneous* counts amendments that do not fall into any of the other categories.

Pressure

A review of the level of amending activity captures only part of the role the full House and Senate play in decision making. It is equally important to know the extent to which the parent chambers influence the recommendations the defense committees make. Congress operates heavily on the principle of "anticipated reactions."[15] "The Hill is totally success-oriented in measuring power and influence. . . . Whatever else the committee and its staff accomplish, they must draw up legislation that will be approved. Defeats on the floor for whatever reason must be avoided like the plague."[16] When the House and Senate routinely defeat amendments by large margins, the defense committees are free to report bills as they see fit. Conversely, when the House and Senate demonstrate that they will reverse committee decisions, the defense committees have an incentive to incorporate strongly held floor views into their recommendations. To do anything else would risk having the bill written on the floor, thereby making the committee irrelevant.

The debate over the Safeguard ABM system illustrates the role of anticipated reactions. In 1970 SASC considered a motion by Sen. Edward Brooke (R-Mass.) to limit Safeguard to two sites instead of the eight requested. The Brooke proposal enjoyed substantial support on the floor. Most members of SASC opposed the motion, however, fearing that it would undermine the entire ABM program. They prevailed upon Sen. Howard Cannon (D-Nev.) to offer a motion to delete without prejudice the funds for four of the eight sites. This left open the possibility of funding all eight sites in future years.

> Knowing that the Brooke scheme presented a credible alternative to the Administration's recommendation, the pro-Safeguard committee majority felt obliged to make some movement toward accommodation on the issue. The chairman and his allies were aware, of course, that any proposal they sent to the floor would come under attack. . . . For the Armed Services Committee leadership, therefore, the palatable middle ground lay with the Cannon amendment. . . . By adopting Senator Cannon's amendment, the committee was able to ward off the more far-reaching Brooke provision and to improve its position for justifying the committee recommendation as a reasonable compromise which did not go as far as the Administration had recommended.[17]

The full Senate narrowly rejected the Brooke amendment. Aware its parent chamber would insist on the Cannon amendment, SASC convinced HASC to fund only four Safeguard sites. Thus even though Senator Brooke lost his battle, his actions forced SASC to modify the administration's plans.

With the importance of anticipated reactions in mind, then, table 3-3 shows the "contestedness" of amending activity. Floor pressure on the defense committees clearly increased in the 1970s and 1980s. During the 1960s contested amendments were rare in both the House and Senate. In the 1970s, however, HASC and SASC faced different environments on the floor. Contested amendments remained uncommon in the House, where only 12 percent of the amendments offered between 1970 and 1979 resulted in votes split 60–40 or closer. In the Senate, however, contested amendments were more common, with 34 percent of the amendments between 1970 and 1979 being contested.

House floor debates became much more heated in the 1980s. Contested votes jumped in both absolute and relative terms; compared to the 1970s the absolute number of contested House votes recorded between 1980 and 1988 jumped more than twelvefold, and the number of contested amendments rose to 30 percent of all amendments. The increased contestedness of House floor debates stripped HASC of its previous position of unchallenged supremacy. The percentage of contested amendments declined somewhat in the Senate, drop-

Table 3-3.
Contestedness of Nuclear Weapons Amendments to the Defense Authorization Bill, 1968–1988

| Year | House | | Senate | |
	Number of Contested Amendments	Number of Voice & Unanimous Votes	Number of Contested Amendments	Number of Voice & Unanimous Votes
1961	0	0	0	0
1962	0	1	0	0
1963	0	0	0	0
1964	0	0	0	1
1965	0	0	0	0
1966	0	0	0	0
1967	0	0	0	0
1968	0	0	1	0
1969	0	1	2	0
1970	1	0	2	1
1971	0	1	2	3
1972	1	2	1	0
1973	0	2	1	0
1974	0	1	1	3
1975	1	1	3	1
1976	1	0	3	0
1977	0	0	0	1
1978	0	1	0	2
1979	0	4	0	1
1980	0	1	2	2
1981	1	3	1	3
1982	2	3	1	4
1983	3	3	4	7
1984	10	12	5	13
1985	4	25	4	9
1986	10	13	4	10
1987	10	8	5	18
1988	11	4	4	6

Note: An amendment is defined as contested if it was subjected to a division, teller, or roll call vote *and* the outcome was split 60–40 or closer.

ping to 23 percent of all amendments. Still, in absolute terms SASC faced more contested votes in the 1980s than it had in the 1970s.

The changes in the contestedness of amending activity correspond to the degree to which the armed services committees pared the president's initial budget requests. During most of the 1970s, SASC recommended far larger budget reductions than HASC did (see table 2-3). During these years SASC faced substantial floor pressure while its counterpart in the House did not. Conversely, in the 1980s, HASC faced greater pressure from its parent chamber and it recommended deeper budget cuts. Moreover, in the 1980s both HASC and SASC recommended dollar reductions in nuclear weapons funding that were sizable when compared to budgetary changes they recommended in the 1970s. Once again, both committees faced as much if not more floor pressure in the 1980s as they had in the previous decade. In short, the armed services committees (and the defense appropriations committees indirectly) did pay attention to sentiments on the floor.

Yet contested amendments did not grow as fast as the number of amendments that passed on voice or unanimous votes. The increase in voice and unanimous votes partly reflects the growing number of position-taking amendments in the 1980s. Many amendments targeted "Apple Pie" themes or other uncontroversial issues. Voice and unanimous votes also increased because the defense committees were under greater pressure from the floor. The defense committees often accepted amendments they did not like because they believed the motion might win if it were taken to a vote. Thus Sen. Sam Nunn (D-Ga.) complained: "The House and Senate tend to accept floor amendments rather than take them on and defeat them."[18]

If floor amendments became more contested after 1968, they also became more successful, as table 3-4 demonstrates. Successful floor challenges were rare in the 1960s, and they became only slightly more common in the 1970s. As with the level of amending activity, the Senate defense committees found themselves under more pressure than their counterparts in the House. The Senate adopted its first nuclear weapons amendment in 1970, and it accepted 33 percent of all the amendments offered to the authorization and appropriations bills between 1970 and 1979. In contrast, no one successfully challenged either of the House bills until 1976, and the House adopted only 16 percent of the amendments brought before it between 1970 and 1979. The fate of floor amendments changed, however, in the early 1980s. In both chambers the number of successful amendments exploded in both absolute and relative terms. To some extent the rise in successful amendments was exaggerated by the increased use of second-degree and substitute amendments. When these parliamentary maneuvers succeed the amended version of the original amendment is usually adopted. Even when overcounting is eliminated, however, the number of successful amendments still rose.

Although amending activity became both more contested and more likely to succeed in the 1970s and 1980s, table 3-5 shows that Congress did not treat all amendments alike. (The figures for amendments to appropriations bills are excluded because of their relative infrequency.) All of the report amendments and most of the policy statement amendments were adopted. Moreover, the report

Table 3-4.
Success of Nuclear Weapons Amendments to the Defense Authorization and Appropriations Bills, 1961–1988.

Year	Authorization Bills		Appropriations Bills	
	House	Senate	House	Senate
1961	0	0	0	0
1962	0	0	0	0
1963	0	1	0	0
1964	0	0	0	0
1965	0	0	0	0
1966	0	0	0	0
1967	0	0	0	0
1968	0	0	0	0
1969	0	0	0	0
1970	0	1	0	0
1971	0	1	0	0
1972	0	0	0	0
1973	0	0	0	3
1974	0	2	0	0
1975	0	1	0	1
1976	0	1	3	0
1977	0	1	0	1
1978	1	2	0	0
1979	3	1	0	2
1980	1	2	0	0
1981	1	4	0	3
1982	4	5	3	1
1983	3	9	0	3
1984	15	16	0	0
1985	23	13	0	0
1986	15	12	0	0
1987	12	21	0	0
1988	16	6	0	0

Note: The figures include all amendments, amendments to amendments, and substitute amendments on nuclear weapons that were voted on. The figures do not include committee and technical amendments, amendments that were offered for consideration but subsequently withdrawn, or amendments that sought to cut defense spending across-the-board.

and policy statements were nearly always adopted on a voice vote, another sign that much of the amending activity in the 1980s involved position taking. In contrast to report and policy statement amendments, very few reduction amendments passed, and those that did usually precipitated contested votes. Even the limited success for reduction amendments did not develop until the

Table 3-5.
Success of Nuclear Weapons Amendments to the Defense Authorization Bill
by Objective, 1968–1988

Amendment Objective	Number That Were Successful	As % of Those That Were Offered	Number That Were Contested	Number Adopted on Voice Vote
House				
Reduce Funds	13	16%	12	1
Add funds	6	43	0	6
Restriction	39	58	14	21
Request report	15	100	0	15
Policy statement	12	92	1	11
Miscellaneous	10	50	1	9
Senate				
Reduce funds	4	9%	1	2
Add funds	7	47	0	5
Restriction	19	51	3	15
Request report	27	100	0	25
Policy statement	29	78	0	19
Miscellaneous	11	61	0	10

1980s; sixteen of the seventeen successful reduction amendments were adopted after 1982. Restriction amendments fared better, with roughly half gaining congressional approval, but they did not do nearly as well as report and policy statement amendments. The greater resistance to reduction and restriction amendments no doubt occurred because they do constrain weapons development thus, the armed services committees generally fought these measures.

Finally, SASC was more successful than HASC in rebuffing floor attempts to reduce spending. SASC fared better because Republicans controlled the Senate in the 1980s when virtually all of the reduction amendments passed. Because most Senate Republicans felt a responsibility to defend a Republican president's agenda, and because many of them were hawks, SASC could count on a majority to support its bill. Democrats controlled the House, and they had no party allegiance to President Reagan. As a result, HASC had to defend its bill in a more hostile environment.

Changing Games

In the 1970s and 1980s the defense committees and the parent chambers all became much more active on nuclear weapons issues. The defense committees held more hearings, requested more reports, and recommended more changes to DoD's budget proposals. The floor debated more amendments on nuclear weapons programs, and at times it overruled the defense committees. But what did the changes in committee and floor behavior mean for the nature of *congressional* decision making on nuclear weapons policy?

During the 1960s congressional activity on nuclear weapons acquisition issues, and defense policy more generally, was an inside game, a closed decision-making style with relatively few participants. Congressional rules gave the chairs of the defense committees the power to create subcommittees, set committee agendas, choose committee staff, and manage defense bills on the floor. Congressional norms held that junior members would see their role as an apprenticeship and defer to committee leaders. Floor challenges were infrequent, and when they did occur they garnered little support. As a result, the senior members of the defense committees for all intents and purposes made the decisions for Congress on nuclear weapons issues.

The ABM debate was the first major challenge to the inside game. Although several members of the defense committees joined the anti-ABM coalition, the debate was initiated and led by senators who did not sit on either SASC or SADS. The ABM debate ultimately culminated in a fifty to fifty vote in the Senate. The anti-ABM movement, however, made no progress in the House. HASC and HADS defeated moves to extend debate on Safeguard, and anti-ABM amendments never garnered the support of more than a quarter of the representatives.

The ABM debate also did not translate immediately into a willingness to challenge the defense committees on other programs. Congress's failure to scrutinize the MIRV program illustrates the point.[19] Senator Brooke, a junior member of SASC, first brought the MIRV issue to the attention of his colleagues in 1969. He argued that in the long term MIRV would be more destabilizing than ABM because MIRV technology would eventually enable the Soviets to destroy the U.S. ICBM force while using only a fraction of their own ICBMs. Despite Brooke's trenchant criticisms, few in Congress wanted to mount an anti-MIRV campaign. Many ABM opponents agreed that MIRV was destabilizing, but they believed that attacking MIRV would divert attention from the Safeguard fight. Some also thought that the MIRV program helped win votes in the battle to block Safeguard. One of the reasons the Nixon administration justified proceeding with MIRV development was that MIRVs would enable the United States to overwhelm any strategic defense the Soviet Union might erect. Faced with these sentiments, Brooke's only success came in April

1970 when the Senate adopted a nonbinding resolution that urged the Nixon administration to halt MIRV testing unilaterally. Still, because Congress did not order MIRV development delayed, Senator Brooke's resolution was, as President Nixon put it, "irrelevant."[20]

In the 1970s congressional decision making shifted toward a decentralized variant of the inside game. The greater power of the armed services subcommittees, modest increases in staff size, and intercommittee competition all pushed the defense committees into deeper examinations of the budget requests for nuclear weapons. Again, the House lagged behind the Senate. Despite these changes, however, the defense committees continued to support administration requests. Moreover, despite the weakened powers of the committee chairs, the locus of congressional influence over nuclear weapons policy remained within the defense committees. Nuclear weapons drew more attention on the floor, but the defense committees almost always sustained their positions. Between 1970 and 1979 the House and Senate adopted only one amendment over committee objections that reduced weapons funding. The exception was an amendment offered in 1977 by Sen. John Stennis (D-Miss.), chair of SADS, to approve President Carter's decision to cancel the B-1 bomber.

The controversy over nuclear counterforce programs illustrates the changed nature of congressional debate in the 1970s. In January 1974 Secretary of Defense James Schlesinger announced the United States had altered its targeting policy to include Soviet military facilities. (The United States had targeted Soviet military installations since the early 1950s, but the Nixon administration was the first to develop a doctrine for targeting military posts.)[21] To make counterforce targeting feasible, the defense budget requested $77 million to initiate three programs for improving missile accuracy. The shift to counterforce targeting marked a major shift in U.S. strategic doctrine that caused some consternation in Congress. Less than three years earlier the Nixon administration had publicly disavowed one senator's effort to increase the counterforce capability of the Minuteman III and Poseidon missiles because the improvements "could reasonably be construed by the Soviets as having a first-strike capability."[22]

As happened with ABM, the Senate took the lead in scrutinizing counterforce programs. Within two months of Schlesinger's announcement, the Foreign Relations Committee held hearings on the foreign policy implications of the new doctrine, and SASC's Subcommittee on Research and Development held hearings on the $77 million request. The Research and Development subcommittee denied the funds, but it was overruled in full committee. In the House the Foreign Affairs Committee did not hold hearings on the counterforce doctrine, and HASC routinely approved the budget request.

After the armed services committees approved the $77 million request, counterforce critics shifted their attention to the floor debate on the authorization bill. Although several members of the Foreign Relations Committee opposed the new doctrine, they refused to sponsor an amendment because they "were unwilling 'to take on Senators Tower and Jackson' on this issue."[23] Senators Brooke and Thomas McIntyre (D-N.H.), both members of SASC, eventually offered an amendment. After a vigorous debate that included a secret session to discuss classified information, the Senate rejected the Brooke-McIntyre provision by a vote of 48 to 37. The House rejected a similar amendment by a 370 to 34 margin. In 1975 and 1976 other amendments were offered to cancel or delay the counterforce programs, but the motions were defeated by similar margins. Counterforce warheads were developed despite the controversy in Congress.

In the 1980s the balance of power between the defense committees and the floor changed again as an outside game emerged in Congress. Much of the congressional activity on nuclear weapons issues bypassed the traditional committee system. Unlike preceding decades, nonmembers mounted credible challenges to the positions taken by the defense committees. In both chambers, and especially in the House, the floor accepted amendments to reduce the funding levels the defense committees had recommended for nuclear weapons. Moreover, the increased contestedness of amending activity forced the defense committees into more aggressive reviews of the defense budget.

The most visible example of the outside game in the 1980s was the MX debate. The defense committees, which supported President Reagan's decision to deploy MX missiles in existing Minuteman missile silos, failed to convince the full House and Senate to support fixed silo basing. With the program teetering on the edge of outright cancellation by Congress, leading members of HASC and SASC convinced the administration to create the Scowcroft Commission to review the status of the U.S. land-based missile force. The decision to throw the MX problem to a presidential commission tacitly recognized that Congress's specialized committee system could not handle the missile basing issue.[24] The Scowcroft Commission eventually recommended the deployment of one hundred MX missiles in fixed silos and the development of the Midgetman single-warhead missile. The defense committees, however, failed to sustain the commission's recommendations on the number of MX. In 1985 Congress capped the number of MX in fixed silos at fifty, even though all four defense committees supported full procurement.

Other examples illustrate how the floor curbed the power of the defense committees. The armed services and appropriations committees initially supported acquisition of a satellite interceptor. Under pressure from the floor, however, Congress banned tests of ASAT weapons against targets in space. The curb derailed development of the program. The floor also repeatedly reduced funding for SDI. And, as the data on the contestedness of the floor debates show (see table 3-3), the defense committees' decisions received greater scrutiny in the 1980s than ever before. Since the defense committees had their recommendations reversed in the 1980s for the first time, they had much greater incentives to incorporate floor views into the bills they reported.

The outside game advanced further in the House. There the Democratic Caucus played the key role. Throughout much of its history, the caucus was relatively inactive on legislative issues.[25] In the 1960s it met only at the start of each Congress to elect the House leadership. In the late 1960s, however, liberals seized on the caucus as the mechanism with which to attack the centralized decision-making process on Capitol Hill, and most of the major reforms adopted in the 1970s were developed by a committee of the caucus. The caucus also took stands on several legislative issues; though, with the exception Vietnam, it refrained from involvement in defense policy. The caucus drifted toward inactivity in the late 1970s, only to be revitalized by the results of the 1980 elections. With Republicans in control of the Senate, House Democrats found that coordinated action was needed to respond to President Reagan's policy initiatives.

The newly aggressive caucus first turned to nuclear weapons issues in 1983 during the controversy over the MX. In May the House voted 239 to 186 to release funds for flight testing of the MX, which Congress had "fenced" the previous December. In the May vote, Speaker Thomas P. "Tip" O'Neill (D-Mass.) was the only member of the House Democratic leadership to oppose the program. In a caucus meeting held shortly thereafter, MX opponents castigated the Democratic leadership for breaking with the majority sentiment of House Democrats. Some spoke privately of working to unseat members of the leadership who supported the missile in the future.[26] This veiled threat apparently had its intended effect. In another MX vote in July, only Majority Whip Thomas S. Foley (D-Wash.) voted to build the missile. In May 1984, however, he joined the rest of the House Democratic leadership in active opposition to the MX.[27]

The caucus's more aggressive posture did not stop with the MX controversy. In the early 1980s, many doves and moderates began to complain that HASC was too hawkish and too eager to concede House positions in conference negotiations with the Senate. In an unprecedented move in 1984, the caucus forced Rep. Melvin Price (D-Ill.), the chair of HASC, to accept dozens of special delegates to the House-Senate conference on the authorization bill. Each "bullet vote" conferee was responsible for defending the House position on one or two issues, in effect wresting responsibility from HASC for negotiating with the Senate.

Emboldened by its success, the caucus removed Price as chair of HASC in January 1985. It took this unusual step despite the active opposition of the House leadership. Despite the leadership's intense pro-Price lobbying, many House Democrats believed that his age and declining health had left the committee leaderless. Unlike the removal of Representative Hebert a decade earlier, however, the decision on Price's successor reflected ideological concerns.

In violation of the cherished norm of seniority, the caucus passed over the next five ranking Democrats, all of whom had decidedly hawkish records, to make Rep. Les Aspin (D-Wis.) the new chair. The choice sent the unmistakable signal that House Democrats wanted the chair of HASC to be closer to the mainstream of the Democratic Party.

After removing Price, the caucus kept a close watch on Aspin. It quickly voiced displeasure with his handling of several defense issues; in caucus meetings in 1985, doves upbraided Aspin for his support of the MX and for failing to defend the House's position in conference.[28] The MX issue was especially acrimonious as several members charged that Aspin had broken a promise, made while he was seeking votes to oust Price, to oppose further MX funding. Discontent with Aspin's performance continued to rise, and in mid-1986 Rep. Marvin Leath (D-Tex.), a hawk who ranked fourteenth in committee seniority, announced he would challenge Aspin for the chair of HASC. Leath drew support from an odd coalition of doves and hawks disillusioned (for different reasons) with Aspin.

The rising dissatisfaction of the caucus impressed Aspin. In the 1986 defense authorization debate he sponsored a package of nuclear weapons amendments previously sponsored by doves. Aspin's leadership helped several of the amendments win House approval. To restrict the power of the hawkish members of HASC in conference negotiations, Speaker O'Neill, backed by the caucus, appointed a set of exclusive conferees to negotiate with the Senate on the various arms control provisions. O'Neill could appoint exclusive conferees because the Speaker of the House has unassailable power to appoint the conferees and House "rules and precedents require that a majority of the conferees must have 'generally supported' the bill."[29] The exclusive conferees, who effectively constituted a negotiating body independent of the standard House conferees, were moderate and dovish members drawn from both HASC and the full House; hawkish members of HASC were deliberately excluded because they opposed the arms control provisions in the House bill.

Despite Aspin's attempt to rebuild his ties to doves and moderates, the caucus removed him as chair of HASC in January 1987. After two weeks in political purgatory and a confession of his errors to the assembled caucus, Aspin won reappointment to the chair. Still, the caucus kept Aspin and HASC under scrutiny. When the House passed the FY 1988 defense authorization bill, the new speaker, Rep. Jim Wright (D-Tex.), followed former Speaker O'Neill's precedent and appointed a set of exclusive conferees, again consisting of several moderate-to-dovish members drawn from both HASC and the full House, to negotiate with the Senate on arms control matters. The House moved away from using exclusive conferees in subsequent years, but the lesson was not lost on members of HASC.

The intervention of the caucus into affairs previously considered to be

HASC's rightful domain had clear implications for members of HADS. The subcommittee generally avoided reopening issues where the floor had overturned HASC, and instead chose to incorporate the legislative provisions agreed to in the House version of the authorization bill into its report on the defense appropriations bill.[30] This occurred even though more often than not a majority of the members of HADS agreed with the positions that the Armed Services Committee had staked out and though the chair of HADS passed in 1986 to the hawkish Rep. William Chappell (D-Fla.) on the death of the dovish Rep. Joseph Addabbo (D-N.Y.). Members of HADS privately admitted that they kept HASC's problems with the caucus in mind when marking up the appropriations bill.[31] At the same time, the growing use of continuing resolutions (CRs) in the 1980s curbed the power of hawkish members of HADS. When defense appropriations bills are incorporated into a CR the conferees are drawn not from HADS but from the entire Appropriations Committee, and these members tend to be more dovish.[32] For both reasons, then, HADS maintained much better relations with the caucus than did HASC.

The outside game did not develop to the same extent in the Senate that it did in the House. The Senate defense committees suffered fewer reverses on the floor. Unlike their counterparts in the House, SASC and SADS could count on a coalition of Republicans and hawkish Democrats to sustain most of their positions. Nonetheless, because many of the amendments on nuclear weapons were bitterly contested in the Senate, the ability of SASC and SADS to insist on their positions in conference was weaker than it would have been otherwise. This was one of the reasons, for example, that the Senate defense committees could not force the House to accept their positions on the procurement of one hundred MX and continued testing of ASAT weapons.

The Senate also never produced an analog to the House Democratic Caucus. This failure reflected the more individualistic nature of life in the Senate. An administrative assistant to a senior member of SASC commented: "There's a lot more of an ego problem over here, and a bit less of a willingness to fall in behind a leader. They're bigger players over here. They make louder sounds when they walk. Some senator wants to offer an amendment and another doesn't like some of the language or says he wants to offer it."[33] Although business in the Senate was always more individualistic than in the House, individualism accelerated in the 1970s and 1980s. As demands on each senator's time increased, they frequently used their personal staff to communicate with their colleagues. A decline in collaboration resulted.[34]

Although the appearance of the outside game is important, it did not make the defense committees irrelevant. The committees remained the most powerful congressional actors on defense issues. The size of the defense budget precluded the floor debate from addressing most of their decisions. Further, members of the defense committees still carried extra weight in debates because many legislators continued to see them as "experts" on defense policy. None-theless, the outside game ended the hegemony the defense committees long wielded on nuclear weapons issues in Congress.

Conclusion

The review of floor activity lends support to the policy lens. Although the defer-ential lens explains why the floor seldom debated nuclear weapons in the 1960s, it offers little insight into the dramatic rise of amending activity in the 1970s and 1980s. The parochial lens also does not account for the floor's newfound enthu-siasm for debating nuclear weapons policy. Most amendments in both the House and Senate seek to reduce spending on these weapons rather than to increase it. The policy lens offers a plausible explanation for the floor's in-creased attempts to shape the nuclear force acquisition process. Simply put, the floor became more involved in decision making because a considerable number of members wanted to change the direction of U.S. nuclear weapons policy.

4 ≫ ≪

Selected Cases

CONGRESS'S ACTIVITY ON nuclear weapons policy increased in the 1970s and 1980s. That much is clear. But how did congressional activism affect the development of individual weapons systems? What follows are brief histories of Congress's deliberations on the MX missile (1974–85), the Trident submarine (1968–74), the Pershing II missile (1974–83), and the ASAT program (1977–88). These four weapons systems are not representative of congressional decision making in a strict sense—we do not know which weapons programs are most typical of how Congress acts. But the MX, Trident, Pershing, and ASAT programs are balanced along several dimensions that might influence congressional decision making. The weapons represent all three services, different price tags, and different levels of salience among the mass public. Moreover, all four weapons entered development after 1968 and essentially completed production by 1990, making it possible to examine Congress's actions across the entire life cycle of each weapons system.

The MX, Trident, Pershing, and ASAT programs illustrate several broader lessons about Congress's handling of nuclear weapons policy. One is that Congress does not give all weapons the same amount of attention. While MX and ASAT encountered tremendous opposition on Capitol Hill, Trident and Pershing II enjoyed strong congressional support. Another lesson is that the full House and Senate are more skeptical of DoD programs than are the defense committees. The battles against the MX and ASAT programs were fought on the floor and not in committee. Last, Congress is not a synoptic decision maker that carefully reviews each weapons proposal as it emerges from the Pentagon. Legislators generally do not intervene in nuclear weapons policy until relatively late in the development of individual weapons systems.

MX

The MX missile program dates back to the air force's search in the late 1960s for a missile to succeed the Minuteman ICBM. Because Minuteman was relatively new, research on a successor missile remained a low priority until the early

1970s. During this time, however, the air force established two criteria that would govern the MX program. First, the missile would carry more warheads, each with a greater ability to destroy hardened targets (so-called hard target capability), than Minuteman. Second, MX would be less vulnerable to Soviet missiles. Since the air force had given up on "superhardening" silos, the MX would use some type of mobile basing scheme.

In 1973 the MX gained a patron in newly appointed Secretary of Defense James Schlesinger, a proponent of counterforce targeting. MX, with its promise of greater hard target kill capability, fit the new strategic doctrine perfectly. In 1974 Schlesinger requested funds to study mobile basing schemes for the MX, which Congress approved. The research, however, quickly ran into technical difficulties and soaring cost estimates. The problems convinced the air force in 1976 to propose that the MX be placed in existing Minuteman silos until a permanent basing mode could be found.

The decision to abandon mobile basing, even if only temporarily, produced the first skirmish in Congress over MX. After repeated air force briefings on the threat the new generation of Soviet missiles posed to U.S. ICBMs, the defense committees had become stalwart supporters of mobility. Piqued by DoD's about-face on the subject, the conference report on the FY 1977 defense authorization bill stated flatly: "Providing a survivable system should be the only purpose of [the MX] effort, that the design of this system should not be constrained for silo basing; that none of this program's funds shall be expended in fixed or silo basing for M-X."[1] Faced with united opposition by the armed services committees, neither the air force nor DoD challenged the ban on fixed silo basing.

The MX program encountered a new obstacle in 1977 with the inauguration of Jimmy Carter. The new president was skeptical of nuclear weapons; "in a briefing at Blair House shortly before his inauguration, he astonished the Joint Chiefs of Staff with a suggestion that [the United States] could make do with a retaliatory force of 200 nuclear weapons."[2] Carter and his senior defense advisers initially questioned the need for MX. They believed that U.S. ICBMs would not be vulnerable for at least a decade and that deploying MX would threaten arms control objectives.[3] For both reasons, Carter reversed an air force decision to move the MX into full-scale development. He also offered in March 1977 to cancel the MX program if the Soviet Union reduced the size of its "heavy" missile force. But the administration soon began to waver on the MX issue. The swift Soviet rejection of the March 1977 proposal weakened the arms control argument against the MX. Matters worsened in late 1977 when the U.S. intelligence community concluded that Soviet missile accuracy had increased; hence, the U.S. ICBM force would soon become vulnerable to a Soviet first strike.[4]

Carter also felt growing pressure from some members of Congress to proceed with MX. These members favored deploying the missile in a Multiple Protective Shelter (MPS) basing system in which the missile would be shuttled among a series of protective shelters. In theory the Soviet Union would not be able to pinpoint which shelters contained missiles and therefore it would be deterred from attacking. In April 1979 Congress directed DoD to proceed with full-scale engineering development of MPS basing unless the president certified that the "system is not consistent with United States national security interests."[5] Mindful of the criticism that greeted the decision to cancel the B-1 bomber and aware that opposition was mounting against the soon-to-be signed SALT II Treaty, President Carter announced in June that the United States would deploy two hundred MX missiles in a mobile basing mode. Three months later the White House announced it had selected MPS as the new basing scheme.

Carter's decision to proceed with MX in the MPS basing mode did not sit well with all members of Congress. Before 1979 few in Congress had criticized the MX; Rep. Ronald Dellums (D-Calif.) had offered the only anti-MX amendment and he had garnered the support of only ten of his colleagues. Yet as it became clear that MX would be based in Nevada and Utah, legislators from the Great Basin began to organize against the program. These legislators had no complaints about the missile itself. Their objection lay instead with what they (and their constituents) saw as the unacceptable social and environmental costs of MPS basing.[6] In 1979 and 1980 Reps. James Santini (D-Nev.) and Dan Marriott (R-Utah) offered amendments that sought to frustrate development of MPS. They lost decisively. The anti-MPS coalition in the Senate had more success. Sens. Jake Garn (R-Utah) and Paul Laxalt (R-Nev.) convinced SASC in 1980 to recommend that construction of MPS be slowed until the air force studied the feasibility of using other sites. The conference committee, however, reworded the provision to allow DoD to waive the prohibition if economic or military factors demanded it.

President Carter's defeat in the 1980 election threw the MX program into uncertainty. Candidate Ronald Reagan had attacked MPS basing as expensive and unworkable, a view probably influenced by his friendship with Senator Laxalt and a desire not to alienate voters in the Great Basin. Reagan was committed, however, to deploying MX in a survivable basing mode, and he repeatedly attacked President Carter for failing to close the "window of vulnerability." Support for the missile itself was also strong in Congress. Anti-MX amendments offered to the FY 1981 defense bills were overwhelmingly rejected.

Upon assuming office, then, the Reagan administration had to find a survivable basing mode for MX other than MPS. The White House at first stalled on the issue. In March 1981 Secretary of Defense Caspar Weinberger reaffirmed support for the missile but stated that the basing issue needed further study. The administration's indecisiveness angered many in Congress because the FY 1982 defense budget contained a request for the first substantial financial commitment to MPS basing. Rep. Paul Simon (D-Ill.) and Sen. Carl Levin (D-Mich.) offered amendments to the authorization bill to require congressional approval of the basing mode the president selected before any funds could be obligated. Although Republican control of the Senate guaranteed defeat of Levin's motion, the Simon amendment failed by only six votes. Support for the missile itself still ran strong, however, and the only amendment seeking to cancel the entire MX program was easily rejected.

In October 1981 President Reagan finally unveiled his strategic force modernization program. As was widely expected, he ended work on MPS basing. To the surprise of most observers, though, he revived the Ford administration's interim basing proposal and recommended that up to forty of a total of one hundred MX missiles be placed in existing silos. To increase the survivability of the missiles, their silos would be superhardened. President Reagan also announced that the air force would continue to research other deployment modes and that he would recommend a permanent basing mode by December 1984.

Legislators from Nevada and Utah applauded the Reagan plan, but much of the reaction in Congress was negative. The defense committees were especially critical. In hearings held in late October, members of SASC disparaged the proposal. Senators complained that silo hardening was an expensive undertaking that would decrease missile vulnerability only slightly. Senators also objected that superhardening threatened to violate the restrictions on silo modifications set down in the SALT II Treaty, which President Reagan had pledged to observe.

The final FY 1982 defense bills reflected the discontent of the defense committees. The authorization bill added funds to study a smaller version of MPS. In debate on the appropriations bill, Sens. William Cohen (R-Maine) and Sam Nunn (D-Ga.) offered an amendment to prohibit the use of more than 5 percent of MX RDT&E funds for work on superhardened silos. The Cohen-Nunn amendment also directed the Reagan administration to recommend a permanent basing mode by July 1, 1983, rather than December 1984. With only four dissenting votes, the Senate accepted the amendment, and it was incorporated into the final version of the defense appropriations bill.

In February 1982 President Reagan abandoned the superhardening portion of the interim basing plan. Reagan's decision did not, however, mollify critics. In May 1982 SASC deleted the funds in the authorization bill for the procurement of the first nine MX missiles and for work on interim basing. In making the budget reductions, SASC mandated that "no further work is to be undertaken in support of fixed-point silo basing of MX."[7] SASC also added funds to the bill to accelerate the search for a permanent basing mode and directed the administration to select a final basing mode by December 1, 1982. The Senate approved the provisions without change. In the House, HASC approved MX procurement funds, but HASC's bill deleted funds for interim basing and contained proscriptions similar to SASC's against work on fixed silo basing. Before the bill could come to a vote on the floor of the House, however, President Reagan dropped the interim basing scheme and agreed to propose a permanent basing plan by the December deadline. The final version of the authorization bill approved production funds for five missiles, but it fenced obligation of these monies until thirty days after the president reported his chosen basing mode to Congress.

In November 1982 President Reagan proposed deploying one hundred MX missiles in a closely spaced basing mode. The plan, popularly known as Dense Pack, met overwhelming skepticism. Meeting in a lame duck session, HADS unexpectedly held hearings on the proposal. Fueled by the results of the recent mid-term elections, widely seen as a rebuff to President Reagan, many Democrats denounced the program. To the air force's dismay, House Republicans also attacked Dense Pack. Rep. Jack Edwards (R-Ala.), ranking minority member on HADS, complained, "I swear the more I sit here and listen to this, the more I wonder what in the world we are up to. . . . This sounds like Dense Pacman."[8] During debate on the defense appropriations bill, the House accepted an amendment sponsored by Rep. Joseph Addabbo (D-N.Y.), chair of HADS, to delete the funds for the first five missiles. The House, however, handily rejected another amendment that sought to reduce RDT&E funds for the MX. Again, Congress showed itself willing to support the missile if an acceptable basing mode could be found.

Any hope the Senate might save Dense Pack evaporated when the chairman of the Joint Chiefs of Staff announced that the heads of the army, navy, and marines all opposed the plan. Senate MX supporters then entered into negotiations with the White House on ways to save MX. The talks produced an agreement under which Congress would appropriate MX funds while fencing virtually all the money until the president submitted a new basing plan. Although the Senate adopted the proposal, the House insisted that more restrictions be placed on the missile. The bill that finally emerged from Congress denied all MX procurement funds, prohibited flight testing of the MX, and barred expenditure of all funds for research and development on a basing mode until both the House and Senate approved the president's selection.

To extricate itself from the impasse over the MX, the Reagan administration in January 1983 established the Scowcroft Commission to review the status of United States strategic nuclear forces. Most of the members of the panel had extensive government experience in national security affairs, and none of them had spoken against the MX. The White House apparently expected that the commission would conclude that the United States needed to deploy the MX in the Dense Pack basing mode.[9] After working closely with several members of

Congress, most notably Reps. Les Aspin (D-Wis.) and Albert Gore (D-Tenn.) and Senator Nunn, the panel released its findings in April.[10] If President Reagan expected the commission to ratify the Dense Pack proposal, he was disappointed.

The Scowcroft Commission made two basic acquisition recommendations. First, it recommended that one hundred MX missiles be deployed in existing Minuteman silos while research continued on developing a more survivable basing mode. The commission argued that the United States had to match the Soviet Union's lead in hard target kill capability. "Our ability to assure our allies that we have the capability and will to stand with them, with whatever forces are necessary . . . is in question as long as this imbalance exists."[11] Second, the panel recommended that the air force begin development of the Midgetman SICBM. According to the commission report, "a single-warhead missile . . . may offer greater flexibility in the long-run effort to obtain an ICBM force that is highly survivable, even when viewed in isolation, and that can consequently serve as a hedge against potential threats to the submarine force."[12]

By recommending that MX be deployed in Minuteman silos, the Scowcroft Commission eliminated the main public argument for developing the missile, namely, that it would redress the problem of ICBM vulnerability. The commission explicitly justified MX instead in terms of its contribution toward reaching agreement at the Strategic Arms Reduction Talks (START). The value of MX as a bargaining chip had attended all the previous justifications for the missile. Now, however, it became the primary reason for the program. The bargaining chip argument proved sufficient. Congress approved the new basing proposal in May, thereby releasing MX research funds and allowing the air force to conduct flight tests.

Support for MX in the Senate continued to run high throughout 1983. In the House, however, the pro-MX coalition began to unravel after the May vote. Committed anti-MX representatives formed the Wednesday Group (named so because it met each Wednesday) to coordinate legislative strategy.[13] A key tactic was to focus criticism on the House Democratic leadership for failing to make the MX flight-test vote a party issue. MX critics gained fresh support when the administration failed to develop a new position for the START talks as it had promised. A sign of the rising discontent came in July when an amendment to delete MX procurement funds lost by only thirteen votes. MX opponents renewed the fight when the appropriations bill came to the floor. This time the pro-MX forces won by only nine votes.

MX opposition in the House gathered steam when the Soviet Union withdrew from all arms control negotiations in December 1983 over the deployment of the Pershing II in Europe. As it became more likely that the House would not authorize MX funds in 1984, a group of moderate legislators led by Representative Aspin hammered out a proposal to save the program by tying it to progress at START. Under the Aspin plan, Congress would authorize funds for fifteen missiles, twenty-five fewer than the administration had requested and half the number HASC had approved, but bar the obligation of funds for six months. If the Soviets returned to the bargaining table during that time, then funds would remain fenced. If, however, talks did not resume, or the president certified that the Soviets were not bargaining in good faith, the fence would be lifted.

The Aspin proposal became a centerpiece of debate on the FY 1985 defense authorization bill. For their part, MX opponents offered an amendment to delete all MX procurement funds. After intense White House lobbying and a whirlwind of parliamentary maneuvers, the House adopted the Aspin proposal on a voice vote. The House then rejected the anti-MX motion by six votes. After the defeat, however, MX opponents regrouped to draft an amendment to modify the language of the Aspin amendment. The revised language gave Congress and not the president the power to approve the release of MX funds. On three separate votes, by margins no greater than three votes, the House accepted the revised Aspin amendment.

The impasse at the START negotiations also enabled MX foes to make headway in the Senate. Sen. Lawton Chiles (D-Fla.), a moderate who doubted the MX's military value but who believed it provided some bargaining leverage, crafted an amendment to delete MX production funds. To retain the missile's potential as a bargaining chip, the amendment provided funds to keep the missile production line warm. Sen. J. Bennett Johnston (D-La.) put the rationale for the Chiles amendment succinctly: "It puts you in the posture to have a bargaining chip without buying it, at least without paying the full price; of having a bargaining chip at the only time when a bargaining chip can work. That is when you have a demonstrated resolve, a demonstrated ability to build it but you have not yet built it."[14] After lengthy debate, the Chiles amendment fell on a tie vote. The Senate reaffirmed its support for the missile itself, however, when it handily rejected an amendment to cancel the entire MX program.

The different House and Senate positions on the MX program necessitated complex conference negotiations. The compromise which emerged contained two basic parts. First, Congress would authorize production of twenty-one missiles in FY 1985, the figure contained in the Senate version of the bill. Second, the procurement funds would be fenced until April 1, 1985.

In December 1984 the Soviet Union announced it would return to the bargaining table. Speculation immediately arose over whether Congress would vote to release the MX funds. As was widely expected, the Senate gave its approval in March 1985. Attention then shifted to the House, which many believed would refuse to de-fence the funds. Fearing just that, the Reagan administration applied a full-court press on swing voters. To bolster the argument that MX was needed as a bargaining chip, Max Kampelman, the chief U.S. START negotiator, returned to Washington to brief members on the progress of the talks. The administration's lobbying effort paid off as the House narrowly agreed to release MX procurement funds. Many swing members immediately announced, however, that they had cast their vote as an endorsement of arms control negotiations and not of the missile itself.

Proof came less than three months later during action on the FY 1986 defense authorization bill. In May, Senator Nunn, previously a supporter of MX, introduced a sense of the Senate amendment that only fifty MX should be deployed. Nunn's stature as the Senate's leading defense expert virtually guaranteed the amendment's passage. Faced with the prospect of defeat, President Reagan endorsed Nunn's proposal, which the Senate then adopted. A month later the House voted to limit the number of MX in fixed silos to forty missiles. In the House-Senate conference on the authorization bill, the conferees agreed on a binding limit of fifty missiles. The decision ended, at least for the time being, the congressional debate on the MX program. (DoD subsequently requested that the fifty MX missiles be based on railroad cars, but the rail-garrison basing proposal did not spark debate in Congress comparable to that seen between 1981 and 1985.)

Congress played a critical role in the evolution of the MX missile program, intervening at several junctures to define what constituted an acceptable new ICBM. Over seven years, legislators ordered three presidents to develop some form of survivable basing for the MX. When the search proved quixotic, Congress temporarily accepted the Scowcroft Commission's logic that MX was needed as a bargaining chip in arms control negotiations. When even this failed to bear fruit, Congress forced the most popular president of the postwar era to accept a permanent cap on the number of MX missiles that could be deployed in fixed silos.

Nevertheless, Congress's objections to MX revolved around the basing mode and not the missile itself. To be sure, many doves denounced MX because of its hard target kill capability. These legislators believed that MX had no value except as a first-strike weapon. Yet arguments about the destabilizing effects of a larger, more accurate missile did not appeal to many legislators. For most, MX's flaw was that there was no way to make it survivable. If DoD had produced such a plan, Congress would have funded it. In the end, however, that goal proved to be beyond grasp.

Trident

The Trident program emerged from the Strat-X planning exercise, a paper competition DoD initiated in 1966 to encourage cost-effective designs for new strategic weapons. Originally dubbed the Undersea Long-Range Missile System

(ULMS), Trident was envisioned as the successor to the Polaris and Poseidon ballistic missile submarine (SSBN) force. The rationale for the new system was twofold. First, the Polaris and Poseidon submarines would reach the end of their projected twenty-year service lives in the early 1980s. Given the long lead time needed to construct submarines, it was necessary to begin development work on a new SSBN. Second, Trident would carry a larger submarine-launched ballistic missile (SLBM) capable of being fired from greater ranges than existing SLBMs. Extending missile range would increase the area in which the submarine could patrol and thereby further complicate Soviet anti-submarine warfare (ASW) efforts.

In early 1968 the navy initiated detailed studies on Trident. Over the next three years DoD and navy officials fought over Trident's size and performance specifications.[15] Congress, however, played no role in the design of the submarine. Between 1968 and 1971 Congress made only minor changes to the funds the administration requested for Trident studies. HASC strongly supported the project in the belief that "as we draw back our forces from overseas, it is all the more important that we get our strategic systems safely located at sea."[16] SASC criticized some aspects of how the program was managed, but the committee recommended nearly all the funds the navy requested. HADS and SADS regularly appropriated the funds that had been authorized.

The Trident program received a major boost in October 1971 when the White House directed Secretary of Defense Melvin Laird to increase spending on strategic systems, and especially spending on Trident. The White House decision reflected political rather than military concerns. President Nixon wanted to gain additional bargaining leverage for SALT, and he hoped to assuage the fears of allies abroad and hawks at home that the strategic balance had tipped in favor of the Soviet Union.[17] In December Secretary Laird unveiled plans to accelerate Trident production. DoD then submitted a $35 million supplemental appropriations request. In hearings on the request, however, several senators suggested that Trident's design was not sufficiently in place to merit an accelerated timetable. Eventually SASC chose to defer action on the supplemental request until it could consider the proposal in conjunction with the FY 1973 defense budget, thereby allowing a review of the entire Trident program. In March President Nixon incorporated the supplemental request into the FY 1973 budget.

Despite its sympathy for the Trident program, HASC was also leery about the accelerated program. In hearings on the FY 1973 budget request, DoD officials admitted that Trident cost estimates had risen by more than three billion dollars in only four months. A HASC staffer expressed the sentiment of committee members when he complained: "The ULMS program is going to be most controversial when we go to the floor, and many members are intuitively in support of the program, but they still do have some questions and some misgivings. One of these, of course, is the lack of credible figures, cost estimates, on what the program will really mean dollar-wise."[18] HASC swallowed its qualms, however, and approved the request. It specifically rejected building more Poseidon SSBNs because "there are many new ways of quieting the submarine which cannot be built into the present design."[19]

The administration's request faced tougher sledding in the Senate. Members of SASC's Subcommittee on Research and Development doubted the need to accelerate Trident development. Senators complained that the navy had failed to provide specific information about the Trident's performance characteristics and the state of Soviet ASW capabilities. The subcommittee eventually recommended that all Trident procurement funds be deleted. After strenuous lobbying by administration officials, however, the full committee split evenly on the issue and funds for the program remained in the authorization bill. In its report SASC warned: "The need for the Trident program is not at issue. The principle [sic] need is to make sure that the management of this program avoids the problems of concurrency which could result from the fact that this program is being accelerated."[20]

Trident became an issue on the floor for the first time in 1972. In the House Rep. Robert Leggett (D-Calif.) sponsored an amendment to delete Trident construction funds, but the motion gained little support. Senate debate over an amendment similar to Leggett's proved to be more contentious. Trident critics complained that the submarine's design was not sufficiently intact to justify accelerated development. Proponents argued that full funding was necessary to ensure the availability of long lead-time items. After two days of debate the Senate voted forty-seven to thirty-nine to authorize accelerated development. The Trident program drew more complaints when the defense appropriations subcommittees met to consider the appropriations bill. Both HADS and SADS criticized the navy's management of the program, and they recommended a small reduction in Trident funding to emphasize that "the ULMS submarine be developed on a competitive basis."[21]

The 1973 Trident debate mirrored that of the previous year. HASC again endorsed the navy's plans, which included funds for building the first SSBN and the purchase of long lead-time items for three more submarines. Representative Leggett offered a floor amendment to pare back the navy request to the construction of only the first Trident submarine. The House rejected Leggett's amendment on a voice vote after brief debate. In the Senate, SASC's Subcommittee on Research and Development recommended that the navy return to the initial Trident construction schedule. At first SASC voted eight to seven to accept the subcommittee's recommendation. Later that same day, however, Sen. Strom Thurmond (R-S.C.) announced that he had mistakenly cast the proxy vote of Sen. Barry Goldwater (R-Ariz.) against the navy request. (Administration pressure on Goldwater rather than a misunderstanding about proxy instructions produced the reversal.)[22] With the vote switch SASC recommended full funding for the Trident program. Sen. Thomas McIntyre (D-N.H.) subsequently offered a floor amendment to return to the initial Trident schedule. Under considerable White House pressure, the Senate rejected the McIntyre amendment forty-nine to forty-seven.

The Trident program encountered even stronger opposition in the defense appropriations subcommittees. HADS recommended that the navy return to the original Trident construction schedule. HADS explicitly rejected the navy's argument that the accelerated schedule was needed to demonstrate American commitment to a strategic deterrent. The committee argued that "the mere fact that this country has an on-going Trident program . . . is clear evidence to any potential enemy that this country is committed to maintaining a strong nuclear deterrent posture."[23] HADS also noted that if the navy managed to adhere to the accelerated timetable, some Poseidon and Polaris submarines would have to be retired early to remain within the SALT limits. HADS concluded by criticizing the navy's failure to develop a competitive bidding process for the Trident program. SADS endorsed the return to the original construction schedule without comment, and the restriction was incorporated into the final version of the defense appropriations bill.

The passage of the 1973 defense bill marked the end of the congressional debate on the Trident SSBN program. Did Congress have a significant long-term impact on the Trident program? No. The focus of debate in 1972 and 1973 was the pace at which Tridents would be built. Congress did reject accelerated development, but subsequent management problems and production delays prevented the navy from even keeping to its initial development schedule. In focusing on management issues, Congress ignored the question of whether Trident was needed. "No one, in any of the congressional records examined, ever questioned the desirability of modernizing the FBM [fleet ballistic missile] system."[24] Some members of Congress, especially those on SASC's Subcommittee on Research and Development, questioned the navy's arguments on issues such as the presumed Soviet ASW threat and the aging of the Polaris SSBNs. Nonetheless, unlike the case of the MX missile, Congress never attempted to pressure the navy or DoD to reconsider the need for or design of the Trident SSBN. Those decisions, whatever their merits, were made in the Pentagon.

Pershing II

The army initiated advanced development of the Pershing II missile in 1974. The purpose of the development effort was to modernize the Pershing I short-range missile by incorporating new guidance technologies. The refinements would enable the new missile to destroy hard targets while at the same time reducing collateral damage, which was important given the high population density of Central Europe. Pershing II immediately ran into trouble in Congress. HASC approved Pershing II funding without comment, but SASC deleted the request. Although the missile had not figured prominently during SASC's hearings on the FY 1975 defense budget, the committee criticized the army on several fronts. SASC argued that the new guidance system had not been adequately tested, that no cost estimates had been done for the program, and that the army had no plan for using tactical nuclear weapons in Europe.[25] The authorization conferees subsequently split the difference on Pershing II funding.

The Pershing II encountered more difficulties during consideration of the appropriations bill. Once again the Senate proved to be the stumbling block. HADS accepted the authorization reduction without comment. SADS, however, followed SASC's lead and recommended that no funds be approved for the missile. SADS explained its decision tersely: "The Department has not adequately justified the need to modernize our current Pershing system."[26] The appropriations conferees subsequently approved less than one-fifth of the original request, a decision that still allowed the army to begin work on the Pershing II.

In 1975 the army requested funds to develop two prototype missiles. HASC again approved the request without discussion. For its part, SASC approved funding for one missile, but then retreated from this position in conference. The appropriations committees also approved the army's request in full. In doing so, SADS dropped its argument that there was no military requirement for the Pershing II. SADS reversed its position largely because the Soviet Union had begun to deploy a new intermediate-range missile, the SS-20, in Eastern Europe.

In 1976 and 1977 Congress approved the army's request for Pershing II research and development funds in full. None of the defense committee reports discussed the missile in either year. In 1978, however, HASC raised its first objections to the program. The committee complained that DoD had two other intermediate-range missiles under development in addition to the Pershing II. To encourage a more rational selection from among the various missile programs, HASC directed that the Pershing missile program be placed under the management of the air force, which was seeking to develop a mobile theater ballistic missile. Congress accepted HASC's recommendation. DoD ignored Congress's directive, however, arguing that the army should retain management of the Pershing program. After venting their pique at the Pentagon's failure to comply with congressional guidance, the defense committees relented.[27]

In 1979 the army requested funds to initiate development of an extended-range version of the Pershing II. For several years the army had been quietly exploring the possibility of doubling the Pershing II's range to allow it to carry out long-range theater nuclear missions. The army's interest in an extended-range missile flowed from a desire to obtain a role in NATO's evolving plans to acquire an intermediate-range nuclear force (INF) capability.[28] (The possibility that the Pershing's range would be extended was the main reason HASC had sought to place the program under air force management.) Both HASC and SASC approved the army's request without discussion. HADS, however, deleted the funds needed to begin work on extending the missile's range. While affirming its support for modernizing theater nuclear systems, HADS complained that it was "unwise to pursue development of a system for which satisfactory deployment arrangements with NATO may not subsequently be forthcoming."[29] SADS restored the funds on the grounds that any reduction "would only serve to slow the missile development and add to the cost."[30] SADS prevailed in conference.

The question of Pershing II deployment was settled in December 1979 when NATO unveiled its "dual-track" policy.[31] The proposal called on the United States to deploy 108 Pershing II missiles in West Germany and 464 ground-launched cruise missiles (GLCMs) in several other NATO countries. NATO further stated it would negotiate limits on intermediate-range nuclear weapons in Europe. The NATO announcement necessitated acceleration of the Pershing II development effort. To meet the initial operational deadline of late 1983, the army cut the normal development cycle by eighteen months, which it achieved by moving the missile into production before development work was completed. Although the defense committees had previously opposed such concurrency, they did not object this time given the high priority of NATO's deadline. In 1980 and 1981 the defense committees recommended approval of the army's requests for the Pershing II.

In 1981 Pershing II became an issue on the floor of Congress for the first time when Representative Addabbo sought to delete procurement funds for the missile. He justified his opposition on management grounds: "I do not propose to stop the Pershing II program. That can be stopped in the strategic armaments talks. What we are stopping are the waste and overruns [caused] by procuring before development is completed."[32] Addabbo's colleagues were unpersuaded; they rejected his amendment on a voice vote after only ten minutes of debate. In 1982 HASC and SASC again recommended full authorization for the Pershing II. When the bill came to the floor, Representative Dellums offered an amendment to delete the funds earmarked to buy ninety-one missiles. Dellums, however, challenged the Pershing II on policy grounds. He argued that Pershing II gave the Soviet Union an incentive to strike first in a crisis because unlike the Pershing I it could reach Soviet soil and do so in four to six minutes. Most representatives found the crisis destabilization argument unconvincing, and the House overwhelmingly rejected the Dellums amendment.

The day after the House vote the army conducted the much-awaited first test flight of the Pershing II. Because NATO's decision to deploy Pershings and

GLCMs had triggered a firestorm of criticism in Europe, members of both the international and national news media attended the test. To the army's embarrassment, the test flight was a spectacular failure. Only fourteen seconds after the launch began the first-stage engine failed, and army officials had to destroy the missile. Although missiles often flunk their maiden test flights, television coverage of the missile veering wildly off course before exploding fueled skepticism about Pershing.[33]

The failure of the test flight strengthened Representative Addabbo's claim that the Pershing II was not ready to enter production. When HADS released its report on the FY 1983 defense appropriations bill, it stated that it saw "little merit in continuing to fund production of Pershing II until the army can document a series of successful tests."[34] HADS went on to emphasize, however, that it still supported the missile, and that it had recommended a production halt "to send the unmistakable signal that the system when fielded will operate exactly as required, without doubt."[35] For its part, SADS overlooked the test failure and recommended full funding. Senate conferees agreed to deny procurement funds only after the House agreed to add funds to the O&M account to ensure that the army could meet the initial operational capability date of December 1983.

Opponents continued to battle the Pershing II during consideration of the FY 1984 defense authorization bill. Both HASC and SASC approved the army's request for procurement funds. Representative Dellums again offered an amendment to cancel the program. After an hour of debate that featured the same arguments and counterarguments aired a year earlier, the House overwhelmingly rejected the Dellums amendment. Dellums later offered an amendment to authorize the requested funds but to bar deployment of the missile for one year. The second Dellums motion also was defeated handily.

The FY 1984 defense budget presented the last opportunity to prevent the deployment of the Pershing II. In November 1983 NATO deployed the first Pershing IIs and GLCMs in Europe. When the FY 1985 defense budget reached the floor of the House, Pershing opponents offered three different amendments to prohibit further INF deployments. The House easily rejected each one. In 1985 Congress approved the procurement of the final batch of missiles, and they were deployed in West Germany as planned.

The Pershing II missile never became controversial in Congress. The defense committees occasionally objected to aspects of the program. Yet with the exception of SADS's initial complaint that the army had not justified the need for the missile, the defense committees focused on the management of the program. The committees seldom questioned the missile's military or political implications, even after its range was more than doubled. Attitudes differed only slightly on the floor. The Senate never debated the missile, despite heated opposition in Europe to the INF deployment and complaints at home that President Reagan had no intention of negotiating an INF agreement. Representatives questioned the Pershing II deployment only as the missile entered procurement. Even then, their efforts garnered little support. Decisions about the Pershing II missile were made solely within the executive branch.

ASAT

The United States developed its first crude ASAT weapon in the mid-1960s, but the program was operational in name only.[36] American interest in ASAT weaponry was rekindled in 1976 when the Soviet Union resumed testing its own ASAT weapon after a five-year hiatus. In his last month in office President Ford directed the air force to begin development of a new satellite interceptor, a decision President Carter subsequently ratified. Carter hoped to create bargaining leverage for an eventual agreement on ASAT weapons. The Soviets agreed to the U.S. proposal for ASAT talks, and three rounds of negotiations were held in 1978 and 1979. The talks produced no agreement, however, and they did not resume after the Soviet Union invaded Afghanistan.

While the ASAT talks were under way, the Carter administration made several decisions about the characteristics of the ASAT program. The first was the choice of the Miniature Homing Vehicle (MHV) as the primary focus of development work. The MHV originated in earlier research on strategic defense. It was a small (twelve-by thirteen-inch) cluster of rockets that used heat-seeking sensors to track its target. The MHV would destroy the target satellite by ramming it. The air force initially considered using ground-based missiles such as the Minuteman III ICBM as the launch platform for the MHV. The Minuteman option was later rejected in favor of the F-15 fighter because aircraft allowed "more attacks per day."[37]

The decision to develop the MHV did not attract comment on Capitol Hill during the Carter years. None of the defense committee reports issued between 1977 and 1980 discussed the program, and Congress approved DoD's request for funds in full for all four years. The first defense committee mention of the ASAT program came in 1981. SADS complained that cost estimates for the MHV interceptor had grown by over $100 million, and the committee asked "whether the program is receiving proper direction."[38] Rather than mandate changes in the program, however, SADS added $20 million to explore the use of advanced lasers as ASAT weapons. Congress accepted the appropriations add-on.

The first anti-ASAT legislation came in 1981 and 1982 when resolutions urging the president to reopen ASAT talks with the Soviet Union were introduced. ASAT opponents argued that if the air force were allowed to develop a satellite interceptor then a space weapons race would result. The mobility and prompt kill capability of the proposed American ASAT weapon made it far superior to its Soviet counterpart. If past history were a reliable indicator, the Soviets would seek to match and surpass the American innovation. Moreover, once the United States tested the MHV system, the Soviets would have no choice but to regard every F-15 as a potential platform for launching ASATs, thereby virtually eliminating the possibility of negotiating a verifiable ban on ASAT weapons. ASAT opponents also warned that the United States had the most to lose if ASAT weapons were deployed because the United States depended much more on satellites than the Soviet Union did.[39]

Whatever the merits of the arguments against the ASAT program, Congress adjourned without taking action on the bills. In January 1983 Sens. Larry Pressler (R-S.D.) and Paul Tsongas (D-Mass.) and Rep. Joe Moakley (D-Mass.) each introduced resolutions that again urged President Reagan to initiate talks with the Soviet Union on banning space weapons. All three bills at first appeared headed for the same legislative oblivion that had greeted earlier anti-ASAT efforts. Then, on March 23, 1983, President Reagan delivered his famous Star Wars speech. Although the ASAT program was separate from ongoing ABM programs, the president's speech whetted congressional interest in research on weapons capable of destroying targets in space.[40]

Concern about the ASAT program soon turned to the debate over the defense authorization bill, which contained the first request for ASAT procurement funds. In May 1983 Rep. George Brown (D-Calif.), a member of the HSTC, offered an amendment to delete the request. Even though the House had not yet held hearings on ASAT weapons, Brown convinced 176 of his colleagues to oppose the weapon. In July Senator Tsongas sponsored an amendment that barred tests of the MHV against targets in space unless the president certified that he was endeavoring in good faith to negotiate a ban on ASAT weapons or that the tests were necessary to avert harm to U.S. national security. After a series of exchanges to establish what constituted "good faith," the Senate adopted the amendment ninety-one to zero. The Tsongas language was then incorporated into the final version of the authorization bill.

Fresh off victory on the authorization bill, ASAT opponents sought to enact the Tsongas proposal as a separate piece of legislation. Unlike the case with defense authorization bills, whose provisions expire after one year, a limit on ASAT tests enacted separately would remain binding until Congress chose to repeal it, thereby sparing ASAT opponents from having to battle annually with the administration. ASAT supporters, however, kept the Tsongas bill off the floor. ASAT opponents then turned to the House Appropriations Committee. Here they won a temporary victory when the committee agreed to add the Brown amendment to the defense appropriations bill. The joint House-Senate conference, however, restored the request for ASAT funds in full. Still, the conferees mandated "that these funds not be obligated or expended until 45 days following submission to the Congress of a comprehensive report on U.S. policy on arms control plans and objectives in the field of ASAT systems."[41]

President Reagan sent the report to Congress in March 1984. The report essentially dismissed any hope of negotiating limits on ASAT weapons. In a cover letter accompanying the report, Reagan stated: "No arrangements or agreements beyond those already governing military activities in outer space have been found to date that are judged to be in the overall interest of the United States and its Allies. . . . I do not believe it would be productive to engage in formal international negotiations."[42] The administration based its conclusion on the claim that without a matching ASAT ability the United States could respond to a Soviet attack on American satellites only by escalating the conflict. The administration also argued that verifying limits on ASAT weapons was impossible.[43] The verification argument insured a new confrontation with Congress. To reach its conclusion the administration had interpreted the proposed ban to mean any weapon, however unlikely, that could be used against satellites. Although Senator Tsongas agreed this was "a clever tactical move," it irritated many members of Congress.[44]

When the defense authorization bill came to the floor in May, Representative Brown again challenged the ASAT program. Rather than seeking to cut procurement funds for ASAT as he had in 1983, Brown proposed a ban on ASAT tests. Brown wanted to take advantage of the Soviet Union's recent announcement that it would observe a unilateral moratorium on ASAT tests against targets in space. After rejecting several amendments offered by ASAT supporters, the House adopted the Brown amendment. Brown's proposal had no chance of passing in the Senate. So Senator Tsongas instead introduced a motion to tie ASAT tests to a serious administration effort to limit ASAT weapons. Fearful that Tsongas's motion might pass, Sen. John Warner (R-Va.), the chair of SASC's Subcommittee on Strategic and Theater Nuclear Forces, authored a compromise measure. Warner's proposal barred ASAT tests against targets in space until thirty days after the president certified that he was endeavoring in good faith to negotiate ASAT limits. After rejecting attempts by hawks to weaken the amendment, the Senate accepted the compromise.

Shortly after the Senate adopted the Warner compromise, the Soviet Union proposed reopening arms control talks on space weapons. As part of the proposal, the Soviets offered what amounted to their version of the Brown amendment: a mutual moratorium on testing ASAT weapons against objects in space. President Reagan replied that the United States would negotiate limits on ASAT systems, but he pointedly failed to respond to the Soviet offer of a joint moratorium. Reagan also did not mention other space weapons, a deliberate tactic chosen to avoid subjecting SDI to arms control talks. Despite several efforts, the United States and the Soviet Union failed to agree on an agenda for the proposed negotiations.

The failure of ASAT negotiations to materialize shaped the progress of the conference on the authorization bill. The conferees finally hammered out an agreement that barred obligation of any of the authorized funds until the president certified to Congress that he was trying in good faith to negotiate "the strictest possible" limits on ASAT weapons. Two weeks after Congress received notification the air force would be free to conduct two "successful" tests of the MHV. To ensure the provision would not give the air force an incentive "to create options for near misses of the target," the conferees ordered DoD to report to Congress immediately should any test be judged a failure.[45] HADS retained this language in its version of the defense appropriations bill, but SADS omitted it entirely. In the conference to negotiate a continuing appropriations resolution, Representative Addabbo insisted that the conferees impose a test moratorium on the MHV interceptor. Addabbo's stand was part of a conscious strategy to limit DoD to two ASAT tests against targets in space, regardless of whether they were deemed successful.[46] In the end, the conferees crept closer to the position the House had taken with the adoption of the Brown amendment; the continuing resolution delayed tests of the MHV interceptor until March 1985, and it limited the air force to at most three tests.

The ASAT battle resumed again in 1985. In reporting their versions of the authorization legislation, neither HASC nor SASC placed any restrictions on the ASAT program. When the authorization bill came to the floor in May, the Senate rejected an amendment to bar all tests of the MHV interceptor against objects in space. Senator Warner then submitted an amendment to allow the air force to conduct tests as it saw fit if the president certified the United States was attempting to negotiate limits on ASAT weapons. Warner's motion retreated from the language adopted the year before, and the Senate accepted the amendment. Defeated in the Senate, ASAT opponents turned to the House. Representative Brown reoffered his amendment to ban tests of the MHV interceptor against space targets so long as the Soviet Union did likewise. He repeated his argument that the MHV interceptor presented verification nightmares because its small size meant that the Soviets would have to treat every F-15 as a potential launch platform. Representative Brown also argued that because the air force had not yet tested the weapon against a space target there was still time to prevent a new round of the arms race. ASAT supporters countered that the United States needed an operational MHV system as a bargaining chip in future negotiations with the Soviet Union. When the debate concluded, the House again adopted the Brown amendment.

The House-Senate conference on the authorization bill eventually agreed to allow the air force to conduct up to three tests of the MHV interceptor against objects in space. The conferees also reduced ASAT procurement funds because of concerns over technical problems and slippages in the test schedule. The conference report directed the air force "to review and, if necessary, to restructure the program."[47] Representative Aspin, completing his first conference as chairman of HASC, defended the decision to recede from the House position on the grounds that the ASAT program was needed for bargaining leverage at the recently resumed START negotiations. Aspin's explanation did not mollify House ASAT critics. Angry over the ASAT issue and other concessions, doves kept the House from considering the conference bill for three months.

In September the air force conducted the long-delayed test of the MHV interceptor against a target in space. The ASAT weapon successfully destroyed an obsolete satellite. Despite the setback, ASAT opponents continued to lobby against the program. Both HADS and SADS endorsed the positions their parent chambers had staked out during the authorization debates. As part of a larger compromise in the conference on the appropriations bill, however, Senate conferees agreed to bar tests of the MHV system against objects in space so long as the Soviet Union adhered to its moratorium. Although the provision did not prohibit other types of tests in space, the ban effectively derailed the ASAT program.

The ASAT ban survived an administration effort in 1986 to allow more tests against objects in space. Both HASC and SASC repealed the language contained in the FY 1986 continuing resolution in their reports on the FY 1987 defense authorization bill. The Senate rejected an attempt to restore the language, but the House again adopted the Brown amendment. In the authorization conference, Senate conferees agreed to accept essentially the same agreement ironed out the year before. The FY 1987 and 1988 defense legislation reaffirmed the moratorium. In 1988 the air force finally acknowledged political reality and declined to request funds for the MHV interceptor, effectively canceling the program.

Two factors helped ASAT opponents to impose a test moratorium. One was that the air force at times was lukewarm in its support for the MHV interceptor. In testimony before HADS in 1984, General Charles A. Gabriel, chief of staff of the air force, was asked if he supported development of ASAT weapons capable of reaching satellites in high (geosynchronous) orbits. General Gabriel replied: "I would not anticipate using it nor would I recommend that we build such a system. I would rather both sides not have a capability to go to geosynchronous with an ASAT. *In fact I would like to be able to agree with the Soviets that we not have any ASATs if we could verify it properly.*"[48] Opposition to ASAT weapons in the military and among some civilian DoD officials stemmed from the belief that the United States depended more heavily on satellites than the Soviets did, and, hence, it had more to lose.

ASAT opponents were also helped by the cost and technical problems that plagued the program. In November 1982 the air force estimated that it would cost $1.5 billion to develop the MHV system. By June 1985 cost projections had escalated to $4.1 billion, an increase of over 150 percent, and it was anticipated that total costs including deployment might exceed $10 billion.[49] Technical problems produced extensive delays in the ASAT test schedule. The air force restructured the program in late 1985 at the behest of the armed services committees to minimize development problems. The move, however, changed few minds in Congress.

The moratorium on tests of the MHV system against targets in space was not a total victory for ASAT opponents. Despite the ban, Congress continued to appropriate funds for the program until the air force canceled it in 1988. Nor did the ban prohibit the air force from conducting other tests of the MHV interceptor. Nonetheless, the ban made it impossible to conduct operational tests. Without the tests, the air force could have little confidence that the ASAT program would be able to accomplish its mission. For those legislators who opposed the ASAT program, that was victory enough.

Lessons

The histories of the MX, Trident, Pershing II, and ASAT programs demonstrate that Congress does not treat weapons equally. Both MX and ASAT triggered protracted congressional debates. Legislators challenged the two programs primarily on policy rather than on cost or management grounds. At first their criticisms won few supporters, but after several years of debate they won over a majority of members to their positions. In the end, the anti-MX coalition succeeded in limiting the number of missiles deployed to one-fourth what President Carter requested and one-half of what President Reagan requested. Although ASAT critics never convinced Congress to delete funds for the MHV program, the test moratorium effectively prevented the air force from deploying an operational satellite interceptor.

The Trident and Pershing II programs attracted relatively little attention. The House overwhelmingly rejected efforts to reduce Trident funding. In 1972 and 1973 some senators challenged the decision to accelerate development of the submarine. They based their opposition on management concerns, however, rather than on the need for a new SSBN. Once the Trident program returned to its initial timetable, major debate over the submarine ended, even though it later encountered severe production delays and cost overruns. As for Pershing II, the defense committees periodically criticized management of the program, but they did not explore the military implications of the missile. Pershing II was debated only on the floor of the House and even here no more than 125 representatives opposed it.

A glance at other weapons programs supports the conclusion that Congress does not treat all weapons alike. The Sentinel/Safeguard ABM system was a heated topic of debate in the Senate from 1968 to 1971. The Nixon administration's request to begin development of counterforce programs triggered intense opposition in the Senate. In the 1980s both the House and Senate furiously debated the merits of SDI. On the other hand, the Trident I and II missiles, GLCMs, the B-1B, and the Stealth bomber (among others) attracted few critics on Capitol Hill.

Chapter 5 addresses the question of why some weapons become the focus of heated debate and others do not. Here it is sufficient to say that in the 1970s and 1980s program cost was not the answer. (As chapter 5 discusses, program cost became more controversial following the collapse of the Iron Curtain in 1989.) Although Trident cost more than $30 billion, the program never attracted the attention given to ASAT, which cost considerably less. Counterforce programs drew more congressional criticism in the mid-1970s than did the B-1 bomber, even though they cost far less. Divisions within the executive branch also do not explain why some weapons become controversial. In the MX, Trident, Pershing II, and ASAT cases, the executive branch was unified. Some air force officers were indifferent or hostile to developing ASAT weapons, but opposition to the MHV program unquestionably originated in Congress and not in the Pentagon. Review of controversial programs indicates that splits within the executive branch are not a major source of congressional debate. The only instances from 1968 to 1988 where "losers" in DoD exported their fight to Congress were the air-launched cruise missile (ALCM) and B-1 programs.[50]

The second lesson about Congress's review of specific weapons systems is that the parent chambers display much more skepticism of DoD's requests than do the defense committees. The defense committees tend to approve the administration's requests, often without question or reservation. The eagerness of the defense committees to ratify Pentagon decisions stems directly from the hawkishness of committee members; most of defense committee members are far more pro-defense than the average member of Congress (see table 2-1). Defense committee members simply are ideologically predisposed to follow DoD's lead on defense policy. As Rep. Charles E. Bennett (D-Fla.) once argued: "When we are making a judgment on what is needed for our national defense, then obviously we ought to listen to the people who have to carry out that judgment and who have to fight for our country."[51] The defense committees often rally around the services, especially when defense programs are under attack on the floor.

But the defense committees are not the rubber stamps they once were for DoD's plans. "Once over lightly" no longer describes the work of the committees. After all, the armed services committees blocked the air force's interim basing proposal for MX and forced the army to prepare a better justification for the Pershing II. In the mid-1970s SASC's Subcommittee on Research and Development also questioned counterforce programs and pushed the air force to develop cruise missiles.[52] In the mid-1980s the defense committees refused to fund several navy tactical nuclear programs when the navy failed to show there was any need for the weapons.[53] Nevertheless, the defense committees lean heavily in the direction of management oversight. The committee hearings and reports on Trident, Pershing II, and ASAT dealt overwhelmingly with issues such as cost overruns, schedule slippages, and production efficiency. The committees gave much less attention to the need for the programs. Even a casual review of committee work on other programs suggests the same conclusion.

The hawkishness of the defense committees ensures that the floor is the most hostile environment weapons programs face in their journey through Congress. On no occasion has the floor fought to save a program while the defense committees attempted to cancel it. House and Senate rules enable members to challenge any program and such challenges are an accepted legislative practice today. Of course, most floor challenges do not threaten the weapon in question. The history of the Pershing II shows that floor amendments may be routinely offered and just as routinely rejected. The willingness of legislators to offer amendments that are regularly rejected may strike some as a *pro forma* exercise. But even successful floor challenges can take years to gain momentum. Three years passed, for example, before any amendment seeking to cut MX funds gained the support of even 25 percent of the House or Senate.

Rank-and-file legislators labor at a disadvantage relative to the defense committees when it comes to challenging DoD requests. To succeed, rank-and-file legislators must first persuade a majority of their colleagues to overrule the defense committees. Beating the defense committees can be a daunting task because many legislators regard members of the defense committees as experts. As Representative Aspin once observed: "Senators Barry Goldwater (R-Ariz.) and Howard W. Cannon (D-Nevada), who are both pilots and staunch airpower advocates, regale their colleagues with stories about the fighter planes they have test flown replete with the jawbreaking jargon of the profession. Other members sit in awed silence, unable to respond because they lack the expertise and the jargon."[54] When floor challenges succeed, critics must then convince the other chamber to go along. Winning in conference is easier said than done. As the 1985 ASAT battle shows, the defense committees may drop provisions they dislike in conference.

The third lesson about Congress's review of specific weapons systems is that Congress is not a synoptic decision maker. Congress does not scrutinize each new weapons proposal. Of the MX, Trident, Pershing II, and ASAT programs, the defense committees took an early interest only in MX and Pershing II. The navy squabbled over the design of Trident for nearly three years without eliciting any comment by the defense committees. The defense committees were silent about the MHV interceptor for the first four years the program was in development. The full House and Senate are even less likely to question weapons early in development. The Trident submarine was the only one of the four programs that was debated on the floor within one year of entering advanced development. Divisions within SASC, however, account for Trident's early floor consideration. The first MX amendment came three years after the missile entered advanced development. The ASAT and Pershing II programs were not challenged until *after* DoD requested procurement funds.

Yet oversight of new weapons is one area where Congress's performance improved in the 1970s and 1980s. In the 1960s legislators, particularly those on the defense committees, knew few details about nuclear weapons. During the first major debate over the ABM system, for instance, critics questioned several aspects of the program. "It became apparent quickly that [SASC's] members did not understand the questions, much less know the answers."[55] SASC's members lacked knowledge about ABMs even though the army had been conducting research on strategic defense for a decade. Similarly, none of the defense committees held extended hearings on the B-1 bomber until 1971, four years after the program began. Members knew even less about smaller programs. Take, for example, the subsonic cruise armed decoy, which preceded the ALCM program. During its first years in development, "neither the Congress nor the public paid much attention to the program."[56]

In the 1970s Congress's willingness to review new weapon starts increased.[57] In addition to MX, the defense committees took an interest in counterforce programs and cruise missiles. Neither of these programs would have drawn any comment from the defense committees a decade earlier. The trend toward increased scrutiny continued into the 1980s. The most obvious example is SDI, which attracted Congress's attention from its conception. The defense committees also reviewed several less well known programs, including Trident II, the E-6A strategic communications aircraft, navy tactical missiles, and several types of battlefield nuclear weapons. The floor debated Midgetman, the Trident II missile, navy tactical nuclear missiles, and the army's Tactical Missile System (ATACMS) during the early 1980s, although none of these programs would enter procurement until the late 1980s or even the 1990s.

Congress still falls short of being a synoptic decision maker. Many programs, especially smaller ones, fail to draw much attention. The failure to scrutinize weapons early on occurs for several reasons. With the defense committees, it is partly by inclination. Many of these members begin with the premise that DoD is justified in its requests. But even members who want to question programs are quickly overwhelmed by the sheer number of new weapons starts contained in the defense budget each year. The early history of the Trident SSBN program illustrates the problem. The first identifiable piece of budget information Congress saw on the program came in 1968. Under the heading "Missiles and Related Equipment" was an entry that read, "G.32.06.47N Advanced Sea-Based Deterrent. Project U15-09X, Undersea Long-Range Missile System." The entry was one of more than four thousand items listed in the RDT&E account.[58]

Another reason the defense committees fail to scrutinize weapons early on, and the main reason the floor does not, is that members want to hedge their bets. Weapons typically take from seven to fifteen years to develop. Promising technologies may or may not bear fruit in the interim, DoD may alter a program's intended mission (as happened with the Pershing II), or threat assessments may change (as happened in the late 1980s). Members know that a research proposal is not a production commitment, and the history of military development is "strewn with the skeletons of canceled systems—one only has to recall the nuclear-powered aircraft, the Navaho missile, Skybolt, Dynosaur, the B-70 bomber, the manned orbiting laboratory (MOL), and literally hundreds of other smaller projects."[59] Legislators recognize that the most productive use of their time is to allow research to proceed relatively undisturbed until it becomes clear that the weapon will be procured. The one exception to this rule is basic research; many members believe that basic research programs produce little of military value.[60]

The virtue of Congress's reluctance to act while weapons are in early development is that programs are not ended prematurely. The danger in waiting is that it enables momentum to build up behind flawed programs. Constituencies invariably develop within DoD and in the defense industries in favor of weapons, regardless of the merits of the programs. The appearance of constituencies makes it more difficult for Congress (and the administration) to modify the proposal. Several years of RDT&E expenditures typically become the basis for arguments about "sunk costs." Members recognize that their reluctance to make quick decisions creates problems, but they prefer waiting to acting too hastily in determining the fate of a new weapons system.

Conclusion

The histories of the MX, Trident, Pershing II, and ASAT programs provide additional evidence for the policy lens. The deferential lens clearly cannot explain the protracted debates surrounding the MX and ASAT programs. After all, it suggests that Congress rubber-stamps DoD's requests. The parochial lens fares only marginally better. Although bile barreling triggered opposition to MPS basing of the MX missile, little else about the MX or ASAT controversies corroborates the parochial lens. In contrast, the MX and ASAT debates support the main prediction of the policy lens, namely, that members of Congress, at least on occasion, debate the substance of nuclear weapons policy. Admittedly, policy oversight is not systematic. One question that needs to be answered is why Congress at times scrutinizes the merits of nuclear weapons programs.

5 ≫ ≪

Agendas

WHY DO SOME nuclear weapons programs sail through Congress while others spark heated debate? The deferential, parochial, and policy lenses all suggest that programs attract criticism when they suffer management problems, though only the deferential lens holds management problems to be a primary factor behind agenda setting. As the history of the Trident submarine attests, however, programs frequently experience severe production delays or cost overruns without triggering significant congressional opposition. The parochial lens contends that programs become controversial when they are canceled or when they impose substantial social costs on some groups. Despite the intuitive appeal of the parochial lens, pork barreling seldom pushes nuclear weapons onto Congress's agenda, and bile barreling shapes the agenda only occasionally. Rather than being driven by management or parochial concerns, nuclear weapons battles on Capitol Hill revolve around the substantive merits of the programs in question. In particular, weapons systems that depart from declaratory doctrine or threaten to cross major thresholds in weapons development generate significant congressional opposition.

Agenda Setting

In a trivial sense nuclear weapons are almost always on Congress's agenda. At almost any point in the year the defense committees or the full House and Senate are making or about to make decisions on nuclear weapons. The observation that nuclear weapons are always on the agenda is hardly illuminating. It is also misleading. As the most cursory review reveals, most programs attract little attention. True, in any given year Congress may change up to half the funding requests for nuclear weapons. Yet, as table 5-1 shows, changes typically are made as part of a general push to reduce defense spending and not because of anything peculiar to the programs in question. Much the same may be said of floor debates. Although any legislator can offer an amendment, most floor amendments are rejected handily. So the fact that Congress changes funding for a program or debates it on the floor does not mean the weapon has moved onto the congressional agenda in any meaningful way.

Table 5-1.
Reasons for Defense Committee Changes to the President's
Nuclear Weapons Budget, 1974–1988

Committee	Fiscal	Management	Policy
HASC	61	20	19
SASC	57	23	21
HADS	57	29	15
SADS	63	19	18

Note: Figures were drawn from an examination of committee reports. All changes were measured against the president's initial budget request. A budgetary change was coded as fiscal if the report stated that it was made "without prejudice," for "budgetary reasons," or if no reason was given. Changes were coded as management when program concurrency, mismangement, or schedule slippage were mentioned. Changes were coded as policy if questions were raised about the need for the weapon, mission overlap, and undefined missions. Where more than one reason was given, the change was credited to the explanation given the most emphasis in the committee report. Figures may not sum to 100 because of rounding error. Values are given as percentages. *Abbreviations:* HADS, House Appropriations Defense Subcommittee; HASC, House Armed Services Committee; SADS, Senate Appropriations Defense Subcommittee; SASC, Senate Armed Services Committee.

By the same token, Congress occasionally passes amendments and resolutions that deal with nuclear weapons programs but which have no effect (directly or indirectly) on U.S. policy. In 1970, for example, the Senate overwhelmingly adopted Sen. Edward Brooke's (R-Mass.) nonbinding, sense of the Senate resolution urging President Nixon to ban MIRV testing unilaterally. The MIRV program nonetheless proceeded apace. In 1988 the House voted to prohibit for one year the testing of depressed trajectory ballistic missiles, so long as the Soviet Union refrained from testing as well. Yet DoD had no plans to test depressed trajectory missiles. Because legislative efforts such as the Brooke proposal and the depressed trajectory ban typically are made for symbolic purposes — indeed, both the sponsors of the legislation and the rest of the members of Congress know the motion will have no practical impact on U.S. acquisition plans — it would be misleading to suggest that such programs are on Congress's agenda in any meaningful way.

Given these observations, the term *agenda* is used here in a more restricted sense. A program is considered to be on Congress's agenda only when, for whatever reason (fiscal, management, or policy), it encounters substantial opposition within the defense committees or the parent chambers. Although such a definition leaves room for dispute about what constitutes "substantial," it highlights the distinction between substantive and theatrical congressional debates.

That said, why do most weapons systems never become controversial? It is certainly not because the defense committees or parent chambers thoroughly assess each program and agree with DoD's request. Congress does not systematically review each weapons request to ferret out those that are questionable on the merits.[1] Instead, the presumption that guides decision making on Capitol Hill is that DoD's requests are innocent until proven guilty. In other words, the burden lies with critics to show that the military does not need a new program rather than with the military to prove it does.

The Pershing II missile illustrates the point. When the army first proposed modernizing the Pershing IA, none of the defense committees explored the substantive merits of the proposal in depth, and the issue never came up on the floor. When the army extended the Pershing's range to enable it to hit targets in the Soviet Union, the defense committees did not reassess the program to determine if this raised new military or political issues. Only when the program was about to enter production, and after President Carter had committed the United States to deploy medium-range missiles in Europe, did some members of the House (but not the Senate) take to the floor to question the contribution Pershing II would make to U.S. national security.

What explains Congress's willingness to treat weapons programs as innocent until proven guilty? Until the early 1970s the answer could be found largely in norms. By all accounts, in the 1960s most members of Congress trusted DoD and recoiled from the notion that they should be skeptical of military advice. Members across the ideological spectrum saw military officers as *the* experts on defense policy. Senior members of the defense committees saw their responsibility as ensuring that the services received the weapons they requested. The few members who questioned the need for weapons systems often found themselves ostracized if not punished outright. At the same time the norm of committee specialization ran strong; the floor almost always deferred to the defense committees.

The deferential norm collapsed under the weight of the events of the late 1960s and early 1970s. By 1980 many members, both off and on the defense committees, were willing to scrutinize DoD budget requests. Yet legislators quickly discovered that they lacked the time, resources, and expertise to review the entire defense budget. Even members of the defense committees find they must specialize to be effective, and, given the size of the defense budget, many DoD programs have no legislator overseeing them. Congressional staff increased in the 1970s, but it remains minuscule compared to DoD's staff and to the task at hand; a single committee staffer might oversee upward of $20 billion in expenditures. Finally, DoD often makes it difficult for critics to obtain information that discredits its requests.[2]

In sum, "the pressing necessity of managing limited time and potentially overwhelming amount of information pushes members in the direction of relative policy passivity."[3] Congress lacks the institutional wherewithal to rewrite the entire defense budget, even if its critics sometimes hold it to this standard.

Moreover, because Congress cannot review the budget systematically, most members assume DoD is justified in making its requests. If a mistake is made, it is better to fund a bad program than to withhold funds from one that might be needed. As Sen. Henry Jackson (D-Wash.) once phrased it, "Always in areas of Defense, if I err, let me err on the side of strength."[4]

Nevertheless, some programs do face scrutiny. The rest of the chapter assesses three explanations for why this happens: management problems, parochialism, and policy objections. Of course, sometimes programs become controversial for idiosyncratic reasons. The neutron bomb gained notoriety in 1977, for example, when the media publicized it as a weapon that killed people but left property intact.[5] Still, absent management problems, parochialism, or policy objections, programs will not remain on the agenda for long no matter how they came to be there. In the case of the neutron bomb, it disappeared from Congress's agenda almost as quickly as it appeared.

Management Problems

The deferential, parochial, and policy lenses all suggest that management concerns shape congressional deliberations on defense policy. Regardless of what motives one postulates for legislative behavior, members of Congress dislike test failures, production delays, and cost overruns; hence, management problems are a major focus of the work of the defense committees. As table 5-1 shows, between one-fifth and one-third of the line-item changes the defense committees recommend can be traced to management issues. The defense committees worry about management problems because schedule slippages and cost overruns mean wasted spending. The defense committees know that when cost overruns come to light, and they seemingly always do, they undermine public support for defense spending. Since committee members generally favor greater levels of defense spending, they have good reason to resolve management problems before the problems turn into public relations disasters.

If management concerns figure prominently in the work of the defense committees, the same cannot be said of the full House and Senate. Even severe management problems convince few rank-and-file members to oppose a weapons system. Take for example the Trident submarine, which ran into repeated production delays in the late 1970s. Despite serious reservations about Electric Boat's ability to build Tridents, no opposition to the program developed on the floor of the House or Senate. Likewise, in 1981 Rep. Joseph Addabbo (D-N.Y.), chair of HADS, sought to delete procurement funds for the Pershing II because excessive concurrency plagued the program. Few of Addabbo's colleagues shared his concern, however, and his amendment fell on a voice vote.

An even more striking example is the B-1 bomber. Beginning in the late

1950s Congress pressed the White House to build a successor to the B-52 bomber. In 1967 President Johnson finally acceded to congressional demands and authorized work on the B-1 (then known as the Advanced Manned Strategic Aircraft). But not everyone, however, believed the United States needed a new bomber. In 1969 Sen. George McGovern (D-S.D.) sought to derail the program. McGovern and his supporters did not challenge the plane on management grounds—the program was still in the early stages of development—but on the grounds that other forces in the U.S. inventory could accomplish the B-1's mission at far less cost. Despite his arguments (and even though SASC had not held hearings on the new bomber), the Senate rejected the McGovern amendment fifty-six to thirty-two.

The B-1 soon met a series of production problems. Work on the plane rapidly fell behind schedule and estimated unit costs ballooned. To hold down costs the air force reduced the plane's performance specifications and mission requirements. Yet even as problems with the B-1 mounted, congressional opposition to the bomber did not grow. The House handily rejected every anti–B-1 motion offered. The Senate debated seven anti–B-1 amendments between 1970 and 1976, but only two garnered more votes than the 1969 McGovern amendment. In one of these only thirty-three senators opposed the B-1. The other amendment, debated in 1976, passed on a forty-four to thirty-seven vote. This motion authorized B-1 production funds but barred obligation of the bulk of the monies until after the presidential election. The motion passed only because Democratic senators were reluctant to embarrass their party's eventual nominee; none of the major Democratic presidential candidates supported the B-1.

Although management problems by themselves do not push weapons systems onto Congress's agenda, critics do use cost overruns and schedule slippages to supplement other arguments against particular weapons. McGovern and his supporters seized on the B-1's escalating cost estimates in their efforts to kill the program. Opponents of ASAT weapons were quick to point to the rising costs of the MHV satellite interceptor. Critics of Pershing II argued that excessive concurrency provided an additional reason to delay the program. But management problems alone, even serious ones, do not provoke substantial congressional opposition to a weapons system. Most members prefer to let the defense committees handle management problems. And typically the committees trim funding and issue stern warnings, but decline to cancel programs.

Why do legislators defer to the Pentagon on management problems? Primarily because of what is nearly an "iron law" of Washington life, namely, that the Pentagon cannot build weapons systems on time and within budget. No matter how much legislators hate management snafus, they expect cost overruns and production delays to occur. As one member of HASC put it, if Congress canceled every weapons system that had management problems, "nothing would ever get built."[6] And legislators are least likely to become excited about cost overruns and schedule slippages when they agree that a weapons system fulfills a legitimate mission. Canceling such a program might not solve the problem, and it may even cost additional tax dollars since money will have to be spent to develop a weapon that will accomplish the mission. So "an argument about sunk costs is very powerful if the mission is uncontroversial."[7]

Parochialism

The parochial lens holds that nuclear weapons become controversial in Congress for two reasons. The first is when the executive branch cancels a program. A production halt means constituents lose jobs, and members will fight to protect the economic interests of constituents. The other (less common) instance is when a program entails significant social costs for some communities. When this occurs, members representing the affected areas will seek to have the program modified or canceled. Both arguments are intuitively plausible. But do they accurately describe congressional agenda setting?

The Carter administration's battle to kill the B-1 bomber is frequently offered as evidence that parochialism shapes the weapons agenda in Congress. In June 1977 President Carter canceled the B-1. The Senate approved the decision after some debate, but the House initially refused to go along. Faced with an embarrassing defeat, the administration applied tremendous pressure on wavering representatives. The effort paid off in September when the House narrowly voted to delete B-1 procurement funds from the defense appropriations bill. Nonetheless, the bill contained nearly half a billion dollars to continue research on the four prototype planes that had been built with prior-year funds.

Carter encountered more trouble in December when he asked Congress to rescind the $462 million that had been appropriated in 1976 to begin construction of planes number five and six. Once again the Senate approved the administration's decision. B-1 supporters in the House, however, argued that the funds would keep the B-1 production line open until late 1979, which would allow Carter to change his mind should events warrant it. The warm production-line argument found wide appeal, and the House rebuffed the rescission request. Not to be deterred, Carter forced a second House vote in February 1978. After intense White House lobbying the House voted to rescind the production monies. Although the program continued to receive some funding for research and development, the February vote marked the last major floor battle over the B-1.

On the face of it, the battle over the B-1 fits the parochial lens precisely. Whenever a project is canceled, especially one as expensive as the B-1, members representing affected districts fight doggedly to save the program. In the case of the B-1, many representatives had parochial interests in mind and did not hesitate to mention them on the floor. During the February 1978 debate, for example, Rep. Robert Dornan (R-Calif.) urged his colleagues to "consider that there will be over 7,000 workers fired if we stop this production line."[8] Dornan had good reason to worry about unemployed B-1 workers; he represented the district where the plane was assembled. Nor does the Senate's willingness to sustain Carter's decision to cancel the B-1 necessarily contradict the parochial lens. House members represent smaller and more homogeneous constituencies, so they generally feel more pressure to defend the economic interests of their constituents.

Still, the battle over the B-1 had as much to do with policy as it did with parochialism. In the 1950s and 1960s, Congress exhibited an almost mystical belief in the manned bomber, and it repeatedly tried to force the president to build a successor to the B-52. Some legislators supported a new manned bomber for parochial reasons. Yet by all accounts, the senior members of the defense committees, who for all intents and purposes were Congress on defense issues until the early 1970s, pressed Presidents Eisenhower, Kennedy, and Johnson to build a new bomber because they believed U.S. national security demanded it and not because they were looking to deliver benefits to constituents.

Disinterested legislators also had good reason to question the decision to cancel the B-1. Senior air force officers uniformly supported B-1. Although air force testimony might be dismissed as self-serving, many of Carter's own appointees in DoD favored building the B-1, and they communicated their views to members of Congress.[9] Even the wider defense and scholarly communities were split over the merits of B-1; for every article that decried the plane as a boondoggle, another praised it as a bulwark for deterrence. In short the B-1 issue divided Congress just as it did the administration and the civilian defense community.

Whatever the relative importance of parochial and policy concerns in the fight over the B-1, additional evidence that economic interests shape Congress's nuclear weapons agenda is missing. To start with, the defense committees demonstrate little parochial behavior on nuclear weapons. Between 1968 and 1988 the defense committees recommended that a new nuclear program be started on thirty-six different occasions, or less than twice a year. Congress actually appropriated funds in only sixteen of these cases (44 percent), and in more than half of the cases funding lapsed after a year. Finally, even where Congress did add new line items to the budget, it is not clear that parochialism rather than policy views motivated the changes.

Constituency interests also do not play a significant role in how the defense committees handled DoD's budget requests for nuclear weapons. The defense committees mostly recommend budget cuts. From 1974 to 1988 authorization and appropriations add-ons constituted only 9 percent of the budgetary changes

HASC made to the requests for nuclear weapons and 6 percent of those HADS made. As for SASC and SADS, the figures were 13 and 11 percent, respectively. The relative infrequency with which the defense committees recommend increased funding is surprising since the committees presumably contain members whose districts have the most at stake in defense spending (at least according to the parochial lens). Nor do budgetary limits explain why add-ons are not more common. Even when the defense committees must cut *total* spending they can increase spending on *individual* programs so long as these additions are offset by cuts elsewhere in the budget.[10] Of course, defense committee members may advance parochial interests by protecting local programs against budget cuts rather than by adding funds. It is impossible, however, to assess this claim given the available data.

Of course, these figures do not take into account *failed* efforts by committee members to add funds for programs important to their constituents. Although these cases are likely to be more frequent than successful efforts, they still are not common. Less than 6 percent (four of sixty-eight) of the nuclear weapons roll call votes in SASC between 1971 and 1988 sought to add funds above the level DoD requested. In the case of HASC, only 9 percent (four of forty-five) of the committee roll call votes between 1973 and 1988 sought to increase funds above the level requested by DoD. The figures do not capture informal efforts to convince colleagues to spend more money on particular programs, but presumably parochially motivated legislators have an incentive to place their efforts on the public record, especially if the effort is likely to fail. After all, members cannot advertise their efforts if no written record exists.

Floor amendments also fail to provide support for the claim that members use nuclear weapons programs to advance the economic interests of their constituents. Between 1968 and 1988 only 8 percent of Senate amendments offered to the defense authorization bill and 14 percent of the amendments offered to the defense appropriations bill sought to add funds to the program totals the defense committees recommended. In the House the figures were 7 and 4 percent (see table 3-2). And, as with the defense committees, the fact that members try to add money to the budget does not warrant the conclusion that they are seeking to steer benefits to their constituents. In 1980 and 1981, for example, Sen. Malcolm Wallop (R-Wyo.) offered amendments to increase funding for research on strategic defense. Parochialism did not motivate Wallop. Wyoming lacks the infrastructure needed to benefit from ABM research; it received only $1 million of the $7.3 billion that would be spent on SDI between 1984 and 1987.[11]

Congress's reactions to DoD decisions to close down weapons production lines also cast doubt on the validity of the parochial lens as an explanation of agenda setting. In the early 1970s, for example, the air force replaced 550 single-warhead Minuteman II missiles with MIRVed Minuteman III missiles.

Until the signing of the SALT II Treaty in 1979, the United States was free to replace the remaining 450 Minuteman II missiles with Minuteman III missiles. Yet Presidents Ford and Carter refrained from doing so. When the last Minuteman III rolled off the production line in November 1978, not one member of Congress offered an amendment, either in committee or on the floor, to continue to convert Minuteman IIs into Minuteman IIIs, even though nearly $2 billion and over forty thousand different subcontracts were at stake.[12]

The failure of legislators to fight to keep the Minuteman III production line open contradicts the parochial lens. Even if efforts to continue the program were likely to fail, parochially motivated legislators still had an incentive to fight. After all, if they properly advertised their efforts to procure more Minuteman IIIs, they would have signaled to voters that they were fighting for the district. And because MX would not enter production for years, lost Minuteman contracts could not be made up in the short term with MX contracts. Nor should the SALT talks have deterred parochially minded legislators; members could always argue that additional Minuteman IIIs would strengthen the administration's bargaining leverage.

The B-1B bomber offers another example where Congress did not pressure DoD to keep a production line open. When the Reagan administration resurrected the B-1 in 1981, it planned to procure only one hundred planes, after which it would build the B-2 bomber. Rockwell International, the B-1B's prime contractor, and Rockwell employees stood to be the biggest losers if the B-1B production line shut down. Rockwell was not part of the Stealth project, and because military aircraft programs are few and far between, Rockwell had little chance of winning another major airframe contract for a decade. So when DoD requested final B-1B production funds in 1986, many observers predicted that a "Battle for Pork-Barrel Hill" would be waged as interested members fought to keep the B-1B production line open.[13]

Contrary to expectations, however, no pork-barrel war materialized. The defense committees took no steps to keep the B-1B production line open. No one in the House offered an amendment to procure additional B-1Bs. During consideration of the authorization bill, the Senate rejected, by a four-to-one margin, an amendment by Sen. John Glenn (D-Ohio) to direct DoD to study the best mix of B-1B and Stealth bombers. Glenn's motion was widely seen as an effort to keep the B-1B production line open; Ohio was the second biggest beneficiary of the program. After rejecting the Glenn amendment, the Senate agreed on a voice vote to limit the B-1B fleet to one hundred aircraft.

The absence of a sustained dispute over producing more than one hundred B-1Bs cannot be blamed on fiscal constraints. Budgetary problems should not have deterred parochially minded supporters of the B-1B. A crucial but often overlooked fact of life on Capitol Hill is that legislators need to be on the *right* side of an issue and not on the *winning* side.[14] Win or lose, pro–B-1B legislators would have accrued electoral benefits from being seen fighting to protect constituency interests. Nor can the absence of a "Battle for Pork-Barrel Hill" be blamed on the fact that some states benefited from both programs. The B-1B and B-2 programs had different subcontractor networks; hence, some constituencies "lost" when the B-1B production line closed. And in 1986 the Stealth bomber was still in development, so in many constituencies the B-2 program only offered the *prospect* of jobs. The B-1B, which was in production, provided *actual* jobs. Because voters tend to be more sensitive to losses than to gains, legislators representing B-1B districts had the greatest incentive to fight for their program (provided that they saw the program primarily in parochial terms).[15]

If the parochial imperative did not help the Minuteman III and B-1B programs, it worked *against* Sentinel, MPS, and the extremely low frequency (ELF) communications system. Local residents opposed all three proposals, even though each program would have provided many jobs.[16] The constituencies chosen to host the three programs as bile barrels. Local residents believed that the program's social costs outweighed any possible economic benefit. Residents in turn pressed their members of Congress to block the programs, and most members responded.

Although bile barreling influences agenda setting in Congress, its importance is limited. Bile barrels occur infrequently. Most programs do not impose significant social costs on any constituency. Also, local concerns alone do not explain why Sentinel, ELF, and MPS basing became controversial. Policy objections were also important. For example, of the senators who held seats in both the Ninetieth and Ninety-first Congresses (1967–70), twenty-seven opposed Sentinel in 1968 (that is, voted against it more than half the time). If anti-ABM senators based their opposition solely on local concerns, they should have supported Safeguard. Yet all but two of the anti-Sentinel senators opposed Safeguard in 1969 and 1970. As for ELF and MPS basing, members who opposed the programs on parochial grounds would not have made much headway if they had not been able to count on the support of members who opposed the programs on policy grounds.

Might more complex links exist between constituency interest and agenda setting? Members of Congress may, for example, rotate the benefits of defense spending among themselves.[17] Legislators may agree (tacitly or otherwise) that fairness dictates that the major defense contractors should each have the opportunity to be the prime contractor for a weapons system. Since defense firms have plants and subsidiaries in different geographic locations, such a system of queuing would enable a wider array of districts and states to benefit. If true, this would explain why no pork-barrel battle was waged over the B-1B (though it would not explain the absence of a fight to continue the Minuteman III production). Legislators from B-1B districts knew they had already had their turn at the defense trough.

Yet if such a queue system existed in Congress, it would have attracted a great deal of attention by now, which it has not. Even if a queue system could be kept quiet, a system of rotating defense contracts could not survive in Congress if the parochial imperative is as powerful as alleged. Given the number of dollars at stake, some members would defect from the arrangement. After all, most voters do not know (much less care) that they must wait their turn. Because legislators need to be on the right side and not the winning side, they could reconcile the parochial imperative with a queue system. A legislator could offer an amendment to save a program, thereby satisfying constituents, without working hard for its passage, thereby obeying the "wait your turn" edict. But legislators seldom seek to add money for nuclear weapons.

The parochial imperative might also shape the agenda by keeping weapons systems off the agenda rather than by pushing them onto it. Members who want to remain in Congress have an incentive not to criticize weapons that employ sizable numbers of their constituents. Rep. Robert Leggett (D-Calif.), a DoD critic, acknowledged the point bluntly: "I've got to be picky and choosy about what I try to terminate, because if I've got a large submarine with 8,000 people working on it in my district, I'm not about to terminate the contract and put 8,000 people out of work."[18] Members know they face political hot water if they challenge programs important to their constituents. The bottom line, then, as the argument goes, is that Congress would debate more weapons if parochialism were absent.

Like any counterfactual, it is impossible to refute the claim that Congress's agenda would look different if the parochial imperative were tamed. Nevertheless, parochialism probably does not keep weapons systems off Congress's agenda. Even if members believe they must support weapons systems that employ their constituents, most constituencies have nothing at stake on any given program. As table 5-2 shows, most of the benefits from the production of a weapons system go to a handful of states. Take the case of the B-1, where the air force maximized the spread of contracts to increase congressional support for the plane.[19] Only seventeen states gained more than five hundred jobs from the B-1 program. In the case of the MX missile, twenty-eight states benefited from the program but only eight received more than five hundred jobs. "SDI is basically a Los Angeles, San Francisco, Seattle, Albuquerque, Huntsville, Washington, D.C., Philadelphia and Boston program."[20] We lack data for other programs, but no reason exists to believe that spending is distributed more widely on other weapons systems. Thus most legislators do not risk constituency interests by challenging a weapons system.

Nor is every weapons system destined to be controversial. Most weapons programs draw no criticism outside of Congress where no parochial imperative exists to dampen opposition. For example, DoD's decisions to develop cruise missiles, a new short-range attack missile, and a variety of improved command and control systems met with little criticism, even in the scholarly literature. To

Table 5-2.
Distribution of Contracts by State, Selected Weapons

ABM				B-1			
State	Funds	% Total	% CUM	State	Funds	% Total	% CUM
NJ	$708m	49.3%	49.3%	CA	$7,317m	30.9%	30.9%
NC	172	12.0	61.3	OH	4,421	18.7	49.6
PA	171	12.0	73.3	WA	2,279	9.6	59.2
MA	109	7.6	80.9	NY	2,040	8.6	67.8
CA	99	6.9	87.8	NJ	972	4.1	71.9
FL	70	4.9	92.7	OK	830	3.5	75.4
NY	54	3.8	96.5	MD	793	3.3	78.7
TX	16	1.1	97.6	KS	759	3.2	81.9
AZ	9	0.6	98.2	TN	642	2.7	84.6
AL	9	0.6	98.8	TX	599	2.5	87.1
DE	8	0.6	99.4	GA	489	2.1	89.2
MN	5	0.3	99.7	MA	446	2.0	91.2
CT	4	0.3	100.0	IL	343	1.5	92.7
NE	2	0.1	100.0	FL	319	1.4	94.1
WA	1	0.1	100.0	CT	251	1.1	95.2

MX				SDI			
State	Number of Jobs	% Total	% CUM	State	Funds	% Total	% CUM
CA	14,473	45.0%	45.0%	CA	$4,964m	45.4%	45.4%
MA	4,942	15.4	60.4	NM	1,354	12.4	57.8
UT	2,956	9.2	69.6	MA	1,028	9.4	67.2
CO	2,653	8.3	77.9	AL	663	6.1	73.3
NY	1,403	4.4	82.3	WA	511	4.7	78.0
FL	1,250	3.9	86.2	TX	416	3.8	81.8
PA	903	2.8	89.0	VA	301	2.7	84.5
NH	546	1.7	90.7	PA	230	2.1	86.6
AZ	466	1.5	92.2	DC	230	2.1	88.7
NM	370	1.2	93.4	NY	221	2.0	90.7
NV	241	0.8	94.2	CO	194	1.8	92.5
TX	238	0.7	94.9	MD	189	1.7	94.2
VA	196	0.6	95.5	FL	120	1.1	95.3
OK	177	0.6	96.1	CT	115	1.1	96.4
OH	161	0.5	96.6	UT	67	0.6	97.0

Note: The figures for the ABM and SDI programs are for monies actually spent. The B-1 data are the expenditures projected before the program was canceled. The MX data are the estimated number of jobs created if one hundred missiles were built. *Abbreviations:* ABM, antiballistic missile; SDI, Strategic Defense Initiative; CUM, cumulative.

Source: ABM data are from "Battle over ABM Switches to Nation's Grassroots," *Congressional Quarterly Weekly Report,* 30 May 1969, pp. 848–49. The B-1 figures are from *Congressional Record,* 94th Cong., 2d sess., 1976, 122, pt. 12:14144. The MX figures are from *Congressional Record,* 99th Cong., 1st sess., 1985, 131, pt. 4:5031. SDI data are from "Where Does the SDI Money Go?" *Space and Security News* 4 (December 1987): 19.

the extent that these programs were noticed at all, they were applauded. So Congress's failure to debate programs does not in itself provide evidence that parochialism keeps programs off the agenda.

Finally, time and resource constraints limit the number of issues Congress can place on its agenda. Of course, members of the defense committees have more time to delve into the details of the defense budget than do nonmembers. Yet any reluctance on the part of the defense committees to challenge DoD programs stems from a pro-defense bias and not parochialism. After all, when the defense committees come under attack on the floor for failing to discharge their oversight responsibilities, they typically respond with more rigorous reviews of the budget, which would not be the case if they were motivated by parochialism.

Policy Concerns

Most discussions of Congress and defense policy dismiss the claim that members care about the merits of weapons programs. But congressional battles over nuclear weapons revolve primarily around policy issues. Idiosyncratic forces sometimes drive these policy concerns. An individual legislator or committee may move to change DoD plans without eliciting much comment from Congress as a whole, as was the case in the mid-1970s with ALCM and again in the mid-1980s with the army's nuclear-armed version of the ATACMS program.[21] But in these and other cases the weapons system appeared on the agenda either because powerful groups within the administration wanted to change the policy (ALCM) or the service was lukewarm about its proposal (ATACMS).

Only seven nuclear weapons became the subject of heated debate in Congress in the 1970s and 1980s in the face of a unified and interested executive branch: ABM, the B-1 bomber, counterforce weapons, MX, ASAT, Midgetman, and SDI. Management or parochial concerns helped push several of these programs onto Congress's agenda. Parochialism infused congressional efforts to stave off cancellation of the B-1 bomber. The anti-ABM movement was helped early on when the protests of citizens living near proposed Sentinel sites convinced some senators to oppose deployment of an ABM system. The MX missile drew fire on Capitol Hill because legislators from Nevada and Utah did not want it based in their states. Opponents of the MHV satellite interceptor frequently pointed to the cost overruns the program had encountered.

Nonetheless, with the exception of the B-1, policy concerns were the primary reason these seven programs appeared on Congress's agenda. In January 1969 President Nixon abandoned Sentinel's goal of area defense in favor of Safeguard's goal of silo defense. If constituent complaints explain why anti-

Sentinel amendments won the support of as many as thirty-four senators in 1968, then the Senate should have routinely approved Safeguard. Instead, the debate intensified. Much the same happened with the MX; the anti-MX coalition grew after the MPS basing mode was dropped. Finally, although opponents of the MHV interceptor often charged that the program was poorly run, they never offered legislation to fix the management problems. Nor did ASAT supporters. The entire battle turned instead on whether DoD should develop a satellite interceptor. Even in the B-1 case. policy concerns rivaled the parochial imperative in keeping the bomber on Congress's agenda after President Carter canceled the plane.

These seven cases show, however, that only two specific types of policy objections carry much weight in Congress. The first is when an acquisition program breaks with a major tenet of *declaratory doctrine*, the public logic that guides the U.S. nuclear arsenal.[22] Declaratory doctrine matters in weapons development because it answers several key questions about nuclear forces: What types of offensive nuclear weapons are needed for deterrence? How and where should weapons systems be based? Are strategic defenses stabilizing or destabilizing? Yet declaratory doctrine is not static; over time administrations revise it as technology and inclination warrant. Doctrinal changes as well as administration failures to act according to doctrine were what propelled counterforce weapons, MX, SDI, B-1, and Midgetman onto Congress's agenda.

President Nixon's decision in 1974 to develop counterforce weapons departed from a long-standing policy that missiles which threatened Soviet nuclear forces were undesirable.[23] (DoD began targeting Soviet military installations in the early 1950s, but inaccurate warheads made it impossible for United States missiles to destroy large numbers of hardened Soviet targets.) In 1969 and 1970 the Nixon administration reaffirmed that the United States did "not intend to develop counterforce capabilities which the Soviets could construe as having a first-strike potential."[24] In keeping with this, Congress in 1970 acted with White House approval to bar the air force from beginning work on counterforce weapons. The following year the Senate, again with White House approval, easily rejected three floor amendments that sought to initiate development of more accurate ICBMs. Finally, at his confirmation hearings in June 1973, Secretary of Defense James Schlesinger reaffirmed that it was U.S. policy not to develop substantial counterforce capabilities.[25]

The MX missile violated the cardinal tenet of declaratory doctrine that ICBMs should be survivable. Almost as soon as the first Minuteman was deployed, ICBMs became the backbone of the U.S. nuclear deterrent. Yet, by the late 1960s DoD recognized that ICBMs in fixed silos would eventually become obsolete. "The task for those responsible for strategic policy was to find an alternative basing scheme for the growing vulnerability of Minuteman, but particularly for the air force's follow-on system, the MX."[26] Thus, in justifying

work on MX, the air force argued that the new missile would be mobile and, hence, survivable. Even when DoD reversed itself in 1976 and sought to place MX in fixed silos, it did not abandon survivability in principle; it described silo basing as an interim measure until a survivable basing mode could be found. When Congress rejected the proposal, no more was heard of it until President Reagan resurrected the idea and the MX debate.

SDI contradicted the principle that missile defenses are destabilizing, a principle enshrined in the ABM Treaty. The United States did conduct ABM research during the 1970s, but the research was a relatively low-priority effort designed to provide a hedge against a Soviet breakout from the ABM Treaty. In 1976 Congress closed the only ABM site in the United States with little opposition and despite a $6 billion investment.[27] President Reagan for one understood that his vision of rendering nuclear weapons "impotent and obsolete" broke sharply with the positions that Presidents Nixon, Ford, and Carter had taken.

> My predecessors in the Oval Office have appeared before you on other occasions to describe the threat posed by Soviet power and have proposed steps to address that threat. But since the advent of nuclear weapons, those steps have been increasingly directed toward deterrence of aggression through the promise of retaliation. This approach to stability through offensive threat has worked. We and our allies have succeeded in preventing nuclear war for more than three decades. In recent months, however, my advisors, including in particular the Joint Chiefs of Staff, have underscored the necessity *to break out* of a future that relies solely on offensive retaliation for our security.[28]

The ferocity of the reaction to Reagan's speech testifies to the radical nature of his proposal. Rep. Les AuCoin (D-Ore.) was one of Reagan's more restrained critics when he complained, "I have regrettably come to the conclusion that this President is not content with deterrence."[29]

Unlike the preceding cases, the battles over B-1 and Midgetman were congressional efforts to add programs. The B-1 controversy hinged on the accepted concept of a triad. With the development of ballistic missiles in the late 1950s, a consensus emerged among nuclear strategists that if the United States wished to ensure robust deterrence of a Soviet missile attack, it had to maintain nuclear forces on land, sea, and air. John Ford, a staff director of HASC, captured the importance of the triad in strategic thought when he commented, "Everyone treats the Triad like the Holy Trinity. Everybody says it is sacred, including the secretary of defense."[30] For many of Carter's critics, particularly members of the defense committees, the decision to cancel the B-1 marked a retreat from the triad.[31] The existing strategic bomber, the B-52, was over twenty years old and vulnerable to Soviet air defenses. Although Carter argued that cruise missiles would eventually carry out the B-1's mission, he had no coherent plan for deploying ALCMs. His subsequent proposal to build cruise missile carrier aircraft enjoyed lukewarm support among his own advisers and none at all in the air force. When Carter failed to produce a viable proposal to modernize the air leg of the triad, congressional pressure for resurrecting the B-1 grew. The Carter administration sought to derail the B-1 bandwagon by leaking a story in August 1980 that DoD had begun development of a highly sophisticated Stealth bomber. (Until then fewer than ten members of Congress knew about the Stealth program.)[32] The leak failed to quiet Carter's critics, and in late 1980 Congress added $300 million to the budget to begin work on a new manned bomber based on the B-1.

The Midgetman SICBM appeared on the congressional agenda because the Reagan administration failed to produce a plan to redress the vulnerability of the U.S. land-based ICBM force. That Congress even considered the Midgetman proposal seriously, let alone funded it, testifies to the centrality of the concept of survivability to strategic doctrine. After all, before Midgetman, Congress had never sought to initiate a major weapons program over DoD's objections. Unlike other proposals for redressing the vulnerability of the land-based missile force, Midgetman did not violate any other aspect of strategic doctrine. The shallow underwater missile and continuous patrol aircraft—two basing modes that received consideration in defense circles but not in Congress—would have abandoned the land leg of the triad.

If many members of Congress are skeptical of weapons that break with declaratory doctrine, many are also wary of weapons that cross thresholds in weapons development. Many members fear weapons systems that introduce revolutionary changes in the capabilities of U.S. nuclear forces, provided, of course, the Soviet Union has not already crossed the same threshold. (The American reaction to the launch of Sputnik episode suggests the threshold argument would lose its appeal to legislators if the Soviets introduced a major new weapon first.) ABM, SDI, and ASAT, for example, were all programs that proposed to add major new capabilities to the U.S. nuclear arsenal. In the case of the two missile defense programs, the United States lacked any capability to destroy incoming missiles when both programs were started. Yet a decision to build ballistic missile defenses, as nuclear strategists frequently point out, poses dramatic consequences for nuclear deterrence.

At first glance the ASAT program does not appear revolutionary. After all, in the mid-1960s the United States developed a satellite interceptor with nary a protest from Congress. Still, this weapon was operational in name only and DoD retired it "in view of the unlikelihood that the U.S. would even use . . . the system."[33] In contrast, the MHV interceptor made it possible for the first time to destroy enemy satellites rapidly and in large numbers. From the perspective of ASAT critics, the MHV program opened the door to an arms race in space. As then-Rep. Albert Gore (D-Tenn.) argued, "If we cross this threshold, then the sky is the limit, it is 'Katie, bar the door.' "[34] Many ASAT critics also opposed SDI and believed the MHV project was intimately related to the work on strategic defenses.

Of course, other policy-based criticisms were leveled against all seven programs. But no other objections were crucial to the debates that developed. For example, questions about the technical feasibility of Safeguard figured prominently in the 1969 Senate ABM debate. But anti-ABM senators focused on the question of feasibility because it appeared to be more objective than political critiques of the system would have.[35] In 1970 the feasibility issue clearly gave way to political and military critiques of missile defenses; revelations of major technical problems with the Safeguard program "made little more than a mild ripple in the chamber."[36]

In the case of MX, some members charged it was a first-strike weapon. The hard target kill argument, however, did not win over many legislators. Counterforce capability *had* been a hotly contested issue in the mid-1970s. Yet once Congress approved development of more accurate warheads, further arguments over the merits of counterforce became moot. The development clock could not be turned back, particularly since the Soviet Union also increased the accuracy of its missiles. As a result, hard target kill became an accepted part of U.S. strategic doctrine, and several weapons systems were explicitly justified on the basis that they would place Soviet hard targets "at risk."

Comparison of the MX and Trident II missiles is useful in this respect. The D-5 was not contested on Capitol Hill even though it, like MX, had significant hard target capability. Where Trident II differed from MX was in its survivable basing mode. As a congressional critic of D-5 observed, legislators voted for Trident missiles because "they were on submarine based platforms that were not particularly controversial, which most members of Congress see as retaliatory. Now the MX was fraught with controversy because of the basing mode and the vulnerability of fixed-silo basing."[37] Some argue that members voted for Trident II because they did not want to be accused of being antidefense. Rep. Les Aspin (D-Wis.), for example, argues that members "begin to get a little uncomfortable if they've gone too far one way and start looking for a way to pop back the other way."[38] But this argument fails to explain why members voted for MX and against Trident II rather than the other way around. Nor does it explain why MX opponents, most of who voted to ban ASAT tests, chose to prove their defense credentials on Trident II and not on ASAT.

As for Midgetman, some proponents argued that it would help stabilize the nuclear balance. Representative Gore, who helped popularize the SICBM concept, argued that a single-warhead missile made sense on arms control grounds: it would be less threatening to the Soviet Union and it might encourage the Soviets to "de-MIRV" their own ICBM missile force.[39] For most Midgetman supporters, however, the missile made sense only if it solved the vulnerability problem. Both Sen. Sam Nunn (D-Ga.) and Representative Aspin, who persuaded the Scowcroft Commission to endorse SICBM, eventually approved a MIRVed version of Midgetman. As Aspin bluntly stated, "I've got no hang-up about the number of warheads that it has. I do have a hang-up if you make it so big it can't be mobile, and that's what worries me."[40]

The only program that did not move onto the congressional agenda even though it raised one of the two policy concerns just discussed was MIRV. Multiple warheads clearly were a revolutionary development. Why then did they fail to become an issue on Capitol Hill? The answer is simple: most members of Congress in the late 1960s were reluctant to challenge DoD. Although the ABM debate broke the tradition of congressional acquiescence, the notion that robust congressional defense debates were proper was still not entrenched. Even though most ABM critics also opposed MIRV, they declined to attack the program because they feared it would hurt the anti-ABM fight.[41] Yet, in failing to become an issue in 1969 and 1970, MIRV became a symbol in the 1980s. During the debates over MX, SDI, and ASAT, critics frequently pointed to MIRVs to warn of the dangers of congressional deference.

MIRV, then, is the exception. No subsequent weapon that received routine congressional approval departed from strategic doctrine or crossed a major technological threshold. Take the Pershing II missile. Although in the 1970s the United States possessed no equivalent intermediate-range nuclear weapons, strategic weapons provided identical target coverage. Whatever gains the Pershing II represented in terms of accuracy, they were incremental when compared to other missiles. At the same time, Pershing II was entirely consistent with strategic doctrine, which nowhere stated (or had stated) that missiles with short flight times were undesirable. Although Pershing II's counterforce capability would have been controversial in the early 1970s, hard target kill capability was an established doctrinal tenet by 1979.

The same may be said of other programs. Rail-garrison basing for the MX stirred relatively little controversy in Congress because, unlike earlier MX basing modes, it addressed (however well or poorly) the problem of ICBM vulnerability. Efforts to block production of the B-1B bomber went nowhere despite claims that the plane cost too much, contributed little to national security, and lacked a defined mission. Congress supported the B-1B because maintaining the air leg of the triad was an entrenched part of strategic doctrine. Efforts to bar procurement of SLCMs made no headway either. Critics charged that SLCMs made treaty verification impossible, but for most members verification difficulties meant that SLCMs were survivable, precisely what strategic doctrine called for in new weapons. Finally, with the exception of ELF, which angered local residents, command and control programs seldom draw opposition in Congress. Although strategists argue that deterrence depends on robust command and control, none of the communications programs DoD requested after 1968 broke with strategic doctrine or crossed a threshold in the arms race.

Why are members sensitive to arguments about declaratory doctrine and thresholds but not to other policy arguments? Because as Representative Aspin writes, "Congress as an institution is conservative, cautious, and reluctant to initiate change. It responds to old stimuli more quickly than to new ones."[42] When faced with issues on which they know little and on which no pressing need for change exists, many members feel most comfortable with the status quo. That is why weapons that look like those already in the arsenal do not appear dangerous. Many members found it hard to see Pershing II as destabilizing because it had the same basic performance characteristics as other missiles already deployed; ICBMs, SLBMs, and cruise missiles provided the same target coverage, and SLBMs could also hit the Soviet Union with little warning. Although critics argued that Pershing's combination of attributes made it special, nonexpert legislators were hard pressed to distinguish these arguments from those the services made to justify the program.

In contrast, weapons systems that break with declaratory doctrine or open new chapters in arms development appear, in the eyes of many legislators, to carry the potential for danger. Members do not need to be well-steeped in the intricacies of nuclear doctrine to appreciate that a drift toward a vulnerable land-based ICBM force weakens the backbone of the U.S. deterrent. Nor do they need to be intimately familiar with strategic doctrine to doubt the rosy scenarios that administrations paint for major breakthroughs in strategic weaponry. Past events warrant skepticism. As the development of MIRV technology attests, major strategic innovations may unsettle the nuclear balance.

Controversy in Congress over nuclear weapons programs need not always stem from departures from declaratory doctrine or efforts to cross thresholds in weapons development. The forces driving agenda setting can and do change with changes in the wider political environment. Indeed, the end of the Cold War in 1989 added a new factor to agenda setting in Congress, namely, acceptable cost. Throughout the postwar era most members of Congress believed that the Soviet threat justified paying enormous sums for individual weapons systems. As the histories of programs like the Trident submarine and the B-1 bomber attest, a big price tag by itself was not sufficient to make a program controversial. In 1990, however, the sea change in Eastern Europe convinced many legislators that the Soviet threat was fading, which in turn made them less willing to support big-ticket defense programs. The scope for controversy inevitably widened.

The debate over the B-2 bomber illustrates how changes in acceptable cost influence agenda setting. Throughout the 1980s legislators from across the policical spectrum supported the B-2 even though they knew the plane would be the most expensive defense program in U.S. history. Efforts to derail the program repeatedly fizzled out, and by the end of 1989 Congress had funded production of fifteen planes. In 1990, however, political support for the plane eroded so rapidly that DoD unexpectedly cut the planned B-2 fleet nearly in half, and Washington geared up for a battle over the remaining planes. Why suddenly was the B-2 controversial? None of the substantive arguments against the plane had changed, no horror stories of B-2 fraud and abuse had appeared in the media, and the federal budget deficit was no worse than in previous years. What had changed was the international climate. The collapse of the Iron Curtain convinced many legislators that the plane now cost too much. And the widespread belief that Mikhail Gorbachev had turned Soviet foreign policy on its head made it likely that big-ticket items would sit less well with Congress in the 1990s than they would have when the Cold War was alive and well.

6 ≫ ≪

Decisions

WHY DOES CONGRESS vote as it does once a nuclear weapons program appears on its agenda? The deferential lens offers no help here; it expects few programs to appear on Congress's agenda. The policy lens provides the best explanation of agenda setting, but it may not explain how Congress decides issues. Agenda setting and decision making are distinct (albeit related) activities. A program may get pushed onto the agenda for policy reasons while votes on the issue split along parochial lines. What determines how members of Congress vote?

Statistical studies reveal that legislators' ideology, as measured by their *public* roll-call voting histories, best predicts congressional voting. Contrary to the parochial lens, constituency interest seldom correlates with voting. These findings support the policy lens, but they do not validate it. Members' publicly expressed views do not *necessarily* derive from their private policy preferences. Members might cast votes to advance their own policy views or to express (what they judge to be) constituent opinion. The accuracy of the competing explanations needs to be assessed, but attempts to do so raise a thorny empirical problem: no mechanism exists for determining the "true" reasons why members vote as they do. Nonetheless, the available evidence suggests that more often than not legislators' votes on nuclear weapons do reflect their private policy views.

The argument that legislators vote their policy views on nuclear weapons issues is fully consistent with Congress's failure to cancel any major weapons program in the 1970s and 1980s. Of course, the conventional wisdom blames the parochial imperative for Congress's willingness to sustain DoD programs. But the available evidence does not support the parochial argument. Congress's failure to kill weapons programs owes to four other factors: the strength of hawks on Capitol Hill; the willingness of the executive branch to modify programs that come under attack; legislative reciprocity; and norms about the role of the president in foreign policy.

Evidence

As chapter 1 noted, political scientists have published numerous studies on the determinants of congressional voting on defense policy. Virtually all studies find that ideology, but not constituency benefit, correlates with defense voting. To take one example, a study of Senate voting on arms control issues concluded: "Senators apparently can and do take a *general* stand with little regard to defense PACs [political action committees] and with even less to defense interests in the state."[1] This and similar findings lend credence to the policy lens. Still, most studies examine congressional voting on defense issues as a whole rather than on individual weapons systems. Do the same results hold when only votes on individual programs are analyzed?

The first published study of congressional voting on a specific nuclear weapons system analyzed Senate voting on the Sentinel/Safeguard ABM program.[2] The ABM study found that a senator's position on a general liberal-conservative scale—as measured by the ideological ratings compiled by Americans for Constitutional Action (ACA) and Americans for Democratic Action (ADA)— provided the best predictor of how he or she voted. The more liberal the senator, the more likely he or she was to vote to cancel ABM. None of several measures of state economic benefit correlated with Senate voting. In particular, liberals from high-benefit states were just as inclined to vote against ABM as were liberals from low-benefit states. Some senators changed their stance on ABM between 1968 and 1970, but virtually all moved from a position that was out of accord with their basic ideological position to one closer to it.

The second published analysis of congressional voting on a specific nuclear weapons system examined Senate voting in the mid-1970s on the B-1 bomber program.[3] Like the ABM study, the B-1 study found that senators' positions on a general liberal-conservative continuum (measured by ADA scores) provided the best predictor of how they voted. Once again, a state's economic interest in the program did not correlate with how senators voted. Conservative senators from low-benefit states voted just like conservative senators from high-benefit states, and liberal senators from high-benefit states voted like liberal senators from low-benefit states. Contrary to the conventional wisdom then, ideology and not constituency benefit explains Senate voting on the B-1.

The findings for the B-1 are the more striking of the two studies. If the conventional wisdom about constituency interests is true, then the B-1 is one weapons systems where parochialism *should* be evident. For over two decades Congress had tried to force the White House to build a new manned strategic bomber, and the air force considered procurement of a successor to the B-52 its highest priority. Any dovish member representing a high-benefit state had an ample record on which to justify a vote for the B-1. To make it doubly difficult for doves and moderates to vote against a new manned bomber, the air force maximized the geographical spread of B-1 expenditures.[4] The work was spread "among 5,200 subcontractors in 48 states and 400 congressional districts."[5] Only Montana and North Dakota missed out.[6] Nor did dovish members fear they would alienate constituents with a pro–B-1 vote. Constituent opposition to B-1 fell far short of that seen in the fight against ABM.[7]

The results of the B-1 study are also surprising because as the Senate decided the B-1's fate in 1977 it was rebuffing President Carter's plan to kill several major water projects.[8] Carter had pledged to halt pork-barrel water projects during the campaign but once in office he discovered that the parochial imperative ran strong in the Senate (and House); senators emphatically defended the projects intended for their state. After a legislative battle that consumed most of his first year in Congress—a time when presidents supposedly enjoy a "honeymoon" in their relations with Capitol Hill—Carter won only 34 percent of the cuts he had sought to make in the budget for water projects. In contrast, the Senate easily sustained Carter's decision to cancel the B-1. Given that projected B-1 expenditures were five times those of the disputed dams, parochial voting should have been evident in the case of the B-1 bomber. But it wasn't.

The ABM and B-1 studies suggest that the policy lens best explains how Congress votes on nuclear weapons programs. But the studies do not settle the issue. One problem is that the findings may reflect the methodologies the studies used rather than reality. Neither study controlled factors such as party affiliation, electoral vulnerability, or presidential popularity that might have influenced Senate voting. Had these factors been controlled, constituency interests might have predicted Senate voting. A second problem with the ABM and B-1 studies is that neither one examined House votes. The reason for the oversight is simple: data are not available on how much each congressional district stood to gain from production of ABM and B-1.[9] Yet it is risky to assume that what holds true for Senate voting also holds true for the House; representatives may be more parochially minded than senators because congressional districts are smaller and less diverse than states.

Recent studies have examined congressional voting on nuclear weapons with these problems in mind. The first examined Senate and House voting on several weapons programs.[10] In the case of the Senate, the multiprogram study analyzed voting on ABM, B-1, MX, and SDI. The study found that senators' hawkishness—measured using the NSI compiled by the American Security Council—provided the best predictor of how they voted. Using more general measures of ideology (e.g., ACA and ADA scores) in place of the NSI did not change the results. Party affiliation also shaped Senate voting in the 1980s but not before then; even when ideology, constituency interest, electoral vulnerability, and presidential popularity (among other things) were controlled, Republicans were more inclined than Democrats in the 1980s to support nuclear weapons programs. The Reagan administration, however, did not cause the rise of partisan voting. Increased partisanship on nuclear weapons in the 1980s instead mirrored a long-term trend in congressional politics toward greater party voting on both defense and domestic issues.[11]

The multiprogram study also found little in Senate voting to support the parochial hypothesis. State economic benefit, whether measured in absolute or per capita terms, did not explain voting on the ABM, B-1, and MX programs. State benefit was related to SDI voting during the Ninety-ninth Congress (1985–86), but the result was produced by a statistical outlier; when one senator's votes were dropped from the analysis, state benefit ceased to explain votes. (Excluding other senators did not restore the significance of the state benefit variable.) The senator in question was Jeff Bingaman (D-N.M.), who generally voted for SDI funding although his defense views were dovish. New Mexico's substantial stake in the program probably explains his votes; it received five times more SDI funds per capita than the next largest beneficiary. Controlling factors that might obscure the constituency benefit-voting link, such as electoral vulnerability, presidential popularity, and unemployment (among others), never produced a robust correlation between state economic benefit and senators' votes. State economic benefit also did not predict the NSI ratings of individual senators, so it was not the case that the hawkishness measure masked parochial behavior. Of course, the results do not mean that no senators voted parochially. Some no doubt did, but these senators seldom determined the outcome of votes; few votes would have had a different outcome if every senator whose hawkishness score fell below the chamber mean had voted against the program in question.

The multiprogram study also examined House voting on the B-1, MX, ASAT, and SDI programs. Lacking complete data on spending by congressional district, the study could not control all the factors that might influence House voting. The study instead used simple correlations and a host of "second-best" tests. These tests produced virtually the same results as those for Senate voting. Representatives' hawkishness correlated strongly with their support for weapons programs; the more hawkish members were the more likely they were to support the program in question. Party affiliation and weapons support also were highly correlated, though in the absence of a multivariate analysis it was impossible to conclude definitively that partisanship contributed to House voting independently of ideology. Moreover, the correlations between party and votes were significantly higher in the 1980s than the 1970s, evidence of the increased partisanship on defense issues in the House in the 1980s.

Finally, the study examined how dovish House members voted in light of data on the location of the major contractors (but not subcontractors) for the B-1 bomber, the MX missile, and SDI. If the parochial lens is correct, then doves should vote their constituency's economic interests rather than their own policy views whenever the two conflict. This relatively crude test produced little evidence that doves voted their district's economic interests. The finding was most dramatic in the case of SDI where the data were the most detailed; looking only at doves who represented a district that hosted a major SDI contractor, these representatives voted by a margin of nearly six-to-one (thirty-four to six) *against* SDI funding. Moreover, those members who voted parochially did not affect the outcome of the votes on SDI or any of the other weapons systems examined.

The results of the multiprogram study support the claim that the policy lens best explains congressional decision making on nuclear weapons programs. This is especially the case with Senate decision making; the study's conclusions about House voting can only be considered suggestive and not definitive. As was the case with the ABM and B-1 studies, the multiprogram study might have missed the relationship between district benefit and support for nuclear weapons systems in House voting merely because the study did not control for influences that obscure the constituency-voting link.

Two subsequent studies addressed the problem of the determinants of House voting. The first applied probit analysis to House voting on the MX missile in 1984 and 1985.[12] Not surprisingly, the study found that ideology—here measured using *Congressional Quarterly's* conservative coalition support scores—was a significant predictor of representatives' support for MX. Party affiliation also influenced House voting on some but not all votes. Last, the analysis produced evidence that district benefits influenced how members voted on some MX votes in 1984. The study found no evidence, however, that district benefits influenced any MX votes in 1985. The divergent findings for votes in 1984 and 1985 are perplexing because two of the amendments up for consideration in 1985 were virtually identical to the 1984 amendments for which there was statistical evidence of parochial voting. Presumably, if members were voting parochially they would do so across time when faced with similar issues. (The study controlled other factors influencing House voting so the inconsistent results cannot be easily blamed on other influences.)

The other study used probit analysis to analyze both Senate and House voting on SDI during the Hundredth Congress (1987–88).[13] Like previous studies, the SDI study found a strong relationship in both House and Senate voting between the hawkishness of members (measured using the NSI) and their support for SDI. Party affiliation also influenced how members voted on some SDI votes. Even more important, the study found little evidence of parochial voting in either the House or the Senate, even though a variety of measures of constituency benefit were examined and though the study controlled other potential influences on congressional decision making that might obscure the parochial imperative. The constituency benefit variable was statistically significant on half of the House votes, but these results were highly sensitive to how a single member, Rep. Bill Richardson (D-N.M.), voted. Richardson, a moderate, was a strong SDI supporter, perhaps because his district was the fourth biggest beneficiary of the program. When Richardson's votes were omitted from the analysis the parochial variable ceased to be significant on every vote save one. (Excluding other representatives did not restore the significance of the constituency benefit variable.) And, on every vote where the constituency benefit variable was significant, the pro-SDI forces *lost*. That is, even if some members voted parochially their efforts did not change the outcome of the vote.

Studies on the determinants of congressional voting on nuclear weapons programs, then, support the policy lens and discredit the parochial lens. Statistical analyses find time and again that legislators' general views on defense policy or their views on a general conservative-liberal continuum provide the best predictors of congressional voting on nuclear weapons programs. Partisan considerations also influence how members vote, particularly since 1980, but party affiliation plays a subsidiary role. Statistical evidence does not support the parochial hypothesis; constituency benefits, however measured, do a poor job of predicting how members vote. Despite popular images to the contrary, members of Congress are not "hustling" pork in their votes on nuclear weapons.

Public Votes and Private Preferences

When members of Congress vote on nuclear weapons issues (or any other policy issue) are they voting their own policy preferences or are they voting constituent opinion? The proposition that members vote the constituency's opinion rather than their own has intuitive appeal. It is often alleged that members either have no policy preferences or are opportunists who seek out the politically advantageous position on any issue. As one wag commented about the "flip-flops" in Rep. Richard Gephardt's (D-Mo.) voting record, "If he thought dressing up like a vegetable would help him win, [he] would appear as a head of lettuce."[14] By most accounts members do worry about constituent opinion, and presumably constituent opinion becomes more important as the issue becomes more salient.[15]

Studies that show that constituency *characteristics* correlate with congressional voting would seem to provide some evidence to support the constituency explanation.[16] But these studies do not establish that legislators vote solely or even largely on the basis of constituency *opinion*. Why not? The fundamental problem is that the personal policy preferences and the constituent opinion explanations overlap to a large extent. When a legislator's policy views coincide with those of the constituency, voting on the basis of private preferences is indistinguishable from voting on the basis of constituent opinion. For all practical purposes, a member's vote in this situation is overdetermined. Consequently, it is possible to tell whether floor votes express personal policy views or constituent attitudes only when legislators' policy views diverge from those of their constituents. This raises an inevitable question, namely, how do members vote when their policy preferences conflict with those of their constituents?

Any attempt to answer this question runs into obstacles. On the one hand, no perfect method exists by which to establish a member's true policy positions. Interviews are the best means available, but even these are flawed. As a (rather cynical) commentator once observed, "Most politicians . . . have no trouble persuading themselves that the politically convenient position is also their heartfelt belief."[17] Presumably, such members are equally adept at convincing their listeners. On the other hand, even if the true policy preferences of members of Congress could be ascertained with some certainty, determining constituency opinion is no small feat.[18] Members might look to the constituency as a whole or any of a wide variety of subgroups. And when groups in the constituency disagree on policy issues it is not always obvious which ones legislators should heed.

What then can be said? The safest conclusion is that members do not always vote on nuclear weapons programs solely to express their private policy preferences. After all, studies repeatedly find that party affiliation influences how members vote. It also would fly in the face of previous research and considerable anecdotal evidence to argue that members of Congress never sacrifice their policy preferences to avoid alienating voters. By the same token, however, analyses of members' ideological ratings find that the ratings cannot be explained as proxies for constituency interests even when those interests are broadly defined.[19] In other words, ideological ratings do appear to measure members' personal views.

Several reasons make it likely that *most* members vote on nuclear weapons issues according to their private policy preferences. First, the legislator who has no policy preferences on the major issues of the day, a category into which nuclear weapons certainly fall, is a relatively rare individual. "When a congressman says, as several did, 'I usually vote my political philosophy,' it is not an idle statement. 'You'll find that most guys are pretty well set most of the time,' said one congressman. 'People have well-formed opinions, and there's not much that can be done to shake them out of them.' "[20] This is not to say that all members are well informed on the issues at hand. Some are, and some are not. But most legislators have opinions of one sort or another.

Second, "it often happens that a congressman never feels pressured by his constituency and in fact never even takes them into account, simply because he is 'their kind of people' anyway."[21] Members often claim their policy views seldom conflict with constituent opinion for just this reason. As one representative put it, "I reflect my district. We agree on most things. That's why I got elected."[22] Of course, such answers may be self-serving. Yet the entire recruitment process for new legislators—residence, coalition building, elections—

makes it likely that members will share many policy attitudes with their constituents. The nature of the recruitment process, of course, is why studies repeatedly find that constituency characteristics correlate with the voting records of members. Moreover, "there is strong evidence that members of Congress vote consistently over time on issues. . . . It seems unlikely in the extreme that a member of Congress could remain so consistent over a career but not be in basic agreement with the reelection constituency."[23]

Third, members of Congress have some freedom to construct a reelection constituency that reflects their own policy views.[24] It is a commonplace that legislators worry less about the opinions of all voters than they do about the opinions of their supporters. This difference between the geographic constituency and the reelection (or support) constituency suggests

> that the effort to separate personal beliefs from constituency is futile and misdirected. A geographic constituency is a smorgasbord of discrete groups that the entrepreneurial politician can select from to form support constituencies that are in accord with their personal beliefs. If these support constituencies are large and powerful enough, the politician wins. And if the politician wins, he/she essentially never changes his/her personal beliefs. . . . Models that do not incorporate a politician's personal beliefs (however arrived at) simply will not work well.[25]

In short, the same geographic constituency may elect individuals with very different defense views. This is especially true of states; "state electorates are able to support a wide range of defense voting in their senators, and, thus somewhat free of restraint, senators can afford to vote ideologically."[26] Thus, states often send one hawkish senator and one dovish senator to Capitol Hill.

Fourth, when members agree with constituents on most issues but disagree with them on some, a vote contrary to constituent opinion often does not pose great costs. Voters generally do not know the specifics of a legislator's voting record, even when a major issue is involved, unless it directly affects the constituency.[27] One member from a moderate-to-hawkish district, for example, offered an anti-MX amendment that received considerable national publicity. Yet when he visited his district later that week, "nobody bothered to ask me about it."[28] Unlike defense policy, however, voters take great interest in constituency service and domestic issues. One member, whose moderate-to-dovish views were at odds with his hawkish district, said his constituents were not concerned about his voting record on nuclear weapons: "The press are the only people that care about it one way or the other. If you answer your mail, attend town meetings, if you are accessible, if you can get social security problems resolved, that's what matters to people."[29]

Even if votes on nuclear weapons are important to constituents (or certain groups of constituents), this does not necessarily mean that a vote contrary to constituent opinion will cause great harm. Members are less concerned with casting an individual vote that will be unpopular at home than they are in compiling a string of votes that alienates voters.[30] Thus hawks (doves) can oppose (support) a weapon their constituents support (oppose) provided that they do not vote this way on all defense issues. For example, Sen. Gordon Humphrey (R-N.H.) opposed the MX missile. Even though New Hampshire was the eighth largest beneficiary of the MX program (see table 5-2), Senator Humphrey won reelection in 1984 by his biggest margin ever. His reputation as one of the Senate's premier hawks protected him from charges of being "soft" on national defense.

Legislators also have considerable (but not total) freedom in how they portray their records. Members know that what matters is not how they vote but how they are *perceived* as voting. As an official of the National Republican Congressional Committee puts it: "Voting at the congressional level does not turn on the issues. There is considerable evidence that people's image of a congressman is more important to their vote than his stand on the issues."[31] Among other things, members know how to use votes on symbolic amendments to offset potentially unpopular votes on substantive amendments.

The role perceptions play in sustaining a legislative career gives members an incentive to put the proper "spin" on their votes. In 1988, for instance, Rep. David Nagle (D-Iowa), a first-term legislator from a traditionally Republican district, sponsored a bill to ban tests of depressed trajectory missiles. Although he had introduced the legislation for arms control reasons, at home Nagle cast the bill as a measure that "saves about $40 billion."[32] The measure actually saved no money; DoD had no plans to test a depressed trajectory missile. But in deficit-conscious Iowa frugality played better than arms control. Another Democrat whose support for the MX missile angered many local party officials chose to neutralize the problem by recasting the issue as an example of his courage to vote his conscience. The member soon found that he had turned the issue to his advantage; "people are pretty proud that I stood up to the Democratic Party."[33] Of course, legislators may not always be able (or inclined) to change constituent perceptions. In these instances, members can seek to highlight their "positives" in other areas. Thus, one representative whose constituents did not share his opposition to ASAT weapons took care to see that voters knew about his positions on issues that directly affected the district. He had discovered that "people will accept my stand, even if they disagree, on the theory that I have some countervailing value on other issues back here."[34]

Finally, references to constituent opinion by themselves cannot explain the fierce and lengthy legislative battles that occur over programs like ABM and MX. If members are motivated by constituent opinion, then their electoral incentive is to be on the right side of the issue and not the winning side.[35] Thus, when legislators disagree with their constituents on an issue (or have no opinion at all) they need not undertake the detailed legislative work needed to push an item onto the agenda, let alone to win a substantial number of votes. These members can satisfy the electoral pressures they face simply by casting their vote in whatever way pleases their constituents. After all, constituents generally know little about how hard their representatives or senators worked any particular issue. Thus, explanations of the Wednesday Group's attempts to block the MX missile program, or Rep. George Brown's (D-Calif.) fight to derail ASAT, or Sen. Malcolm Wallop's (R-Wyo.) efforts to convince his colleagues of the need for strategic defenses must acknowledge the policy preferences of legislators.

Again, members of Congress do not always vote their personal policy preferences. Members themselves admit that they bow to constituent opinion at times in casting their votes. For instance, when Rep. Silvio Conte (R-Mass.) dropped his support for the B-1 bomber he explained his decision to Rockwell lobbyists by noting that "constituent pressure would no longer permit him to vote for the B-1."[36] On almost every major nuclear weapons vote the news media single out a handful of members who are under intense constituent pressure to change their votes. Invariably some of these legislators do switch votes. Yet two points should be kept in mind whenever stories are told about members caving in to constituent pressure. The first is that the fact that *some* members of Congress vote against their private policy beliefs on a particular issue does not warrant the conclusion that *most* legislators do. In telling the story of members who bow to constituent opinion the news media (and scholars too) often overlook the more common story of members who either agree with constituents or resist constituent pressure. Such selectivity produces a distorted view of Congress.

The second point worth remembering is that legislators often use constituent opinion as an excuse to deflect criticism from other political actors. For instance, one Republican House member who held a traditionally Democratic seat frequently irritated the Reagan White House by voting against defense programs. The legislator defended himself against charges of disloyalty by pointing to the makeup of his constituency, even though he based his votes on own policy preferences. Preferring a dissenting Republican to a dissenting Democrat, unhappy White House officials bit their tongues.[37] Likewise, in May 1983 Rep. Mervyn Dymally (D-Calif.) succumbed to an intense lobbying effort by Northrop Corporation and voted for the MX missile. (The Northrop plant in Dymally's district built the inertial guidance system for the MX and employed over two thousand workers.) Given his dovish views, Dymally found the vote distasteful. He then asked SANE, a major arms control group, to solicit anti-MX mail from his district. Dymally presented these letters to Northrop to explain why he could no longer support the MX program.[38]

In the final analysis, it is impossible to establish that the policy lens unequivocally explains House and Senate voting on nuclear weapons policy. The considerable statistical evidence that members' general defense views or ideology best predict how they vote may simply reflect the fact that legislators vote on the basis of constituent opinion. Yet members of Congress appear to be more than mere weather vanes. Although it would stretch credulity to the breaking point to argue that members never sacrifice their policy preferences to satisfy constituents, evidence suggests that members' policy views generally do not conflict with constituent opinion. Even when members find themselves at odds with the constituency, they often can vote their preferences without damaging their electoral chances.

Congress and Nuclear Weapons

Congress has never canceled a major nuclear weapons program. Most observers attribute Congress's willingness to fund all DoD requests to parochialism. Yet statistical evidence discounts the role the parochial imperative plays. At the same time, on several occasions before World War II Congress blocked major defense programs: in 1908 it cut in half Theodore Roosevelt's request for battleships; in 1916 and 1917 it killed two defense programs Woodrow Wilson initiated to prepare the country for war; and in the late 1930s it rejected naval base construction on Guam. Presumably, the legislators involved in these battles also faced the parochial imperative. (Although Guam did not have a vote in Congress, the materials used to build the base would have come from the states, which did have representation on Capitol Hill.) For these reasons, any explanation of why Congress does not cancel major weapons systems must go beyond parochialism.

The first and foremost reason why Congress does not lead on nuclear issues has to do with the strength of hawks in both the House and Senate. As figures 6-1 and 6-2 illustrate, hawks (defined here as those with an NSI score of eighty or more) constituted a near majority in both the House and Senate during the Ninety-first through Hundredth Congresses. Many fewer doves (here defined as members with an NSI score of less than twenty) sit in Congress, although their number grew in the House during the 1980s. Most of the votes used to calculate the NSI ratings involved issues where no constituency benefits were at stake; hence, figures 6-1 and 6-2 do not simply show that most members vote their parochial interests.

The predominance of hawks in Congress means that nearly every defense program begins with a near majority, no matter where the weapon is built. Hawks favor large defense buildups, and many are inclined to support DoD when it clashes with the White House, as President Carter learned firsthand

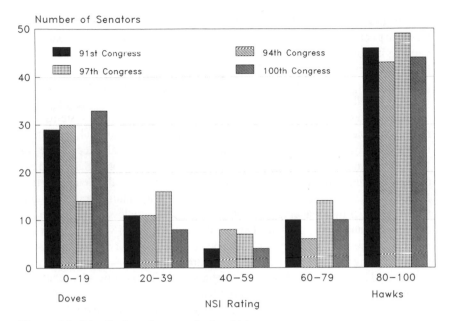

Figure 6-1. Distribution of senators by hawkishness

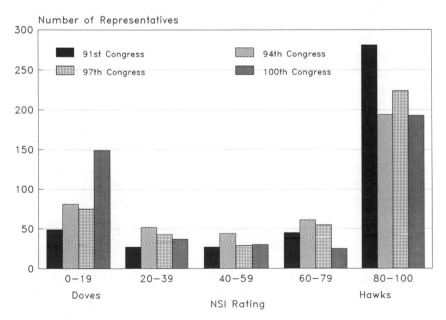

Figure 6-2. Distribution of representatives by hawkishness

with the B-1 bomber. For doves to enact their preferences into policy, however, they must convince large numbers of moderates to join them. But coalition-building is arduous work. Doves have few carrots and sticks with which to enlist the support of moderates, and most moderates initially are disposed to support DoD's requests. Doves generally are left with only the quality of their arguments to fall back on.

The second reason that Congress never cancels major weapons systems outright is that the executive branch generally counters congressional opposition by trying to find a variant of the program that will be politically acceptable. In 1969, for example, President Nixon dropped Sentinel in favor of Safeguard after he determined an area defense would not pass muster in the Senate. When MPS basing came under fire on Capitol Hill, the Carter administration sought to placate critics by advancing alternate versions that were less disruptive to the environment and less expensive. During its push for the MX, the Reagan administration cut the number of missiles and proposed a variety of basing modes to contain congressional opposition. The political success of changes like these is enhanced by the appeal of sunk cost arguments. Like most people, members of Congress dislike canceling programs when billions of dollars have already been spent. They hope that with time, money, and effort the United States can salvage its investment.

Legislative reciprocity is the third reason why Congress does not cancel weapons outright. To begin with, members of Congress have many policy goals. Even those who agree on a particular policy may disagree on how to achieve it or on its priority. Those who place a low priority on a policy will likely sacrifice it if this means they will advance a higher-priority policy. As a result, some members may vote for a weapon they would otherwise oppose if the administration promises to modify policy positions it has staked out, either in areas related to nuclear weapons (e.g., arms control proposals) or in policy domains that have nothing to do with defense.

The most visible example of this sort of legislative reciprocity was the Scowcroft Commission's MX compromise. When the MX's future looked dim at the end of 1982, Rep. Les Aspin (D-Wis.) led a coalition of moderates and doves who rescued the program in return for changes in the Reagan administration's arms control policy. Aspin spoke bluntly about his motives:

> It seemed to me that if Scowcroft came up with a bipartisan package and the President accepted that, the Democrats would not be in good shape if it was voted down. It was clear that most Democrats would vote against it. But if enough voted for it, and Reagan got it, the headline would say "Reagan Gets MX." If not, the headline would be "Democrats Block MX." Reagan could have used that as an excuse. Now that he has the tools he needs, the Administration is in a bit of a hot seat. *It has to produce an agreement.*[39]

Though Aspin's coalition clearly had partisan concerns in mind, it also saw MX as a lever by which to force President Reagan to change arms control policies.

Another form of legislative reciprocity is old-fashioned "horse trading," voting for a weapons system in exchange for administration promises to deliver parochial or personal benefits. To take just one example, in March 1985 Rep. Stephen L. Neal (D-N.C.) dropped his opposition to MX and voted for the missile. Neal's change of heart reportedly came after the White House agreed to lift its approval of a House Republican campaign committee plan "to spend $6 million on an advertising campaign to 'soften' up Neal and 24 other House Democrats prior to the 1986 elections."[40] Some members also see a vote on a controversial weapons system as an opportunity to put the administration in their debt. For instance, after Rep. Tommy Robinson (D-Ark.) voted for the MX in 1985, he denied that he had engaged in any horse trading. Robinson admitted, however, that the vote "gives me a bargaining chip with the White House."[41]

Despite the media's fascination with horse trading, few members trade on any single vote. Moreover, many alleged cases of horse trading more closely resemble extortion. When a weapons system encounters trouble on Capitol Hill, members who support the program often see this as an opportunity to extract concessions from the administration. In 1985, for instance, Rep. Harold Rogers (R-Ky.) opposed White House plans to phase out some price supports for tobacco, an important crop in his district. To underscore his displeasure, Rogers, who had consistently voted for MX, "took a walk" during a crucial MX vote in the House Appropriations Committee. After reassurances from senior White House officials about future tobacco policy, Rogers voted for the MX.[42] Similarly, Sen. Alfonse D'Amato (R-N.Y.), one of the most hawkish members of the Senate, "became notorious for haggling in private with the Reagan White House, pushing what one official called his New York 'shopping lists' before he would agree to support the president on big items such as the MX missile."[43] Bargaining of this sort, although it aggravates White House officials, does not increase legislative support for weapons systems.

Legislative reciprocity, in either its policy or parochial-based forms, highlights the superior bargaining position of the White House. Presidents have power. They can usually convince waffling legislators to vote with them, either by promising to make changes in other policies or by attending to more narrow needs. Critics, on the other hand, have no similar reservoir of influence to which they can turn. They must rely largely on the quality of their arguments. As Sen. Lawton Chiles (D-Fla.) notes, what results is that "It's hard to beat the president. . . . You'd have to have 10 or 15 votes to spare because he can always get one or two [turned around]."[44]

The final reason why Congress does not cancel weapons programs outright is that some moderate members defer to the president on contentious weapons issues when arms control negotiations are involved. In 1970, for instance, four senators reversed their decision to oppose Safeguard after administration officials persuaded them that the program was critical to the progress of the SALT negotiations.[45] Cynics might suggest that these were politically convenient conversions. Yet the following year Sen. John Sherman Cooper (R-Ky.), who had led the anti-ABM movement, voted for the program because he decided "it best that we do not alter the basis upon which negotiations are taking place."[46]

Of course, members do not necessarily believe the program in question is desirable when they decide to defer to the president. In March 1985, for example, Congress released funds for the MX missile, which had been frozen the previous October. The White House triumphed only after it lobbied intensively to convince members that the MX was needed as a bargaining lever at the recently reopened START negotiations. Three months later Congress voted to cap MX deployment at half the planned level. Why the mixed votes? Because many moderates doubted the military utility of MX but did not want to deal the president a major foreign policy defeat just as negotiations began. Once they had symbolically ratified the president's foreign policy supremacy, they felt free to constrain what they believed to be a bad weapons system.

Most observers explain congressional deference to the president on high-level foreign policy negotiations by referring to the electoral connection. To quote Sen. Dale Bumpers (D-Ark.), "A lot of people are just frightened to win one on a weapons system for fear that the President will beat them to death for being weak on defense."[47] Despite the intuitive appeal of the electoral connection argument, attempts to assess it have produced at best mixed results.[48] Nevertheless, fear of the president may tip some moderates who doubt the wisdom of a program in favor of it.

Yet the electoral connection is given too much credit in explaining Congress and foreign policy. To begin with, policy calculations also play a role. Some members place a higher priority on arms control than on limiting what enters the U.S. arsenal. They can point to the ABM and INF treaties for evidence that building weapons can promote arms control, so killing a weapon may impair U.S. bargaining leverage. Even if members do not accept the bargaining chip argument, they still may see stopping a weapon as counterproductive. As Representative Aspin's remarks suggest, some legislators see votes that block weapons development as Pyrrhic victories that reduce the pressure on the president to negotiate. These legislators believe arms control goals are better served by keeping weapons programs alive. So long as a program survives, the White House will have a more difficult time blaming Congress for any failure to produce an arms control agreement.

The electoral connection also cannot explain why members often side with the president on national security matters even when voters do not. "Congress could have ended American participation in the Southeast Asia war at any time

. . . simply by refusing to appropriate money to fight it. However, in the House of Representatives, this was never done, even during the dying days of the war when public sentiment against it was overwhelming."[49] The Senate passed the Panama Canal treaties by the required two-thirds majority even though polls showed over 60 percent of the public opposed the treaties.[50] In September 1983 Congress approved a resolution authorizing American marines to remain in Lebanon for up to eighteen months. Congress took the step even though Americans were divided over the marines' presence in Beirut, and even though a majority opposed any increased involvement.[51] During the early 1980s Congress frequently supported President Reagan's Central America policy even though a substantial majority of Americans opposed it.[52]

Why do legislators often refuse to vote against the president even when they will not alienate constituents? Because many members believe *in principle* that Congress should exercise great caution before it shackles the president's foreign policy powers. The deferential norm, of course, was born in the experiences of World War II, and it dominated Congress until the mid-1960s. Although the Vietnam war severely weakened congressional deference, the deferential norm retains legitimacy among moderates. For them, Congress cannot manage foreign policy effectively, so it must not constrain the president's freedom of maneuver without good cause. Indeed, when weapons systems become controversial, most moderates prefer that the executive branch modify the program rather than forcing that burden onto Congress.

The power of the deferential norm among moderates is why presidents often link troubled weapons systems to arms control policy. The Nixon administration, for example, "linked several strategic initiatives, particularly ABM and MIRV, to success at SALT."[53] In 1970 the White House did not have enough votes to sustain its Safeguard request. To avoid a major policy defeat, President Nixon directed Gerard Smith, the chief U.S. negotiator at SALT, to send a telegram to the Senate "stressing the need for Safeguard for successful negotiations."[54] The telegram convinced several key senators to vote with the administration. In the words of Secretary of State Henry Kissinger, Smith's message "saved the day for 'Safeguard.' "[55]

The Reagan administration also tied procurement policy to arms control negotiations in its battle to save MX. The Scowcroft Commission essentially abandoned any military justification for the missile, arguing instead that MX was needed for arms control leverage. When the Soviet Union suspended negotiations following the initial deployment of Pershing II, the Scowcroft compromise collapsed. To underscore his argument that the missile was necessary for talks, President Reagan ordered chief arms control negotiator Max Kampelman to return from Geneva to lobby members of the House. As with Smith's telegram, Kampelman's visit saved the day for MX.

Presidential efforts to link weapons procurement to arms control negotiations are not necessarily motivated by good faith. Smith's telegram had all the earmarks of a political ploy; whereas his telegram described Safeguard expansion as a "vital bargaining element," six months earlier Smith had told members of SASC, "I don't think I go as far as some people would who think you ought to go ahead faster with Safeguard to step up the bargaining advantage."[56] Thirteen years later many House members doubted Kampelman's claim that success at Geneva hinged on whether Congress funded the MX missile. Nevertheless, when presidents argue forcefully that they need a particular weapons system to succeed at the bargaining table, many moderates find it very difficult to say no. And without the support of moderate legislators, congressional efforts to block weapons development fail.

7 ≫ ≪

Congress and Defense Policy

THE EVIDENCE presented in preceding chapters points to the policy lens as the best explanation of congressional decision making on nuclear weapons policy. Contrary to much of the literature on Congress, members care about the substance of policy and not just where the benefits go. This is not to say that legislators never submit to the parochial imperative, or worry about how votes will affect their reelection chances, or defer to the president's judgment. Most members do at one time or another. Nevertheless, members act largely on the basis of their policy views.

Does the policy lens explain congressional decision making on other defense issues? The conventional wisdom argues that parochialism drives congressional decisions about conventional weapons programs. The available evidence and common sense both suggest, however, that the parochial imperative plays at best a subsidiary role in the conventional force acquisition process. Members do at times try to advance parochial interests, but Congress generally appropriates funds for conventional weapons systems because agreement exists that the nation's security warrants the weapons and not because constituents demand jobs. Most conventional weapons programs would continue to be procured even if Congress dropped out of the decision-making process.

Unlike weapons programs, the parochial imperative clearly motivates congressional behavior on military base issues. Members of Congress, be they Democrats or Republicans, doves or hawks, newcomers or veterans, fight ardently for military facilities in their districts and states. In the 1960s and 1970s Congress enacted several pieces of legislation that effectively suppressed the executive branch's ability to close military bases, regardless of cost or need. Legislators continue to devote considerable time and effort to seeing that DoD invests new monies in the facilities in their constituencies.

Why does congressional behavior vary across defense issues? The answer lies in a basic lesson about life on Capitol Hill, namely, that members of Congress will vote their policy preferences only so long as the costs of doing so are not too high. Legislators essentially pursue their conceptions of good policy subject to a "constituency constraint." Opposition to a weapons system usually poses relatively low electoral costs to members, and it can even be an electoral

123

plus. But legislators who fail to work to protect military facilities in their constituencies run great electoral risks. Norms also shape how members assess
electoral costs. Because weapons have a direct link to national security, legislators evidently are more inclined to evaluate these programs from a national perspective than they otherwise would be.

Nuclear Weapons and the Policy Lens

The policy lens best explains the role Congress played in nuclear weapons policy in the 1970s and 1980s. Members of Congress tried to surface critical issues
in nuclear weapons policy, and they decided those issues primarily on the basis
of their policy views and not parochial interests. To be sure, Congress did not
subject all programs to the same degree of scrutiny. The House and Senate are,
after all, political bodies and not bureaucracies; their efforts are necessarily
limited. Nor did the collapse of the old norms of deference proceed at the same
pace in both chambers. The Senate began its first serious reviews of the merits
of weapons development in the late 1960s, but it took the House nearly a decade
longer. Nonetheless, by the early 1980s legislators in both chambers were willing to grapple with the merits of nuclear weapons issues.

Members of Congress, however, do not operate as Burkean legislators, de-
liberating at great length and with great thoroughness on what course of action
is best for the nation and without regard to all else. Some members vote parochially while others cast their ballots for partisan reasons. Nor do members who
shun parochial and partisan pressures necessarily spend hours evaluating the
arguments for and against a program (though some may), refuse to compromise
(though some may), or decline to exploit political advantages that favor their
preferred policies (though some may). Decision making in Congress is not a
systematic and dispassionate affair given only to pure deliberation. Still, most
members decide on the basis of their policy views.

Members of Congress also do not weigh every possible objection to a policy
equally. As chapter 5 showed, members pay far more attention to weapons systems that depart from declaratory doctrine or which threaten to cross thresholds
in weapons acquisition. Other policy-based criticisms generally do not carry
great weight. Put another way, members of Congress are far more attentive to
the "big picture" than is typically acknowledged. They recognize they are not
weapons engineers or nuclear strategists. Members devote themselves mostly
to assessing proposed changes in the policy status quo and not to dissecting the
performance specifications of individual weapons or the subtle nuances of
strategy.

But the policy lens does recognize that legislators care about reelection. Regardless of their views on nuclear weapons policy, representatives and senators

generally want to be reelected. At times concerns about reelection dissuade legislators from tackling politically difficult issues and encourage them to promote local interests. In 1981, for example, Sen. Howard Metzenbaum (D-Ohio) dropped his opposition to the B-1B. Metzenbaum faced a tough reelection campaign, and the United Auto Workers had "let him know that their support hinged on his backing the B-1B."[1] Yet cases of members abandoning their personal policy preferences to advance constituency interests are more the exception than the rule on nuclear weapons policy. Even when legislators do act parochially, their behavior often has no practical effect. Metzenbaum's switch, for instance, did not matter because Congress strongly favored production of the B-1B.

Electoral considerations also provide members of Congress with positive incentives to vote their policy preferences. A whole host of changes in the American political arena since the 1960s "made it more rewarding, both electorally and personally, for congressional candidates and officeholders to take publicly visible positions on defense issues and to demonstrate an ability to help shape defense policy."[2] The emergence of nuclear weapons policy as a potential source of electoral profit had the biggest impact on defense critics. Whereas members of Congress once declined to criticize DoD because they feared being labeled "un-American," in the post-Vietnam era legislators found that opposing weapons procurement could help build constituent support. During the battles over the MX, for instance, the reelection campaigns of many doves and moderates benefited from the assistance of committed antinuclear weapons activists.

The policy lens also recognizes that DoD and defense firms try to use the parochial imperative to their advantage. DoD and defense contractors at times (how often is debated) widen the geographical distribution of contracts and subcontracts to maximize support for a program on Capitol Hill.[3] The most extreme example is the B-1 bomber, where the air force spread contracts throughout the country to increase the chances for congressional approval.[4] The services and defense contractors also take great care to inform legislators of the constituency's economic stake in particular programs. Again, the B-1 provides the most dramatic example. As criticism of the plane mounted in 1975,

Rockwell and Air Force lobbyists armed themselves with meticulous lists of every B-1 subcontract location, cross-referenced by state, town, and congressional district. The studies, prepared both by Rockwell and by the Air Force comptroller's office, showed how many dollars of B-1 money flowed into a congressional district each month. This information allowed the lobbyists to show members of Congress, down to the last dollar, how their constituents benefited from the B-1. The data became even more potent as subcontractors, mayors, and union leaders were enlisted to lobby their members of Congress.[5]

But such full-court lobbying often does not account for much. Despite the impressive lobbying effort on behalf of the B-1, most legislators, both in the House and the Senate, voted for or against the plane in accordance with their overall policy views and not with their constituency's economic interest.

The policy lens did not always explain congressional behavior on nuclear weapons issues. Most scholars agree that the deferential lens best describes and explains Congress's handling of nuclear weapons issues (and defense policy more generally) from the end of World War II until the late 1960s.[6] The defense committees, and Congress as a whole, seldom intervened in the acquisition process. When Congress questioned particular programs, it usually examined issues of fraud and waste, and not the military and diplomatic merits of weapons systems. Nor did parochialism guide congressional behavior toward nuclear weapons in the 1945–67 period. Whereas Congress devoted considerable time to issues like military pay and base construction, it generally neglected weapons development.[7]

Why did congressional behavior change? The most important reason was Vietnam. The war divided the country on national security matters, raised doubts about the "imperial presidency," and weakened the military's claims of expertise. Vietnam encouraged other trends both in Congress and outside it. Numerous candidates rode antiwar platforms to seats in Congress. These legislators helped energize the reform movement that swept Congress in the 1970s and ushered in the outside game. Vietnam also stimulated the growth of public-interest groups (both dovish and hawkish) dedicated to defense issues, and it convinced existing organizations to enter the defense debate. Again, these developments all combined to lower the electoral costs (or to raise the electoral benefits) facing members who criticized DoD.

Of course, the pattern of congressional politics that held in the 1970s and 1980s occurred in a particular world context, namely, one of peaceful coexistence. Although U.S.-Soviet relations had their low moments during this time —most notably immediately after the Soviet invasion of Afghanistan—they never fell to levels comparable to those seen during the 1950s. If superpower relations had fallen to (and stayed at) such levels following Vietnam, members of Congress, mindful of the World War II precedent, no doubt would have given the president great leeway on nuclear weapons policy. Indeed, in 1980 and 1981 many doves resigned themselves to the political inevitability of higher levels of defense spending over the short term. By the same token, however, the dramatic changes Mikhail Gorbachev made to Soviet foreign policy in the late 1980s raised the possibility of a Congress even *more* willing to question nuclear weapons policy. Less able to use anti-Soviet rhetoric, presidents may find it more difficult to build congressional support for their programs.

Conventional Weapons

Does the policy lens explain congressional decision making on conventional weapons programs? Answering the question is difficult because anecdotes have substituted for systematic analysis in most discussions of conventional weapons. Part of the reason why tanks and rifles have attracted less scholarly attention than bombers and ICBMs is that conventional weapons are less "sexy" than nuclear weapons. The relative lack of systematic study of conventional weapons also stems from a lack of appropriate data. Figures on the geographical distribution of expenditures are even more difficult to obtain for individual conventional weapons programs than for nuclear ones. Only two statistical analyses have been conducted on congressional voting on conventional weapons.

The first study analyzed Senate defense votes cast in 1982.[8] Contrary to the research on nuclear weapons, the study found that ideology did not predict how senators voted on specific weapons systems but that parochial interests did. Two problems, however, cast serious doubt on the validity of the findings. One problem is that the study used state characteristics (e.g., overall per capita DoD spending, degree of unionization of the labor force) to measure state economic interest; data were not available on how much each state stood to gain from the programs in question. The quality of state characteristics as a proxy for actual program expenditures is debatable; hence, the results may be distorted. The other problem is that the study examined mostly votes on O&M programs rather than on weapons programs. Personal ideology should fail to explain voting on O&M votes because it is difficult to say *a priori* how doves and hawks will split over an issue such as whether to allow DoD to hire civilian firms to provide security at military bases. On the three votes that actually involved weapons programs, ideology was significant twice. As for the third vote, neither the ideology *nor* the state characteristics variables were significant.

The second study of congressional voting on conventional weapons examined two House votes on the navy's aircraft carrier program.[9] Unlike the Senate study just mentioned, the carrier study had data on how much each congressional district stood to benefit. When the study examined spending for the House as a whole, it found no evidence that district interest affected how members voted. Only the hawkishness of members had a statistically significant effect on voting. Once representatives were differentiated by region and party, however, a different result emerged. Here the study found that spending levels influenced the votes of nonsoutherners but not those of southerners. Parochialism apparently also shaped how Republicans voted but not Democrats.

The findings of the carrier study merit four comments. First, although nonsoutherners and Republicans voted differently from southerners and Democrats, it is not clear *why* they did. Lacking a theoretical explanation for the difference, it is possible, and perhaps even likely, that the results are a statistical artifact or a quirk of the carrier issue. Second, "because both amendments to delete the carriers lost by such wide margins . . . [spending] could not have had much impact on the final outcome."[10] Third, the lopsided margin of the vote raises the prospect of strategic voting. When members from interested districts know that Congress will fund a program, they have no reason to vote against the request. Legislators are not martyrs. To vote against the carrier would anger some constituents without advancing a member's policy preferences. So legislators are more inclined to vote parochially on lopsided votes so they can afford to vote their policy views on close issues where their votes are likely to matter. Finally, the study concluded that hawkishness "remains the most potent predictor of congressional roll-call voting behavior. A member's party membership or NSI score reveals more about whether he or she will support a weapon than does the amount of local jobs it produces."[11]

The only other evidence about how Congress handles conventional weapons programs is anecdotal. One notable case is the Bigeye binary chemical weapon. Here parochial interests failed to help the program. Sen. David Pryor (D-Ark.) not only opposed production of Bigeye, he led the Senate fight to kill the program. Given Pryor's relatively dovish voting record, this would be unremarkable except that the weapons were to be built in Pine Bluff, Arkansas. During Senate debate in 1987, Pryor confronted the jobs argument directly: "A lot of people in Pine Bluff want to go into the new generation of nerve gas simply because it is going to create something called jobs, j-o-b-s. Jobs drive too many military decisions in this body. I hope these points will be considered as we hopefully vote for the Hatfield amendment to postpone assembly."[12] Arkansas's other senator, Democrat Dale Bumpers, also opposed production of the Bigeye.

Perhaps binary munitions can be dismissed as an exception; given their horrific nature, chemical agents share more in common with nuclear than conventional weapons. Yet other conventional weapons programs also reveal no signs of parochialism. The MBT-70 tank is a case in point. Initiated in the early 1960s, the MBT-70 was designed to replace the M60 as the Army's main battle tank. After several years of technical, managerial, and financial problems, DoD canceled the project. A study of the battle over the tank concluded that "the involvement of a member's district in MBT-70 contracting worked *against* rather than *for* the system."[13] Several key House members, whose districts stood to benefit from production of the MBT-70, opposed the program because they believed it was an inferior weapon. The strongest support for the tank came from senators whose states had no stake in the program.

The history of the Sergeant York Division Air Defense (DIVAD) gun also suggests that parochialism influences acquisition decisions less than is commonly thought. Many legislators criticized DIVAD because it repeatedly flunked development tests. After the army failed to fix the gun, Congress imposed restrictions on the program. When it became clear that DIVAD would never meet the requirements, Secretary of Defense Caspar Weinberger killed the program. If the parochial lens explained congressional behavior, then legislators from affected constituencies should have rallied to the defense of DIVAD. After all, the army planned to spend $2 billion to procure it. Even if members believed the army would develop a replacement for DIVAD, they still had an incentive to attack Weinberger's plan. Putting together a new weapons systems takes time, and a DIVAD-successor might have a different network of contractors and subcontractors. But no "save the DIVAD" campaign materialized on Capitol Hill. Instead, legislators loudly applauded Weinberger's decision.

What about the debates in Congress in the late 1980s over how to pare back defense spending? At first glance the debates clearly support the parochial lens. In 1989 DoD proposed canceling an array of weapons systems to meet fiscal constraints. Congress saved several of the programs, however, from the budget cutter's axe. Parochialism was certainly evident during congressional debates; the most vocal proponents of weapons targeted for cancellation invariably represented districts that stood to lose if the program died. But the more fundamental reason why the V-22 Osprey and a few others escaped immediate cancellation was uncertainty, both inside and outside Congress, over what America's "postcontainment" defense policy should look like, and, by implication, what weapons the United States would need in the future. Most everyone expected, however, that a consensus would develop eventually, and that Congress would approve the cancellation of weapons systems. The changes in the Soviet bloc simply were too large to ignore. As a lobbyist for a major defense contractor acknowledged, "No matter how big your political action committee is, you can't turn back Eastern Europe."[14]

If parochialism is less important in congressional decision making than is commonly alleged, why do conventional weapons seldom become heated issues in Congress? One reason is that Congress can place only a limited number of issues on its agenda. When Congress gives substantial time over to debates on nuclear weapons, it necessarily cuts into the time available for other defense issues. Not even the defense committees have the resources to review DoD's plans with a fine-tooth comb. The defense committees did increase the size of their staff during the 1970s and 1980s, but the committee staff remain small when compared to DoD's staff and to the massive size of the defense budget. In a situation where resources severely limit what can be debated, Congress tends to focus on the most salient issues. In the case of defense policy, nuclear weapons are the most salient because they possess the greatest potential for mass destruction.

A second reason why conventional weapons seldom become heated issues in Congress is that most conventional weapons programs are not inherently contentious. Former HASC subcommittee chair Rep. Richard C. White (D-Tex.)

points out that "probably 95 percent of the items on the defense agenda are not truly controversial."[15] Whether in Congress, the Pentagon, or the civilian defense community, most people believe that DoD should buy rifles, troop transports, fighter planes, and the like. Because a consensus exists that most weapons programs are needed, the number of weapons that are candidates for heated debate in Congress is much smaller than the total number of weapons.

A third reason why conventional weapons seldom become controversial in Congress is that the criticisms most often made about these programs are precisely the criticisms least likely to spark debate in Congress. Attacks on conventional weapons programs almost invariably target cost overruns or inadequate performance. Either or both charges figured in the controversies over the C-5A, DIVAD, the Bradley armored personnel vehicle, the Advanced Medium-Range Air-to-Air Missile, and the F-18, just to name a few. During these disputes no one argued that the United States did not need the weapon, or that acquiring the weapon contradicted long-standing U.S. policy, or that procuring the weapon would cross a threshold in the arms race. But management and performance complaints seldom push Congress into action, even when nuclear weapons are involved. Most members regard management problems as an unfortunate but inevitable part of weapons acquisition.

Of course, parochialism is not entirely absent from congressional decision making on conventional weapons. Some members do try to advance parochial interests. Examples abound of members of Congress touting (or defending, as the case may be) programs that employ their constituents. Also, legislators probably heed the parochial imperative on conventional weapons more readily than they do with nuclear weapons. Rep. Nicholas Mavroules (D-Mass.) helped lead the anti-MX fight even though the warhead for the MX was built in his district. Simultaneously, he fought for other defense contractors in his district. When asked about the discrepancy Mavroules argued: "The argument I put forth is that we have all the nuclear deterrent we require; modernization of conventional weapons is what we need today. That argument sells pretty well."[16] Rep. Tom Downey (D-N.Y.) opposed the B-1 bomber and Trident II missile, two programs that brought jobs to his district. When it came to the A-6 and T-46 (conventional) planes, however, Representative Downey was "eager to promote the programs of Long Island's aircraft manufacturers."[17]

But many of the stories told about congressional parochialism confuse *individual* with *institutional* behavior. Parochially motivated legislators frequently lose their battles to protect or promote a favored weapons systems. In 1986, for example, Sen. Alfonse D'Amato (R-N.Y.) tied the Senate in knots in his effort to save the T-46 fighter trainer. D'Amato's motives were clear. If the program died, Fairchild Republic, the prime contractor, would be forced to close its Long Island plant, putting several thousand people, many of whom were D'Amato supporters, out of work. The T-46 imbroglio drew considerable media attention, including lead coverage by all three major television networks of a shouting match on the floor of the Senate between D'Amato and Sen. Barry Goldwater (R-Ariz.), at the time the chair of SASC.[18] What the media did not play up was that D'Amato's effort failed and the T-46 was canceled. The same may be said of many other stories that grab journalistic and scholarly attention: while individual legislators often act parochially, Congress as an institution usually does not.

Stories about congressional parochialism also perpetuate the myth that parochially motivated legislators invariably foist unnecessary weapons on the military. Yet the services frequently encourage parochialism because it furthers their own ends. For example, Rep. Joseph Addabbo (D-N.Y.) was criticized during his tenure as chair of HADS for forcing the air force to buy more A-10 close-air-support aircraft. Addabbo's parochialism was blatant since the plane was built in his district and the air force had resisted the plane. Yet the story is more complicated. The air force long neglected the close-air-support mission, thereby jeopardizing the safety and effectiveness of army troops in any major battle.[19] Army officials frequently complained about the lack of close-air-support aircraft. The A-10, which "has shown high operational reliability and an excellent armor-killing capability," earned a reputation among experts as one of the best weapons in the U.S. arsenal.[20] Thus, army officials encouraged Addabbo to add funds for the A-10.

Even when parochial politics does succeed and DoD finds itself burdened with a program it does not want, the result may not be terribly significant or costly. Take for example the highly publicized Senate debate in 1982 over plans to upgrade U.S. airlift capacity.[21] The air force initially requested funds for both the C-5B (built by Lockheed) and the C-17 (built by McDonnell Douglas) aircraft. Sen. Henry Jackson (D-Wash.), however, convinced his colleagues on SASC to buy Boeing 747s, which were built in his home state, rather than C-5Bs. Jackson's move touched off a furious legislative battle between partisans of both companies. Congress eventually chose to proceed with the C-5B program, but it also decided to buy three used 747s. While this case is often held up as evidence of the prevalence of the parochial imperative, it remains that the three 747s cost only $145 million, hardly a staggering amount by government standards.

If parochialism fails to explain much of Congress's behavior in the area of conventional weapons, why does it remain such a popular explanation? One reason has already been mentioned, namely, that people often confuse the behavior of individual legislators with the behavior of the institution. Another reason is that members of Congress frequently do act parochially, although their actions usually do not shape the *content* of defense policy. Legislators frequently act as agents or ombudsmen for firms back in the home district. Many members take great pains to inform local companies of contract opportunities and help steer them through the intricacies of the Pentagon's contracting maze. Legislators frequently seek to arrange meetings between constituents and DoD officials, as well as learn why a local firm lost a bid for a defense contract.[22] Besides helping firms on an individual basis, members also pass legislation designed to negate the market advantages some firms have. Thus DoD's acquisition regulations include special provisions for minority businesses, small businesses, firms in economically depressed regions, not to mention "Buy American" requirements. While these activities contribute to higher defense costs, they do not alter the basic composition of the force structure.

Perhaps even more important, members of Congress have an incentive to cultivate the *impression* that they influence DoD's conventional weapons policies to benefit their constituents, even if they have no influence. "Credit claiming" is a valuable electoral tool.[23] Members stand to gain a political payoff whenever they can make the case that they are looking out for the interests of the constituency. Observers typically notice credit claiming behavior and jump to the erroneous conclusion that congressional parochialism shapes defense spending. But the fact remains that "the processes by which contractors are selected and contracts awarded are structured, intentionally or not, so that congressional influence *cannot* play a major role."[24]

If parochialism plays a limited role in congressional decision making on conventional weapons, what about the O&M and personnel accounts, which together account for roughly 50 percent of the defense budget? As with conventional weapons, congressional actions in these two areas have not been adequately studied and only brief remarks can be made about them. The O&M and personnel accounts contain some major items that reflect parochialism.[25] Yet O&M traditionally is the first defense appropriations account cut to meet fiscal constraints. This suggests that legislators generally do not view O&M parochially. As for personnel matters, members of Congress seldom manipulate military pay or personnel levels to deliver local benefits.[26]

Some parochialism affects acquisition decisions for conventional weapons. No doubt at times senior members of Congress use their positions to persuade DoD to continue programs important to their constituents. Some legislators do swallow their policy objections and vote for programs that employ their constituents. Most members at one time or another act as agents for local firms, trying to obtain information about contract decisions from DoD. And Congress has imposed a whole range of procurement regulations on the Pentagon with the sole purpose of negating the market advantages that certain firms or regions possess. Overall, however, parochialism is a subsidiary factor in decisions to acquire conventional weapons. Those decisions hinge mostly on merit.

Military Bases

If the policy lens best explains congressional decision making on weapons programs, the parochial lens appears to best explain how Congress handles DoD's requests on military bases. Perhaps the most obvious sign that basing issues differ from weapons matters is that bases enjoy a special status in Congress. By tradition, legislation for military construction is handled separately from the rest of the defense budget. Until the late-1960s the only budget account the armed services committees marked up with any regularity was the one for military installations, even though it was a tiny portion of total defense spending.[27] The appropriations committees operate in a similar vein; they have long maintained subcommittees for military construction in addition to their subcommittees on defense. None of the Pentagon's other budgetary accounts is so favored.

The importance of military facilities to members of Congress can also be seen in the motives for seeking a seat on HASC. As chapter 2 discussed, most members who seek seats on the committee for parochial reasons do so because the committee has jurisdiction over military installations in their districts. In the case of members of HASC at the start of the Hundredth Congress, for example, all but two of the thirteen members who said that parochial concerns played a role in their decision to seek a seat on HASC mentioned the committee's jurisdiction over military installations (see table 2-2). In short, members of HASC are very interested in military construction matters.

Military bases are important to senators and nonmembers of the defense committees as well. Although many legislators decry defense waste, most reflexively oppose any plans to close or reduce military bases in their constituencies. In 1983, Sen. John Tower (R-Tex.), then chair of SASC, asked his colleagues to list the defense programs in their states that could be trimmed. Only six senators responded. "Their combined proposals for savings in their own states totaled less than $200 million, of which not one penny involved a military facility from their own state or that of any other member."[28] In 1985 Congress responded to concerns about the mounting federal deficit by passing legislation that mandated automatic, across-the-board budget cuts if certain budgetary targets were not met in future years. Yet buried deep in Gramm-Rudman was a provision that forbade DoD to use automatic budget cuts as a reason to close or realign any military bases.[29] The reluctance of members to close military bases, even though most members agree that some bases are not needed, means that "trying to close down bases is not just a job, it's an adventure."[30]

The executive branch did not always find efforts to close military facilities to be an adventure.[31] Until the 1960s few formal constraints limited the executive branch's authority to close or realign bases. There were, of course, some informal constraints; presidents knew that base closings angered members of Congress, and that knowledge probably influenced which bases were closed. Also, members of the defense committees apparently used their positions to deter DoD from closing bases in their districts.[32] Nevertheless, DoD closed 125 major (those employing more than one thousand people) army and air force facilities between 1952 and 1974.[33]

Congress first sought to limit the executive branch's authority to realign bases when Presidents Johnson and Nixon moved aggressively to close military installations. Eventually Congress passed several bills designed to give it a greater role in decisions about base closures. The laws worked as intended. Despite several attempts by DoD, *no* military facilities (major or otherwise) were closed between 1977 and 1988.[34] To quote Secretary of Defense Weinberger, "The restrictions that are presently on the books for closing bases mean that practically speaking we cannot close any facility, no matter how much we want to or how little need there is for it."[35]

Efforts to block plans to close military bases are only the most visible way in which members of Congress protect constituent interests. Legislators also work hard to obtain funds to upgrade local facilities. Rep. G. William Whitehurst (R-Va.), a longtime member of HASC, admits that he and his colleagues often fought to add funds to the budget to finance local projects. In 1973, for instance, Whitehurst succeeded in earmarking $3.4 million for bases in his district by cutting an equal amount from a pollution abatement project in California. He did not worry about the trade-off because "I could stand the smell from California a lot better than the noise I would get from Norfolk."[36] Rep. Roy Dyson (D-Md.), also a member of HASC, defended his bid to add funds to the defense budget for a base in his district with the curt comment, "I was sent here to do that."[37]

Some parochial efforts on military construction involve substantial costs. In 1987, for instance, Rep. Samuel S. Stratton (D-N.Y.), the third ranking Democrat on HASC, wrote to his constituents that he would "continue to be in a crucial position to supply Defense Department funds" for such projects as the "near-billion-dollar" renovation of Fort Drum.[38] But most add-ons to the military construction bill represent relatively mundane projects with small price tags. Most of the local projects Representative Whitehurst fought for involved only a few million dollars. Representative Dyson's efforts were aimed at funding new family housing, a chapel, and a day-care center.

Some members deliberately push for a large investment in local bases because it makes it financially imprudent for DoD to close the facility. In 1970, 1974, and 1979 the Pentagon reduced the size of the staff at Loring Air Force Base (AFB) in Maine, moves widely seen as a prelude to closing the base. To keep Loring open, Sen. William Cohen (R-Maine) used his position on SASC to see that more than $125 million was spent on construction at Loring between 1980 and 1983. In 1985 DoD acknowledged political reality and gave up its fight to close Loring. Assistant Secretary of Defense Lawrence Korb testified that "because of the expenditure of new construction money that was basically *jammed down our throats* by the Congress, it no longer makes any sense to close that installation."[39] In 1979 the Pentagon announced it would seek to close Goodfellow AFB in Texas. Opposition from the Texas congressional delegation, though, forced DoD to drop the proposal, and Goodfellow subsequently received over $25 million in unrequested funds, even though it is a small, single-mission base.[40]

Members of Congress also often seek to influence where planes and ships will be based. Such basing decisions ensure the flow of money and jobs into the district. In the early 1980s Sen. Robert Dole (R-Kans.) reportedly used his position as chair of the Senate Finance Committee to force DoD to base a B-1B bomber squadron in Kansas.[41] Rep. Mickey Edwards (R-Okla.) was widely credited with convincing the navy to base E-6A communications aircraft at Tinker AFB in Oklahoma City, although Tinker was not on the original list of bases considered.[42] Also, legislators often haggle over the provision of new equipment to their state's reserves. One congressional staff member commented: "Members worry a lot about the Air National Guard and Air Reserve. They all fight to make sure that the outfit in their state gets a new allotment of fighter planes. There's a rotation system going on. You got taken care of last year; we should get taken care of this year. All in all, it's a nice political plum to hand out."[43]

Congressional parochialism on military construction matters has its limits. In 1988 Congress authorized the creation of a national commission to determine which military installations should be closed or realigned. The commission subsequently recommended that the Pentagon close thirteen major bases and close or realign 132 other facilities.[44] Congress agreed to the idea of an independent commission because the sponsors of the legislation crafted the bill in a way that insulated members from blame. The measure did not require legislators to vote to close any particular military facility. The legislation also stipulated that the base closings would be enacted unless both the House and the Senate adopted a resolution (which would be subject to a presidential veto) that disapproved the entire list of bases. As the sponsors had astutely calculated, legislators representing affected constituencies failed to muster the votes needed to overturn the commission's recommendations.

Members of Congress also do not support all proposals for military bases or base construction. Legislators from Nevada and Utah lobbied furiously against the Carter administration's proposal to base the MX missile in the Great Basin, and they ultimately succeeded in killing the proposal. The Michigan and Wisconsin congressional delegations fought, with substantial success, to terminate the navy's plan to construct the ELF system across the northern regions of both states. Both the MX and ELF projects threatened massive environmental destruction and substantial socio-economic costs for the local populations. Yet

MPS basing and ELF are the exceptions rather than the rule. More typical is the congressional reaction to the Reagan administration's "homeporting" plan that called for a series of new naval bases. Although critics pointed to fiscal and military flaws in the plan, legislators representing the cities that were candidates for the new naval bases enthusiastically embraced the proposal.[45]

Policy Goals and Constituency Constraints

Neither the deferential, parochial, or policy lens explains how Congress decides all defense issues. Each lens explains congressional decision making on some issues or (in the case of the deferential lens) for some time period. How can the differences in legislative behavior be reconciled?

To develop a broader theory of congressional decision making the most appropriate place to start is with the relationship between legislators' electoral and policy goals. Most observers agree that reelection is the primary objective for all legislators. As former Rep. Frank E. Smith (D-Miss.) once wrote, "All members of Congress have a primary interest in being re-elected. Some members have no other interest."[46] Yet even proponents of the electoral connection model of congressional behavior would grant that members of Congress also hope to advance their conceptions of good public policy (though these observers might see this goal as secondary to reelection).

Members know that voting their personal policy preferences in any given situation will have one of three possible effects on their reelection chances. First, it may hurt their electoral prospects. Constituents may disagree with the policy stance, fear they will lose their jobs if a legislator opposes a program providing local employment (as the parochial lens suggests), or believe the legislator should not question the president's policies (as the deferential lens suggests). Second, members may vote their policy preferences with no effect on their electoral prospects. This might happen if constituents vote on the basis of other issues, if they have no parochial interest in the program, or if they are not concerned with whether the legislator supports the president. Third, members might actually improve their reelection chances by voting their private policy preferences. Constituents may support the policy stand, applaud the effort to protect local jobs, or reward the legislator for standing by the president.

Legislators undoubtedly prefer situations where their policy goals will help, or at least not hurt, their electoral goals. Yet they find themselves at times in situations where the two goals conflict. When this happens, members must assess the costs involved in choosing one goal over the other. In calculating trade-offs, legislators must answer several questions: What are the benefits (costs) of supporting the program in question? What are the benefits (costs) of opposing it? What are the benefits (costs) of logrolling on the issue? Admittedly, members frequently find it easier to ask these questions than to answer them; among other things, constituency preferences for specific policy options (as opposed to broad themes) often are not readily discernible, and members must worry that the intensity of constituency opinion may change in the future as the political salience of the issue rises or falls. Nonetheless, members can and do estimate how a policy position will affect their electoral prospects.

However precise members of Congress are in their cost-benefit calculations, the bottom line remains the same: the greater the electoral costs (or the fewer the electoral benefits) associated with a particular policy position the more likely a legislator is to abandon it.[47] In other words, a constituency sets constraints, sometimes quite broad and sometimes quite restrictive, on the freedom its legislators have to pursue their conceptions of good public policy. But the constituency does not provide a *positive* guide to legislative action. To quote John Kingdon:

> It seems more useful to think of the constituency, not as directing a legislator *to* act in a certain way, but as telling him how *not* to act. The mass public in a district sets rather broad boundaries beyond which the legislator may not go; they are there, but are vague. Attentive people and elites in districts narrow those boundaries; they will allow a narrower range of options than the mass public. The politician's supporting coalition narrows the range of the possible further. But there is still considerable discretion available to the legislator much of the time.[48]

Members of Congress can act on their beliefs within the boundaries laid down by their constituencies.

The view that members of Congress pursue their conceptions of good public policy subject to a constituency constraint explains why the policy lens best characterizes how Congress handles weapons issues while the parochial lens appears to better describe how Congress handles matters involving military installations. Constituency constraints typically are far less restrictive on weapons issues than they are on basing matters. The reason is because the decision to oppose a weapons program may cost a member (particularly a dovish one) few votes, even if it is built locally, and opposition to the program may even enhance his or her electoral chances. The decision to oppose a local military facility, however, usually places a legislator in great electoral jeopardy.

The greater electoral costs associated with opposition to military facilities (hence the less freedom of action for legislators) can be seen in three respects. One is that the closure of a military facility usually hurts a constituency more than a comparable decision to cancel production of a weapons program. Frequently several towns depend on the well-being of the base. A decision to close or realign a military installation can literally turn the surrounding communities into ghost towns as base personnel leave, related businesses collapse, and the tax base dries up. Where this is the likely result of a base closure, political reality demands that members obey the parochial imperative, regardless of the merits of DoD's case. Any other course of action would be electoral suicide. Entire regions of the district or state could quickly throw their support to a political opponent.

Decisions to cancel or scale back defense contracts generally are less devastating. Most constituencies do not depend on defense contracts to the extent that many constituencies depend on military bases, and, hence, the loss of a contract does not cause as much economic dislocation. One member explained his opposition to a nuclear weapons program that employed several hundred of his constituents with the argument: "Defense contracts in my district are spread across the board. It's not like an army or air force base."[49] The economic pain caused by the loss of a contract will also be eased if the firms in question have either (or both) other defense contracts or substantial commercial interests. As a result, legislators who vote against their constituency's interests on weapons matters do not necessarily expose themselves to the same risks they would face if they failed to protect a local military installation.

Of course, constituencies that host prime contractors usually depend on that weapon as much as other constituencies depend on bases. Members representing these constituencies often have little electoral choice but to support the weapon. Thus it makes sense that Sens. Alan Cranston (D-Calif.) and John Tunney (D-Calif.) supported production of the B-1 even when most other doves opposed the bomber: California received nearly twice as much from the B-1 program as any other state (see table 5-2). In the case of the T-46 trainer, Fairchild Republic's ability to remain in business as an aircraft manufacturer depended upon its contract to build the jet trainer. The potential loss of thousands of jobs gave the Long Island congressional delegation an incentive to fight to save the T-46. For Electric Boat, the contractor for the Trident SSBN, submarine construction is its sole business. Since Electric Boat is a major employer in both Connecticut and Rhode Island, members of these congressional delegations are solicitous of its needs.[50]

The second reason why opposition to a local military installation typically poses higher electoral costs to members of Congress is that base closings usually elicit different party and constituency reactions than do efforts to cancel weapons systems. In terms of party reactions, military construction seldom becomes a partisan affair. Legislators generally are free to vote as they see fit on basing issues without any concern about retribution from party leaders. But partisanship at times influences voting on nuclear weapons. Members occasionally find they will have to pay a price if they fail to remain loyal to the party. As chapter 3 discussed, several House Democratic leaders dropped their support for MX after 1983 because dovish and moderate Democrats threatened to oppose any candidate for a leadership post who supported MX.

As for constituent reactions, when DoD threatens to close a military installation, the affected constituents usually rally to save the base. Generally no group arises to demand fiscal responsibility and military efficiency, either because the potential savings to be gained by closing any single base are relatively small or because most people see military facilities as essentially a reasonable middle-class welfare expenditure. The absence of groups lobbying for base closings means that members who fail to support the constituency's interests on basing issues run tremendous electoral risks. They cannot expect offsetting electoral support from other quarters. Consequently, only brave (or foolhardy) legislators resist the parochial imperative on basing matters.

In contrast, controversial weapons systems often trigger the emergence of public-interest groups that lobby against the proposed program. This is especially true for nuclear weapons. For example, the anti-MX missile coalition brought together a diverse assortment of lobbying groups. "There were daily meetings of the lobbyists representing the American Baptist Churches, Americans for Democratic Action, Coalition for New Foreign and Military Policy, Common Cause, Council for a Livable World, Friends Committee on National Legislation, Friends of the Earth, National Association of Social Workers, Network, Physicians for Social Responsibility, Sane, United Church of Christ, Union of Concerned Scientists, and others."[51] When President Reagan unveiled his vision of a strategic defense that would render nuclear weapons "impotent and obsolete," lobbying groups sprung up almost overnight.[52]

The existence of lobbying groups means that members representing constituencies that benefit from the production of a weapons system may offend some constituents no matter how they vote. This matters because members care about whom they disappoint. They much prefer to offend voters who do not belong to their reelection coalition than those who do.[53] While this holds true for all legislators, doves and hawks occupy unequal positions on defense issues. Since hawks typically support greater defense spending, and presumably their supporters do as well, they can usually (but, as the fight over MPS basing shows, not always) satisfy both the parochial imperative and constituent opinion with the same vote. Hawks are likely to alienate only those voters outside their reelection constituency.

Doves, however, face conflicting pressures. If they defend the constituency's parochial interests and vote for the weapons system in question, they may alienate supporters and open themselves up to the politically damaging charge that they are inconsistent. If they vote against the weapon, they risk offending constituents who work on the program. Yet some or perhaps even many workers may not belong to the member's electoral coalition. As a result, doves who oppose a weapons system that employs their constituents do not run the large risks that the parochial imperative suggests. Indeed, if individuals in the reelection coalition feel strongly about the issue, opposition may help a legislator. And here total numbers are not always the most important factor; intensity of support also matters. One congressman relied heavily on support from people in the peace movement, even though the number of peace activists in his district was small. "But 100 activists can do a lot. On Moratorium Day, they had 15,000 people marching up Riverside Boulevard."[54]

The role of lobbying groups shows why it is misleading to suggest that some arbitrary threshold of constituency benefits exists above which members of Congress, regardless of their policy views, find it impossible to vote against a program.[55] Legislators worry not only about what they stand to gain by supporting a program but about what they stand to lose. Thus it is not surprising that Senator Cranston opposed SDI even though it meant many more dollars for California than even the B-1 provided. The anti-SDI lobby in California was large, well organized, and drew much of its support from individuals in Senator Cranston's electoral coalition. The anti–B-1 movement was never strong in California. In short, a decision to support SDI would have alienated key members of Senator Cranston's electoral coalition.

Differences in the intensity of lobbying also explain the difference in the degree of parochialism that motivates congressional decision making on nuclear versus conventional weapons. Arms control and pro-defense organizations care deeply about chemical and nuclear weapons, but they do not display the same passion for conventional ones. Moreover, few public-interest groups lobby on conventional weapons issues. Thus, dovish and moderate legislators may find that opposing a conventional weapons system that employs their constituents is more likely to produce an unacceptable loss of electoral support than opposing a comparable nuclear weapons system; their arms control supporters may not care deeply enough about the conventional weapons system to offset the ire of those constituents who are employed by the program.

The third reason why members of Congress find it more politically costly to oppose constituency interests on basing issues than on weapons issues is that the incentive to logroll is much greater on military construction matters. Every state, and almost 60 percent of all congressional districts, contain or are near some military installation.[56] Also, members of Congress know that DoD wants to close or realign many bases. These two factors create a natural basis for logrolling. Members know if they vote to close a facility in another district today, they will lose potential allies in tomorrow's fight to preserve the base in their district. As a result, even though legislators may believe military installations elsewhere should be closed, they refuse to support those closures in return for a tacit agreement by their colleagues not to close bases in their districts. The response (or lack thereof) to Senator Tower's inquiry attests to this behavior.

In contrast to military installations, DoD rarely lobbies Congress to discontinue a weapons system. Since the cancellation of one weapon does not herald the cancellation of others, legislators have less reason to logroll. They know that they can vote against, say, the MX, without jeopardizing, say, the F-16. Of course, DoD might punish members it sees as hostile by steering contracts to other constituencies (which is often hard to do) or by manipulating basing matters. For example, the air force reportedly declined to base a B-1B squadron at Wurtsmith AFB in Michigan because, as one general put it, "We have legislators in Michigan who have not defended the B-1 program—and those states with B-1 opponents will be the first to be cut."[57] Still, most members contend that DoD seldom attempts to punish its critics on Capitol Hill in this fashion.[58]

The diminished incentive members of Congress have to logroll on acquisition decisions is important because expenditures on most weapons are concentrated on a small number of states. Take the case of the B-1 bomber, where DoD maximized the spread of contracts to increase support for the plane. Before President Carter canceled the bomber, it was estimated that six states would absorb more than 75 percent of all the funds spent on the plane (see table 5-2). The B-1, of course, is one of the largest defense programs in U.S. history; most weapons cost far less and involve many fewer congressional districts. Thus not only do legislators have a smaller incentive to logroll in debates over weapons systems, they also typically have either a very small parochial interest in the weapons system in question or none at all.

Up to this point the focus has been on the potential costs members of Congress face in opposing constituency opinion, but not all members are equally sensitive to the costs of their policy positions. To begin with, the threshold at which a policy position becomes too costly varies among legislators. Some members are election maximizers. They will abandon any policy position likely to hurt their reelection chances. At the other extreme, some legislators are "saints" who would rather risk defeat at the polls than tailor their positions to appease constituents.[59] No doubt most legislators fall somewhere in between. They will offend some constituents to pursue their policy preferences, but they refuse to commit the political equivalent of seppuku.

Besides individual predisposition, norms shape how members of Congress calculate trade-offs between their policy and reelection goals. Notions of proper conduct may make legislators willing to bear more electoral costs on some types of issues than on others. To return to the differences in how Congress handles nuclear weapons versus military construction matters, decisions to acquire weapons have clear implications for national security; hence, legislators may be more likely to look at these issues from a national perspective than is true with basing issues.

Decisions about weapons acquisition are closely related to matters that affect the perceptions of foreign governments—especially potential enemies. While it is immaterial to potential enemies whether the Texas airfield site is chosen over the California site (the same Air Force commands them both) it *is* important that our technological capabilities be viewed with the utmost respect. . . . It is all well and good to boost one's district, but if it is true, as the Defense Department may claim, that the contractor in the other fellow's district makes a better missile, it is best to try again on another slice of the defense pie.[60]

The relative infrequency with which members make explicit appeals to parochial interests during public debates over weapons systems provides some evidence that legislators treat acquisition decisions differently from other defense issues. It was a departure from practice, for instance, in 1985 when Representative Stratton urged his colleagues to vote for the MX missile because it would "put some of the unemployed back to work."[61]

Norms may also make members of Congress more sensitive to criticism that particular programs endanger U.S. national security than to other types of criticism. For instance, whereas critics of the B-1 bomber complained the plane was (or quickly would be) obsolete, critics of SDI argued that strategic defenses would increase the likelihood of nuclear war. Given this difference, a dove such as Senator Cranston might have found it much easier to justify support for B-1 than for SDI, even when both meant large amounts of federal spending for California. Such an argument is not farfetched. In 1981 Rep. Thomas Downey (D-N.Y.), a passionate critic of the B-1, reportedly abandoned the fight against the bomber because it was "merely a waste of money and at least not a destabilizing weapon."[62]

In contrast to debates over weapons systems, members of Congress have long considered it legitimate to discuss military installations in terms of their local impact. (Whether legislators *should* view bases from this perspective is a separate question.) During efforts to prevent DoD from closing bases, legislators proudly justify their positions in terms of defending local interests. Sen. John Glenn (D-Ohio), for instance, opposed DoD's decision to reduce several facilities in his home state because "the State of Ohio is being asked to bear a disproportionately large share of the Defense Department's cutbacks. . . . This disproportion is unfair because Ohio already gets less than its fair share of military spending."[63] Similarly, the FY 1980 military construction bill blocked a DoD proposal to reduce personnel at five bases until DoD had redone the required impact statements to "place special emphasis on socio-economic factors in the affected areas."[64]

Of course, norms cannot override political necessity. To repeat an earlier point, very few members of Congress are saints. Legislators who doubt the need for a particular weapons system learn to live with their qualms when the program employs many of their constituents. Rep. Matthew G. Martinez (D-Calif.), who opposed production of the MX missile, summarized this basic reality of life on Capitol Hill bluntly: "If there were 10,000 jobs for my district from MX contracts, or even 5,000 jobs, I would regard that as positive enough to swing my vote. Unemployment in my district is over 10 percent, and when you have that kind of unemployment rate, 5,000 jobs becomes a very attractive number."[65] Nevertheless, norms do matter. Members often shoulder more electoral costs than they would otherwise simply because they believe it is the right thing to do.

The view outlined here of members of Congress as individuals pursuing their conceptions of good public policy subject to a constituency constraint offers to explain more than just how Congress handles defense policy. It also provides a potentially powerful explanation of congressional decision making on domestic issues. As is the case with military construction, some domestic policies are sacrosanct (or nearly so) on Capitol Hill because legislators see enormous electoral costs in challenging the status quo. Social Security is probably the most frequently cited example of this phenomenon. It is safe to say that most members refuse even to entertain the notion of reducing or taxing social security benefits because they believe the political strength and savvy of the "grey lobby" makes being identified with these positions suicidal.

By the same token, much of congressional decision making on nondefense affairs cannot be explained simply with reference to reelection or self-interest. Studies of congressional voting on domestic issues typically find that ideology is a better predictor of how members vote than is constituency benefit.[66] As is the case with the debate over nuclear weapons, some domestic policies are not "sacred cows," either because legislators do not see sizable electoral costs in challenging the status quo or because they see electoral benefits in these activities. The fight over deregulation in the late 1970s and early 1980s illustrates the point. Proponents of deregulation in Congress were motivated largely by a belief in the need for greater competition. They won the repeal of a variety of regulatory strictures, despite intense, well-organized opposition by the regulated industries. The victories came even though the legislators who voted for deregulation took some electoral risk in doing so. Thus, in supporting deregulation, many members evidently discounted the most compelling electoral considerations to endorse a measure that fit their view of the public interest.[67]

Considerable evidence exists, then, that members of Congress do care about the substance of defense policy, a lesson that probably holds true for domestic policy as well. The dominance of the electoral connection in the study of American politics has led many scholars to neglect to look at how individual policy preferences shape congressional decision making. Much more research needs to be done on the connection between ideas and public policy. What should not be in doubt is that while members of Congress are not altruists, neither are they simply "errand boy-ombudsmen" for their constituents.[68]

8 ⟫ ⟪

Influence

DOES CONGRESS MATTER in nuclear weapons policy making? The answer is not self-evident. Skeptics argue that the pitched battles on Capitol Hill are "full of sound and fury, signifying nothing." After all, despite fervent debates over ABM, B-1, MX, and ASAT, Congress appropriated procurement funds for all four programs. But the cancellation standard is too stringent. Congress may impose restrictions on weapons systems without canceling them, it may strangle programs in their less visible research and development stages, or the administration may fashion its requests in expectation of what Congress desires.

The more appropriate standard for judging congressional influence is whether Congress's participation in policy making changes the substance of policy. By this standard Congress today is a player in nuclear weapons policy. In the 1950s and 1960s Congress was largely irrelevant on weapons acquisition matters. With a few exceptions, the Congress of Carl Vinson and Richard Russell did not affect the substance of DoD policy. In the two decades after 1968, however, Congress's ability to influence defense plans grew. The influence Congress now wields is of two types. First and most prominently, it is *negative*. As the histories of the MX and ASAT programs attest, Congress at times constrains the development and deployment of weapons programs. To a lesser extent Congress exercises a *positive* influence over the process, using its powers to push or (less commonly) require DoD to develop particular weapons. Despite its growing influence, though, Congress operates as a junior partner to the executive branch in policy making.

Short of major changes in congressional norms or in the membership of the House and Senate, Congress will not become a coequal of the executive branch in nuclear weapons policy. The inherent limits on Congress's influence flow directly from the ideological composition of Congress, the procedures and structures of the institution, and the power of DoD. Critics have proposed various reforms to circumvent these obstacles and make Congress more effective in its oversight duties. Yet most reform proposals are unlikely to be adopted or, if they are, they are not likely to work in practice. Congressional oversight will improve only if the hawkishness of the defense committees is moderated.

Congressional Influence

In the 1950s and 1960s Congress was more an observer than a participant in nuclear weapons policy making. The defense committees and their parent chambers seldom displayed interest in defense policy. When Congress did seek to intervene in decision making, its views were brushed aside by the executive branch. Even the defense committees recognized their irrelevance. HASC complained in 1962: "More and more the role of the Congress has come to be that of a sometimes querulous but essentially kindly uncle who complains while furiously puffing on his pipe but who finally, as everyone expects, gives in and hands over the allowance, grants the permission, or raises his hand in blessing, and then returns to his rocking chair for another year of somnolence broken only by an occasional anxious glance down the avenue and a muttered doubt as to whether he had done the right thing."[1]

In the 1970s and 1980s the kindly uncle became boisterous. Congress no longer was content to sit in its rocking chair. Of course, not all the activity on Capitol Hill shaped acquisition decisions. Many efforts to change policy failed. And because members of Congress have an incentive to engage in political grandstanding, not all congressional actions were intended to influence policy (though they may have done so unintentionally as happened with the neutron bomb).[2] Yet even taking failed legislative initiatives and position taking into account, Congress's influence over nuclear weapons policy grew markedly in the 1970s and 1980s.

Congress's greatest influence is negative; it can limit what DoD may develop. At the broadest level, Congress exercises negative influence by shaping what the administration requests. Congressional opposition to a weapons system often prompts the executive branch to revise the program substantially. Several examples illustrate anticipated reactions at work. In 1969 President Nixon replaced the Sentinel ABM program with the Safeguard system. The switch came primarily because it had become "increasingly unlikely that the Senate would approve further deployment money."[3] In the mid-1970s Senate opposition to the B-1 made it easier for President Carter to cancel the program.[4] Carter also advanced several variants of the MPS basing mode to contain growing opposition to the MX missile. Finally, President Reagan abandoned his October 1981 interim silo basing plan for the MX as well as several successor basing options because of opposition on Capitol Hill.

Congressional opposition does not always force the executive branch to modify its programs. President Nixon remained committed to Safeguard even as the number of Senate opponents approached fifty. The Ford administration stood by the B-1 and counterforce programs even though more than thirty senators opposed both. Nearly one hundred members of the House opposed Pershing II, but the Reagan administration never wavered in its commitment to deploy the missile in Europe. The executive branch sometimes risks displeasing legislators to pursue programs it favors.

Whether or not the executive branch redraws its proposals in the face of congressional opposition depends on several factors. One is the length of time during which opposition is feasible. The Ford administration knew in 1974 that if counterforce programs were funded for two years then the research would pass a point of no return, making further debate moot. The size of the opposition coalition is also important. Opposition to Pershing II in the House simply was too small to threaten the Reagan administration's policies. Finally, the perseverance of the administration matters. President Nixon never attempted to save the Sentinel program, even though he supported the concept of area defense. The Reagan administration, however, repeatedly submitted requests for MX missiles even when "informed opinion" on Capitol Hill held that the program was dead.[5]

Besides influencing what the administration requests, Congress also uses its control of the purse strings to constrain weapons development. Many of these limits, especially those on programs in the early phases of research and development, are often little noticed outside the Pentagon. In 1980, for example, Congress deleted funds to develop a cruise missile carrier airplane, a program President Carter had advanced to compensate for his decision not to procure the B-1 bomber. Several years later Congress blocked the navy's tactical nuclear modernization program and prohibited the army from developing a nuclear-armed version of the ATACMS program.[6] Although these constraints may seem marginal, even minor restrictions may have significant long-term consequences. The 1976 congressional decision to prohibit DoD from spending funds on fixed silo basing for the MX missile touched off the protracted search for a feasible mobile basing mode for the MX.

On four different occasions Congress also formally constrained a high-profile weapons system. One occasion came in 1985 when Congress barred the air force from deploying more than fifty MX missiles in fixed silos. This was one-half the number of missiles President Reagan had requested and only one-quarter of the number President Carter proposed originally. The second occasion also came in 1985 when Congress limited operational testing of the MHV satellite interceptor, which effectively forced the air force to forego procurement of an ASAT weapon. Congress resisted subsequent attempts by the Reagan administration to have the MX and ASAT restrictions lifted.

The third instance where Congress curbed procurement of a weapons system was the Safeguard ABM system. Safeguard was initially intended to protect Minuteman missiles and to provide limited population defense. Even though the Senate in 1969 approved the start of construction at two Minuteman sites by the narrowest of margins — an amendment to delay the program fell on a fifty to fifty vote — the Nixon administration returned the next year to request authority to build eight sites, including four for use in an area defense. When several Safeguard supporters announced they opposed expansion of the system, SASC directed that Safeguard be limited to defense of Minuteman bases. After Congress endorsed SASC's recommendation, the Nixon administration agreed to limit Safeguard, and DoD "accelerated work on the so-called Hardsite technology, looking toward precisely the kind of nonprovocative, local defense long advocated by opponents of Sentinel/Safeguard."[7]

The restrictions imposed on SDI testing are the fourth example of how Congress limits weapons development. In 1985 the Reagan administration announced that, contrary to past practice, the ABM Treaty permitted virtually unlimited testing of ABM technologies. After the administration resisted congressional pressure to observe the traditional interpretation of the treaty, the armed services committees recommended in 1987 that the air force be barred for two years—essentially the remainder of Reagan's term in office—from taking any steps to enact the "broad" interpretation of the treaty without prior congressional approval. Even though Senate Republicans filibustered the SDI restrictions, the Reagan administration finally agreed to refrain from tests prohibited by the traditional interpretation.

With the MX, ASAT, Safeguard, and SDI programs Congress restricted DoD's plans. But would the Pentagon's final acquisition decisions have been significantly different had Congress been absent from the process? After all, if left alone the Nixon administration might have limited deployment of Safeguard, the navy might have abandoned its nuclear modernization program, and the air force might have decided that an ASAT weapon diverted funds from programs with higher priorities.

It is impossible to disprove a counterfactual. Nonetheless, the U.S. nuclear arsenal probably would look very different today if Congress were absent from the policy-making process. The momentum that builds up behind weapons programs can prove irresistible even to presidents. To take one example, "had there been no congressional reticence toward Sentinel and Safeguard, by 1972 the United States would have been well on its way to a full twelve-site defensive deployment. With such an infrastructure laid out across the country, it would have been exceedingly difficult, if not impossible, to conclude the Moscow Treaty of 1972 limiting ABM installations to negligible levels."[8] If the two superpowers had deployed larger missile defenses in the early 1970s, subsequent U.S. acquisition decisions would have been much different. Given Reagan's commitment to MX, the air force probably would have pushed for even *higher* deployment levels if not for congressional opposition. Congress's impact on programs such as the navy's tactical weapons, ATACMS, and SDI is more difficult to assess because Congress constrained the programs early in their development. Fiscal, management, or technical problems, as well as changes in administrations, might have derailed any of these programs. The restrictions placed on these programs might also be lifted in the future. Still, at least in the case of SDI, the constraints Congress imposed prevented President Reagan from violating the ABM Treaty and thereby placing pressure on his successor to deploy a strategic defense.

Congress also exercises some positive influence over nuclear force acquisition decisions. At the broadest level, members of Congress can pressure administrations to develop particular weapons and make them pay a price if they do not. This was the one power Congress wielded before the ABM debate. For example, Secretary of Defense Robert McNamara decided to deploy one thousand Minuteman missiles because he believed it was the smallest number that Congress would accept.[9] Likewise, President Johnson approved deployment of the Sentinel ABM system partly because several senior members of Congress advocated it.[10]

Today Congress continues to use its hortatory powers to push the administration in the direction it desires, especially with respect to major weapons programs. In 1978 Congress passed legislation urging President Carter to authorize full-scale development of MPS basing. Although the appeal was not binding, Carter subsequently committed the United States to deploy two hundred MX missiles in the MPS mode. Likewise, in 1980 Congress added $300 million to the budget to begin research and development work on a new strategic bomber. The various committee reports explicitly mentioned the possibility of procuring a variant of the B-1 bomber. When the Reagan administration took office the following year, it knew that Congress had already declared itself in favor of resuming B-1 production, which strengthened the hand of administration officials who favored resurrecting the bomber.

Congressional exhortations are not limited to big-ticket items. In the early 1970s Congress pushed the air force to develop cruise missiles to improve the ability of B-52 bombers to penetrate Soviet air space. Air force officials demurred, however, because they feared that cruise missiles would be used on standoff launch platforms, thereby obviating the need for a new penetrating bomber (a fear President Carter justified when he canceled the B-1 and initiated work on a cruise missile carrier airplane). When the air force continued to drag its feet, HASC deleted all funds for ALCM while authorizing funds for the navy's cruise missile program. Although the ALCM funds were later restored, air force officials understood HASC's message.

> USAF reluctantly and, almost, belatedly hurried to "get on board" to avoid getting "a torpedo rammed up its bomb bay." For a very real and growing possibility existed that if the Air Force did not produce a suitable cruise missile, DoD and Congress would see that the Navy did. . . . Little wonder then that the ALCM program took a different turn in the mid to late 1970s. As a SAC [Strategic Air Command] internal document put it in early 1976, "SAC's

position . . . has mellowed, because of the political atmosphere, and is [now] in line with higher echelon thinking."[11]

With a shove from Congress, the air force found it liked cruise missiles.

Congressional efforts to push DoD in one direction or another are most likely to succeed when executive branch officials, and especially high-ranking DoD officials, share Congress's objectives. Astute bureaucrats can use congressional action to bolster the projects they favor.[12] Proponents of point defense in DoD seized on Senate opposition to the Sentinel and Safeguard programs to argue that the United States should seek to defend only ICBM sites. Officials in the Office of the Secretary of Defense (OSD) used congressional support to force the air force to accept development of armed cruise missiles. Despite strong support in Congress for a new strategic bomber, the B-1 may not have been resurrected if senior defense advisers in the Reagan administration did not believe that the plane was needed to revitalize the U.S. nuclear deterrent.[13]

Only with Midgetman did Congress insist on the development of a nuclear weapons system over the objections of both a service and the civilians in OSD. The Scowcroft Commission endorsed the SICBM concept largely at the behest of several members of Congress. Once the commission issued its report, Congress appropriated funds to initiate research and development on Midgetman. To ensure that the missile would be mobile, Congress also placed a weight limit on the missile. And to prod the White House into proceeding with the program, Congress linked approval of MX funding to progress in Midgetman development.[14]

Midgetman represented a major change in congressional behavior with potentially significant implications for the nuclear force acquisition process. Yet substantial congressional support by no means assured the missile's future. Many senior air force officials opposed the program, partly on doctrinal grounds and partly because they believed a successful Midgetman program would encourage more congressional "meddling" in what was properly the air force's domain of expertise. The OSD and a majority of members of SASC were also unenthusiastic about the program. Even without this opposition, budgetary pressures made the program's relatively high cost potentially unpalatable, especially in light of the growing belief that the Soviet threat was fading.

Congress influences nuclear weapons acquisition, but it remains a decidedly junior partner in policy making. In particular, Congress's influence over nuclear weapons policy falls far short of the power it wielded over U.S. foreign policy in the 1930s. Even taking the Midgetman initiative into account, the executive branch dominates the agenda setting process for nuclear weapons by virtue of its control over information and expertise. Congress might reject a program request and direct DoD to study alternative proposals, but legislators generally lack the time, let alone the expertise, to produce their own alternatives. Congress at times makes a difference in the decision-making process, but it does not dictate outcomes to the executive branch.

The limits of congressional influence can be seen best with respect to strategic doctrine. Few members support *congressional* efforts to change existing doctrine. In 1971, for example, Sen. James Buckley (C-N.Y.) offered three amendments to reverse the stated policy against counterforce weapons. None of the amendments gained the support of more than seventeen senators, and the issue lay dormant until three years later when the Nixon administration revised strategic doctrine to justify counterforce targeting. SDI provides another example. Before President Reagan made his famous Star Wars speech, hawkish legislators failed to win much support for the goal of aggressively developing strategic defenses. Most members refuse to support congressional efforts to change existing strategic doctrine because their knowledge of nuclear strategy is limited; hence, they are most comfortable (all else being equal) with the status quo.

Reluctant to alter strategic declaratory doctrine on its own initiative, Congress restricts itself to responding to executive branch proposals. Even here Congress's influence over nuclear strategy is at best indirect. When Congress refused to fund one hundred MX missiles it obviously hampered the air force's ability to increase U.S. hard target kill capability. Yet the limit on the number of MX did not change the strategic argument for more MX. Indeed, doctrinal matters remained firmly in the hands of the air force, which continued to insist that MX was justified. Of course, Congress could enact its preferred doctrine into law, but, as one defense consultant put it, this would trigger a "donnybrook of unparalleled proportions between Congress and DoD."[15]

Congress's limited influence on strategic doctrine means that the executive branch can propose building a weapons system even if Congress blocked earlier versions. President Reagan initiated SDI despite a 1976 congressional decision to close the sole U.S. ABM base. Even as congressional criticism forced the air force to cancel the MHV program, the Pentagon was researching several more sophisticated ASAT technologies as part of SDI, and the Reagan administration proposed in its final defense budget to authorize the navy to build a new ASAT weapon.[16] The result is a tremendous asymmetry between DoD and its critics. Defense critics often have only a limited time to defeat a new weapon. As the MIRV and counterforce programs illustrate, once new technologies pass a certain threshold, the development clock cannot be turned back. If Congress constrains or blocks a program, however, DoD can always renew its requests at a later time.

If Congress does not lead on nuclear weapons issues, it does restrain the executive branch's freedom of maneuver. As is the case with foreign policy more generally, Congress acts as a brake on U.S. nuclear weapons policy.[17] The administration must pay far more attention to sentiment on Capitol Hill than was the case in the 1950s and 1960s. Congress subjects many weapons proposals to public scrutiny, and in some important instances it forces the executive branch to revise its programs. Even when Congress approves a DoD request, it is now unlikely that a program that has a major impact on the nuclear balance will proceed, as MIRV did, without serious examination of its merits *and* demerits. The end result is that presidents today find their power to restructure the U.S. nuclear arsenal more circumscribed than ever before.

The limits on presidential power apply equally to hawkish (or Republican) and dovish (or Democratic) administrations. Reagan administration officials criticized Congress for blocking the MX, SDI, and ASAT programs, but President Carter, whose political party and views on nuclear weapons both differed from his successor's, received as much if not more "advice" from Capitol Hill.[18] Congress forced Carter to abandon his cruise missile carrier proposal, pushed him to accept the MX missile and MPS basing, and generally pressured him to spend more on defense. Whatever Congress's other failings, it does not discriminate among presidents on the basis of ideology or party.

Limits to Congressional Influence

Although Congress wields more influence over the nuclear force acquisition process now than it did in 1968, its newfound power does not match its increased level of activity. One reason for this is that not all congressional actions are aimed at influencing policy. Yet references to political grandstanding do not provide a complete explanation of why Congress's influence did not grow in tandem with its increased activism. One must look instead to three other obstacles to congressional influence: the ideological composition of Congress, the procedures and structures of Congress, and the power of DoD.

The biggest obstacle to congressional influence is the ideological composition of the House and Senate. No dominant coalition exists in Congress around a particular view of what constitutes a "proper" U.S. nuclear weapons policy. Congress, and especially the Senate, is divided among doves, moderates, and hawks. Members on either end of the continuum need the support of the moderate camp to enact their preferences into policy. But moderates, who see merits (and demerits) in both extremes and who are sensitive to the president's stated need for negotiating flexibility, typically support legislation consistent with past policy. As a result, bold departures from policy, be they those favored by doves (a freeze on new missiles) or hawks (rapid deployment of SDI), will fail to gain a place on Congress's agenda unless they have the president's support.

Congressional decisions would look quite different if ever the dovish or hawkish factions grew dominant. Some indication of how different can be gleaned by examining Congress's role in defense policy in the first half of the twentieth century. In 1908 Congress cut in half Theodore Roosevelt's requests for battleships. In the late 1930s Congress rejected several of Franklin Roosevelt's proposed defense programs. Congress acted decisively before World War II because majority coalitions formed around particular policies, and most legislators did not recognize the argument that Congress should defer to executive branch expertise on defense policy. Less willing to defer to the president, majority coalitions on occasion overcame Congress's institutional inertia and the resistance of the executive branch to shape defense policy.

When a dominant coalition is absent on Capitol Hill, it matters whether the same party controls both the executive and legislative branches. Presidents typically encounter less resistance to their programs when their party controls Congress. President Nixon would have obtained a more sympathetic hearing on Capitol Hill if the Republicans had been in the majority. Much of the legislative success of the Reagan defense agenda owed to Republican control of the Senate; when the Democrats regained control of the Senate in 1987, Congress checked several programs, most notably SDI. This does not mean that presidents who belong to the majority party have a free ride on Capitol Hill. President Carter met strong resistance from a Democratic Congress, and his image as "soft" on defense owed much to the fact that he was being criticized on national security issues by members of his own party.

Congress's ability to influence nuclear weapons policy is also limited by the procedures and structures of the institution. In terms of procedure, the decision process favors DoD's requests. Given the Pentagon's superior technical expertise and the limits on the amount of work Congress can undertake, DoD not only assesses ways to fulfill missions, it also selects one for funding. Congress then decides whether to fund the Pentagon's choice; it does not evaluate the other alternatives. Given the hawkishness of the defense committees, this means that the standard assumption is that a program deserves to be funded unless it is shown otherwise. So unless DoD's critics build a majority coalition (and provided the administration does not reverse its position) a program will go until completion.

The presidential veto and the filibuster are other aspects of procedure that limit congressional influence. Although presidents rarely veto defense bills, the threat of one often forces DoD's critics to abandon their efforts. In 1986 and in 1987, for example, the House voted to ban all nuclear tests above one kiloton. Both times, however, the House conceded its position in conference because President Reagan promised to veto any bill that contained a test ban. In 1988 Reagan actually vetoed the defense authorization bill, ostensibly because Congress had limited spending on research into space-based interceptors. Unable to override the veto, Congress acceded to Reagan's wishes and increased spending on space-based interceptor research. Likewise, the Republican filibuster in 1987 over limits on SDI tests showed it takes only forty-one senators to bring business on Capitol Hill to a halt. Although the Republicans finally conceded the battle, they did so only after the Democrats expended substantial political capital, capital they would not have spent on a lesser issue.

The structure of the institution makes it difficult for Congress to influence the acquisition process. Congress has two houses, two political parties, four different defense committees, and 535 members. Because no one member can impose a decision on the others, Congress accomplishes nothing when widespread agreement is absent. So legislators seeking to rewrite executive branch proposals must build coalitions that cut across institutional, party, and committee lines. Such coalition building is hard work. The task facing defense critics is made more difficult by the need to pass defense bills each year. Threats to block passage of a defense bill until unacceptable provisions are deleted or favored provisions are added simply are not credible. Even sympathetic members do not want to be seen refusing to fund national defense, so DoD's critics frequently find themselves under pressure to compromise. Since the process already favors the Pentagon, compromise often means victory for DoD.

Procedural and structural obstacles plague congressional efforts to constrain weapons development, but they are felt most severely in efforts to compel DoD to initiate programs. Critics, be they from the left or the right, must not only convince a majority of their colleagues in both chambers that DoD's plans are flawed, but also that their proposal is the remedy. This is a daunting task. Members may agree that an alternative program is needed but disagree on which one is appropriate. Among anti-MX legislators, for example, some favored placing the missile on submarines, others argued for ground-mobile launchers, and still others were content with the existing Minuteman force. Even if DoD's critics can rally majority support behind one option, the possibility of a veto or filibuster can render the effort worthless. That is why Congress often fails to force initiatives onto DoD's agenda.

The third factor that limits congressional influence is the power of DoD. To be fair to members of Congress, they are not the only actors in Washington to find it difficult to change Pentagon policy. "The American weapons acquisition process remains essentially service-dominated. The military—as in many other countries—tends to instinctively resist civilian 'intrusion' into this area, partly for fear that this would delay the process and impede its efficiency. Even the secretary of defense and his Office of the Secretary of Defense (OSD) do not exert full control over it."[19] Former Secretary of Defense James Schlesinger lamented that his responsibilities were "not matched by the powers of the office."[20] Former Secretary of State Henry Kissinger, a master practitioner of bureaucratic politics, admitted that the Nixon "White House never achieved the control over defense policy that it did over foreign policy."[21]

DoD frustrates congressional intervention in several ways. First, the Pentagon accepts decisions as final only if they mirror its own position. When Congress refused to base more than fifty MX in fixed silos, air force officials requested funds to develop a railroad launcher for the missile, even though they had dismissed earlier versions of the proposal.[22] Much the same thing happened with ASAT. Even though the House favored the test moratorium, and though the Democrats regained control of the Senate in the 1986 elections, the air force asked again in 1987 for authority to resume testing against targets in space. To improve its chances of success, the air force even reorganized its staff responsible for lobbying the House and Senate on the MHV program.

Persistence does not always produce victories for DoD. Congress agreed to appropriate RDT&E funds for rail garrison basing, but it refused to lift the ban on ASAT testing. But battles like those over MX and ASAT force the Pentagon's critics to expend substantial resources simply trying to maintain victories already won. Since DoD can mobilize impressive resources on its own behalf, efforts to hold onto past triumphs can consume considerable time. As a result, defense critics find it difficult to intervene successfully in other areas of the budget.

DoD also uses its superior information resources to its advantage. In 1971, for instance, Sen. Hubert Humphrey (D-Minn.) sought to delay deployment of MIRVed missiles. He worried, however, that his proposal would hurt the program to convert Polaris submarines to carry the new Poseidon missile; Sen. Claiborne Pell (D-R.I.), whose state benefited from the conversion program, had agreed to support the amendment provided it did not affect submarines already undergoing conversions. For several months Humphrey's staff tried, to no avail, to discover whether DoD had funds on hand to finish the work under way on the submarines already in the yards. On the day of the vote DoD informed Sen. John Stennis (D-Miss.), the chair of SASC, that the Humphrey amendment would stop Poseidon conversion in its tracks. Humphrey later took to the floor to compliment Stennis for being "so well fortified with facts and figures. I wish I had a part of the Pentagon on my side."[23]

The B-2 bomber provides another example of DoD's reluctance to provide information to potential critics. While the air force heavily publicized the B-1 program, for a long time it shrouded the B-2 program in secrecy. Not only did DoD refuse for a decade to list the bomber in the public version of the federal budget, during one public hearing Pentagon officials denied the plane existed.[24] When Rep. Mike Synar (D-Okla.) asked to tour the Stealth assembly plant, DoD insisted he obtain permission from the chair of HASC. Synar did. The air force then insisted he obtain permission from the ranking minority member on HASC. At this point Synar screamed foul. DoD finally relented, but the rules of secrecy prevented Synar from discussing his trip in public.[25]

As table 8-1 shows, the B-2 episode is part of a larger trend in the 1980s toward greater secrecy on weapons programs.[26] Spending on black programs in the strategic RDT&E budget soared during the Reagan administration. The fig-

Table 8-1.

Classified Spending on Strategic Research, Development, Testing, and Evaluation (RDT&E), FY 1978–1989

Fiscal Year	Total RDT&E A($)	Total RDT&E B(%)	Army A($)	Army B(%)	Navy A($)	Navy B(%)	Air Force A($)	Air Force B(%)
1978	1	0	0	0	1	0	0	0
1979	65	3	18	7	1	0	46	4
1980	n.a.	n.a.	n.a.	n.a.	n.a.	n.a.	n.a.	n.a.
1981	50	1	0	0	0	0	50	2
1982	34	1	0	0	0	0	34	1
1983	94	1	43	5	0	0	51	1
1984	1,166	13	44	6	0	0	1,122	17
1985	1,821	21	198	87	0	0	1,623	32
1986	2,270	27	204	87	0	0	2,066	36
1987	2,736	29	249	89	0	0	2,487	35
1988	3,556	36	98	100	0	0	3,458	41
1989	2,910	47	80	100	0	0	2,830	53

Key: Columns labeled "A" list classified spending on strategic RDT&E measured in millions of dollars. Columns labled "B" list classified spending as a percentage of total spending on strategic RDT&E.

Source: Department of Defense, *R,D,T & E Programs (R-1)*, various years.

ures in table 8-1 actually underestimate the total level of secret programs because they do not count classified nuclear expenditures listed elsewhere in the defense budget. For example, the FY 1987 request for the B-2 reportedly was listed under a line item in the procurement account entitled "Other Production Charges."[27] Nor does a single program account for the growth in classified spending. As late as 1982 the strategic RDT&E budget contained classified requests for only two nuclear weapons programs; by 1985 the figure stood at fourteen.

The Pentagon claims that national security necessitates greater black spending. But the way each service classifies its strategic RDT&E spending suggests that programs are put in the black to blunt congressional intervention. The navy, whose programs meet little opposition in Congress, lists all of its strategic RDT&E budget requests. The air force, which is a frequent target of attack in Congress, classifies many of its programs. Legislators know that DoD puts too many programs in the black. Reps. Les Aspin (D-Wis.) and William Dickinson (R-Ala.), the chair and ranking member of HASC, estimate that "fully 70 percent of all the funds that are now obscured under the 'black' umbrella could be listed publicly in the budget without causing any harm to national security."[28]

Secrecy does not prevent legislators from questioning weapons projects. Members, especially those on the defense committees, can obtain classified information, though it may take considerable persistence. Yet black spending makes it more costly in terms of time and effort for members to ask questions. It "clearly hurts attempts to gather information. One cannot build a record about classified information, so the hearings process becomes less useful."[29] Members can request classified briefings, but the services may still not be forthcoming. When asked to describe classified briefings, Rep. Larry Hopkins (R-Ky.), a member of HASC, replied: "You just sit there and get the hose treatment for several hours."[30] The Pentagon's willingness to restrict information deters many members of Congress from asking questions. One member of HASC observed, "They know our attention span is not that long. They hope that we'll move onto a new question. And they know they can hold us at arms length and get away with it. They've done it in the past, and they'll continue to do it."[31]

DoD may also punish members who oppose defense programs. To what extent DoD actually acts in this manner is unknown; the Pentagon is understandably reluctant to admit that it uses threats, while many legislators downplay reports of coercion by the services.[32] Nevertheless, some members point to purported incidents of pressure, such as a 1986 decision by DoD to seek to close military facilities located in the districts of three leading Pentagon critics.[33] Likewise, the air force apparently maintains a dossier on each member of Congress that details his or her "antidefense" votes and public statements.[34] And some members believe representing a district with no military installations allows them to vote strictly on the merits of defense issues. One House Democrat even thanks President Nixon for closing several bases in his state: "He did us a favor. He gave us freedom. As Janis Joplin used to sing, 'Freedom's just another word for nothing left to lose.' We don't have to grovel any more."[35]

Why can DoD often frustrate Congress? One reason is the Pentagon has many allies on Capitol Hill. Many hawkish members approve of the ends DoD seeks, if not always the means, and oppose efforts to punish the Pentagon for supposed transgressions. So DoD officials usually risk little when they refuse to cooperate with members of Congress. Another reason is that DoD differs from every other bureaucracy in Washington. Not only does it dwarf all others in size—making it more difficult to deal with in any event—the Pentagon is the only bureaucracy with both a civilian and military component. The military itself is actually four organizations, each of which has an *esprit de corps* unrivaled on Capitol Hill (no committee in Congress has its own uniform, college, and fight song). All of these attributes make DoD a formidable adversary.

Finally, when dealing with DoD the basic presumptions shift for many members of Congress. As Representative Aspin points out, "To most Congressmen, defense experts are people in uniform, rather than academics in universities or 'think tanks.' Uniforms are identified with expertise: the higher the rank, the greater the expertise."[36] By virtue of their training, military officers lay claim to expertise that few individuals on Capitol Hill or in OSD can match. Unlike private defense analysts, military officials also can claim access to classified information. As a result, when the services testify that the United States needs a weapons system, the burden rests with legislators to prove otherwise.

Reforms

Can Congress improve its ability to oversee and influence nuclear weapons policy? Many observers say yes. One popular view holds that the key to improved congressional oversight lies in formal changes in the way Congress conducts its business. A variety of congressional reforms is possible. On the procedural side, numerous observers urge Congress to adopt multiyear budgeting techniques such as biennial budgets and milestone authorizations.[37] On the structural side, reformers urge Congress to create a joint committee on national security as well as specialized policy subcommittees within the armed services committees.[38] Although the details of the various reform proposals vary greatly, proponents believe that changing congressional procedures and structures will enhance Congress's ability to focus on crucial issues in defense policy.

However well-intentioned these reforms may be they suffer two major shortcomings.[39] One is that any reform effort will meet tremendous political resistance on Capitol Hill. Most reforms, whether procedural or structural, threaten the power and prestige of existing groups or individuals in Congress. This in turn creates opposition because, as former Speaker of the House Thomas P. "Tip" O'Neill (D-Mass.) once observed, on Capitol Hill "the name of the game is power and the boys don't want to give it up."[40] This is why proposals to merge the defense appropriations subcommittees with the armed services committees have never made headway. Members of these panels have long opposed committee consolidation because it would rob some of them of their influence.

The second problem with changing Congress's procedures and structures is that the reforms probably will not work. Proponents of biennial budgeting contend that a two-year budget cycle will give Congress more time to focus on major policy issues. Yet any biennial budget process must provide a mechanism to consider supplemental requests during the second year should changes in the economy, threat assessment, or technology warrant them. If the president or a sizable number of legislators dislike the budgetary allocations made in the first year—a likely prospect—then supplemental requests will quickly begin to look like annual budgets. A similar criticism may be leveled against the call for policy subcommittees. If policy subcommittees are to be more than debating societies, they must have influence over the level and content of defense budget requests. Yet this will trigger turf fights with the subcommittees that already exist.

A different approach to improving congressional oversight holds that Congress should alter the decision-making process within the executive branch, and particularly within the Pentagon, either by redistributing authority among existing actors or by creating entirely new ones.[41] The assumption here is that a changed process will produce policies more in tune with the preferences of members. Congress has employed this strategy on other occasions. In 1961 it created the Arms Control and Disarmament Agency (ACDA) because many members believed that insufficient attention had been given to arms control. Congress established the Office of the Special Trade Representative in 1974 because legislators believed "that the State Department . . . was unsympathetic and unresponsive to domestic interests and that the responsibility should be assigned elsewhere."[42] In 1986 Congress, irate at what it saw as the Pentagon's neglect of commando forces, created the Special Operations Command to "insure that counterterrorism and the special operations forces had an institutional voice in the Pentagon."[43]

Like proposals for changes in how Congress conducts its own business, attempts to restructure the decision-making process in the Pentagon face tremendous political hurdles. The ability and willingness of the services to thwart reform efforts are legendary. To take only one example, during the push in 1986 to strengthen the Joint Chiefs of Staff (JCS), the navy created a "crisis management center on DoD reorganization" whose purpose was to see that reform did not restrict the navy's traditional autonomy.[44] Although Pentagon reform is not impossible—Congress passed a JCS reorganization bill in 1986—the inevitable service resistance means that major reforms will occur infrequently and generally will fall far short of what proponents seek.

Battles to restructure decision making in the Pentagon also do not end with the passage of a piece of legislation. DoD has a proven track record of frustrating reforms. Despite hopes that ACDA would integrate arms control concerns with military objectives, it "has always been either wholly or substantially excluded from that [weapons acquisition] process."[45] In 1983 Congress established an independent office to prevent the services from rigging weapons tests. The General Accounting Office later concluded that the reports issued by the Office of Operational Test and Evaluation "contained incomplete or inaccurate statements" and that "the omissions, inaccuracies, and overall assessments consistently resulted in a more favorable presentation to the Congress of test adequacy and system performance than was warranted by the facts."[46] In 1986 Congress created the post of Under Secretary of Defense for Acquisition to improve the management of procurement programs. After less than a year on the job, the first "Acquisition Czar" resigned, citing his "judgment that the Pentagon was not prepared to move ahead vigorously with the implementation of reforms."[47]

If restructuring the way Congress and DoD operate is not likely to improve congressional oversight, changing the ideological composition of the defense committees offers more hope.[48] This change would address the major deficiency in congressional defense oversight, namely, that Congress delegates its oversight responsibilities to members who are more hawkish than the House or Senate as a whole and who often see their task as defending Pentagon requests rather than examining them. As a result, much of Congress's activity on defense policy is dissipated on internal squabbling as the defense committees square off against their opponents on the floor.

The defense committees would act differently if they reflected the views found in the full House and Senate. Congressional politics is no exception to the notion that competition makes for better products. The defense committees became active in the early 1970s only after they came under attack from members dissatisfied with the content of defense policies. Similarly, the House Democratic Caucus used special "bullet vote" delegates several times in the mid-1980s to prevent HASC from abandoning the House's position in conference negotiations with the Senate.

Efforts to make the defense committees reflect the views of their parent chambers are also politically realistic. In 1985 the House Democratic Caucus made Representative Aspin, a moderate, chair of HASC. In the Hundredth Congress, the House Democratic leadership weakened the hawkishness of HASC by adding five moderate Democrats to the committee. As these episodes suggest, however, membership on the defense committees will change only if rank-and-file legislators push for change. Without pressure from nonmembers, particularly doves and moderates, congressional leaders have no incentive to revise the assignment patterns that produced hawkish defense committees in the first place.

Changing the composition of the defense committees has disadvantages. Because seniority is crucial to influence in both chambers, it will take several years (or more) before new members rise to positions of power within the committees. This is especially true in the House, where a member may serve for a decade and still lack seniority to chair a subcommittee. A potentially more serious disadvantage is that attempts to balance the defense committees ideologically may further polarize their work. For instance, the House Republican leadership responded to efforts to place moderate Democrats on HASC by denying moderate Republicans seats on the committee.[49] But the fear of partisanship hardly justifies maintaining a biased committee system and inadequate congressional oversight.

9 ≫ ≪

Congress and Its Critics

SHOULD CONGRESS PLAY an active role in nuclear weapons policy? Many argue that Congress has become too active on nuclear weapons issues. One line of complaint focuses on the inefficiency of congressional decision making: Congress takes too long to make decisions, and it frequently changes its mind, which in turn upsets DoD's plans and increases defense costs. A second line of complaint holds that Congress should defer to executive branch expertise because legislators lack the technical knowledge needed to make intelligent decisions about nuclear weapons policy. A third line of complaint charges that Congress's constant intervention in nuclear weapons policy interferes with the president's ability to negotiate arms control agreements with the Soviet Union.

The efficiency, guardianship, and bargaining chip critiques are all appealing at first glance. None of them, however, holds up on close inspection. The fixation with congressional inefficiency obscures more than it illuminates. Even leaving aside the question of whether the costs of inefficiency are as great as critics complain, the Framers did not design Congress to be efficient, nor does an efficient Congress necessarily serve the public interest. The guardianship argument fails to recognize that politics often shapes executive branch decisions and that decisions about nuclear weapons require more than mere technical knowledge. The historical evidence about bargaining chips is ambiguous. Bargaining chips frequently are not traded away, and administrations often use the bargaining chip argument as a political ploy to force members of Congress to support new weapons systems.

Congress has its flaws, but they are not sufficient to merit congressional passivity. When Congress intervenes in the policy process, it counters the narrowness and bias that often pervades executive branch decision making. Congress also limits the president's ability to break with the status quo. Observers typically applaud when Congress rejects a policy they dislike and howl when Congress blocks policies they favor. But the constraints Congress places on the president force him to build public support for his policies, a requirement that can only be healthy for democratic government. Last, Congress should be active in nuclear weapons policy because the American political system is based on the idea that both the president and Congress should make national policy. No good reason exists to abandon the bedrock of American politics.

Congressional Inefficiency

The most common indictment of Congress's handling of defense policy is that it is an inefficient decision-making body.[1] Most complaints focus on Congress's inability to approve the defense budget before the start of the fiscal year. Critics also complain that even when Congress finally approves a defense budget, the reliance on annual budgeting means that program decisions can be reopened each year. Legislative vacillation looms large in nuclear weapons policy because nuclear weapons are the most contentious items in the defense budget. As one commentator complained at the height of the MX debate, "By my count there have been thirty-six 'test votes' in the House and Senate on the MX missile since Reagan took office, most of them necessitated by some whorl of the budget process. These test votes have been accompanied by tension, packed press galleries, ringing debate—all the drama of decision, but no decision."[2]

Critics decry congressional inefficiency because it complicates DoD's planning and increases defense costs. The tendency of the House and Senate to alter many budget line items, coupled with often divergent defense committee recommendations, compounds the problem. Defense contractors in turn are hard pressed to schedule efficient use of their production lines because Congress may radically change the size and character of the "buy" that DoD anticipated. As a result, padding is built into the contracting process and some defense spending is wasted.

Criticisms about congressional inefficiency have merit; even Congress's most passionate defenders complain about legislative delay and vacillation. But the inefficiency argument is overstated. Absent total passivity, congressional decision making will always be inefficient. Congress is a *political* institution, not a bureaucratic one. "Congress invariably appears inept and irresponsible from the perspective of anyone who thinks of it as a bureaucracy that can formulate policies, manage operations, or even systematically assess and review programs. Congress does not have the structure of a bureaucracy, it is institutionally incapable of doing what bureaucracies do, and it is unrealistic to expect otherwise."[3] Congress's ability to act expeditiously is further limited when the issue at hand sharply divides its members, as is often the case with nuclear weapons.

Critics also exaggerate how much Congress hurts the Pentagon's ability to plan. Fiscal constraints dictate most budget cuts, and often Congress follows DoD's recommendations on where to cut funding. Only a handful of programs are controversial. Even here the balance sheet on congressional activism is not as clear as critics suggest. When Congress forces the executive branch to withdraw or revise a weapons program, the result may benefit the United States treasury. The United States, for example, spent roughly $6 billion to construct one Safeguard ABM site. Less than a year after the system became operational, the air force dismantled the interceptor missiles because they did not work.

Thus, when Congress blocked President Nixon's proposal for a network of ABM sites, it actually *saved* taxpayers from spending several billion dollars on a worthless weapons system.

Critics also never show why efficiency should be the standard for judging good government. The Framers of the Constitution certainly did not hold efficiency in such high esteem. As Justice Louis Brandeis writes, "The doctrine of the separation of powers was adopted by the Convention of 1787, not to promote efficiency but to preclude the exercise of arbitrary power."[4] Nor does history suggest that efficient governance promotes *wise* governance. By any conceivable indicator Congress was more efficient during the 1950s and 1960s than it was in the 1980s. When the inside game reigned on Capitol Hill few members took part in decision making, it took less time to pass the defense budget, and Congress made few changes to individual line items. Despite its efficiency, however, the inside game neglected oversight. The House and Senate repeatedly failed to question DoD about new weapons. The failure to evaluate new weapons proposals was most serious in the case of MIRV technology. Once the United States developed a MIRV capability, "there went the possibility of preserving the relative invulnerability of American ICBMs into a longer future."[5]

Congress's critics forget that its two primary functions—to make laws and to represent the people—frequently clash. "Lawmaking implies action, decision-making, and choice. Representation implies full consideration, widespread consent, and ample opportunity for various interests to be heard. The two sets of values are not completely exclusive, but the two central thrusts are different."[6] In the 1960s Congress handled defense issues more efficiently, but at the cost of robust debate. Changes in congressional rules and norms in the 1970s and 1980s made robust debate possible. The increased number of participants inevitably complicated congressional decision making.

Can Congress be made more efficient without degrading its ability to articulate diverse points of view? The evidence on this score is discouraging.[7] As with reforms designed to improve Congress's oversight capabilities, any effort to streamline congressional decision making faces tremendous obstacles. Most reforms seek to concentrate power, requiring members to relinquish some of their ability to influence policy. Legislators generally refuse to make this sacrifice, even though they may find Congress's inefficiencies to be maddening at times. Even if a reform proposal is politically feasible, it still may not make Congress more efficient. Reforms often have perverse results. The Congressional Budget and Impoundment Control Act of 1974, for example, sought to rationalize the budget process. Instead the Budget Act spawned a procedural nightmare. Today many members want to overhaul the budget process, though they disagree on how to fix it.[8] Similarly, in 1975 the Senate lowered the number of votes necessary for cloture to make the Senate function more efficiently. An unexpected result was the rise of the post-cloture filibuster, which came to hobble Senate business.[9]

Critics are right: Congress *is* inefficient. It often frustrates both members and observers, it frequently vacillates on questions of great importance, and it undoubtedly complicates DoD's work. Still, the costs associated with congressional inefficiency are exaggerated and the benefits neglected. Critics usually fail to acknowledge that healthy democratic political institutions must balance the need for efficiency against the demand for representation. On decisions of great importance where opinion is divided, debate in Congress *should* be prolonged and repetitive. When they feel deeply about policy issues, members should use the tools available to them to translate their preferences into policy. That is the nature of the American democratic process. As one representative put it, "This is not meant to be a precise system. This place is not meant to run like a Swiss watch. Do you want liberty or do you want order? You can have both. But if you do you're going to get a little less of one or the other."[10]

Guardianship

A second criticism of Congress's role in the nuclear force acquisition process involves what may be called the "principle of guardianship."[11] The guardianship argument begins with the unassailable observation that members of Congress, no matter how well-intentioned, almost always lack in-depth understanding of nuclear issues. After all, few legislators were trained as engineers, scientists, or nuclear strategists. The executive branch, however, possesses substantial technical expertise on nuclear matters; many DoD officials devote much of their adult lives to mastering the intricacies of the nuclear debate. Because of the tremendous disparity in knowledge between the two branches of government, proponents of the guardianship argument believe legislators should defer to the executive branch if they want to serve the public interest.

Although the guardianship argument has some superficial appeal, it suffers two fatal flaws. One is that the argument rests on the claim that the executive branch makes better decisions because it possesses superior technical expertise. But bureaucracies fall short (sometimes very short) of the rational decision-making ideal often attributed to them. "No doubt a very large amount of technical knowledge and scientific study enters into [decisions about military programs]. But so do public fears or apathy, political pressures, service traditions, vested interests, personal abilities or ambitions, the accidental distribution of stupidity at one point or imaginative iconoclasm at another in the vast military-bureaucratic machine."[12]

The weapons acquisition literature provides numerous examples of how nonobjective factors led the services to develop (or not to develop) weapons. The Trident submarine assumed its mammoth dimensions primarily because Admiral Hyman Rickover wanted a platform for a new reactor he had devised and not because of military requirements.[13] In the early 1970s the air force resisted proposals to arm the subsonic cruise armed decoy missile—the predecessor to the ALCM—with a live warhead because it threatened the manned bomber program.[14] The air force blocked research on the continuous patrol aircraft basing proposal for the MX because the plane threatened funding for other aircraft programs and because air force officials wanted fast planes not slow ones.[15] Finally, as the air force's policy on MX mobility shows, DoD often seizes and discards assessments of external threats as they are needed to justify new programs rather than vice versa. The threats "that have bureaucratic power appear to be those that can be ameliorated only by new and expanded weapons systems."[16]

White House officials also have been known to base their decisions on politics. After signing the SALT I Treaty, President Nixon asked Congress to increase spending on strategic programs to win Pentagon support for the treaty; "Secretary of Defense [Melvin] Laird and the Joint Chiefs of Staff made Administration support of a broad program of strategic modernization the fairly explicit condition of their support of the treaty."[17] During development of the MX, disagreement arose in the Carter administration over the size of the missile. The winning faction wanted a ninety-three-inch diameter missile partly to foreclose the possibility that MX would be based on Trident submarines. These officials "knew that the ninety-three-inch MX design was too big to be fitted into the Trident launch tubes."[18] President Reagan unveiled his strategic force modernization program in 1981 without consulting senior military officials. This led Sen. John Tower (R-Tex.), chair of SASC, to complain that Reagan's decision was made "within a small circle, without the coordination of the best military expertise."[19]

The second flaw with the guardianship argument is that decisions to build nuclear weapons require more than technical knowledge. To quote Robert Dahl:

> On a great many questions of policy, instrumental judgments depend on assumptions that are not strictly technical, scientific, or even very rigorous. Often these assumptions reflect a kind of ontological judgment: the world is this way, not that, it tends to work this way, not that. With nuclear weapons, for example, ordinary people . . . are likely to believe in Murphy's famous law. They believe that if things can go wrong, they probably will go wrong. Although supported by a great deal of experience, in fact probably as well supported by experience as most generalizations in the social sciences, Murphy's law is of course not a well validated empirical law in the strict sense. It is a common sense judgment about a tendency of things, an ontological view about the nature of the world.[20]

Samuel Huntington, whose views on nuclear weapons policy are considerably more hawkish than Dahl's, concurs: "The more important a policy issue is, the less important becomes detailed technical information and the more relevant become broad judgments on goals and values, i.e., political judgments, where presumably the congressman's competence is greatest."[21]

Ontological or political judgments are critical to decisions about nuclear weapons because nuclear strategy is not a science. It involves politics. As more than forty years of debate testify, no one can prove what makes deterrence work. While some experts argue that the United States needs a warfighting capability, other, equally respected experts claim the mere possession of nuclear weapons deters. That nuclear strategy rests on ontological and not scientific judgments is why defense experts can agree on the "facts" but still recommend very different policies. Take for example the reactions to the original "nuclear winter" study. Carl Sagan used the findings to argue for "safe and verifiable reductions of the world strategic inventories."[22] Edward Teller used the study to push for more spending on "active defense, civil defense and food storage."[23] Sagan and Teller parted course not on the scientific issues at stake but on their political judgments of the Soviet threat and how to deter Soviet leaders.

Of course, legislators frequently invoke technical arguments to advance their policy preferences. But for most members technical arguments merely provide a useful tool for advancing policy prescriptions that are based on judgments about a program's political and military merits. Take for example the Safeguard debate. While many senators criticized the ABM system on technical grounds, most of "these senators were acting on the basis of a high-level political judgment that the United States could best serve its long-term security interests through attempts to negotiate a standstill in the strategic arms race."[24] Members like to invoke technical arguments for a simple reason: "Technical testimony appears more 'objective' and policy neutral, and it is thus thought to carry more weight with those politicians who have not yet made up their minds."[25] And because politics divides scientists as it does everyone else, members find it easy to play the game of "pick your scientist."[26]

Do experts make better ontological judgments than do members of Congress? The available evidence suggests the answer is no. "Studies have shown that in a great many fields the forecasts of experts are no better, or in some cases only slightly better, than the forecasts of laymen."[27] Members of Congress may even have an advantage over weapons experts because legislators have more experience making decisions based on assessments of risk, uncertainty, and trade-offs, three characteristics of public policy generally and nuclear weapons policy specifically.[28] Experts, on the other hand, often are not forced to view public policy from beyond the confines of their narrow specialty, and so their vision frequently is narrow.

Congress was created in the belief that the elected representatives of the people should participate in the making of public policy. There may be policy questions where Congress should delegate its authority, but the burden rests with the executive branch to show that these questions involve only technical knowledge beyond the reach of the average legislator. In nuclear weapons policy the executive branch has not established such a case. Politics often shapes administration and service decisions. Moreover, the decisions that Congress must make—for example, to authorize one hundred MX missiles in fixed silos —are "political in nature, involving not merely 'scientific' solutions to 'objective' problems, but political values and preferences among a variety of approaches to the nation's security interests."[29] Congress shirks its duties when it leaves acquisition decisions solely in the hands of the executive branch.

Bargaining Chips

The third criticism leveled against Congress holds that Congress limits the president's negotiating leverage. Proponents of the bargaining chip theory contend that the United States should build nuclear weapons if only to extract concessions from the Soviet Union at the negotiating table. According to the argument, the Soviets will bargain in good faith only when they fear the United States is gaining strategic superiority. As a result, congressional efforts to limit weapons development, even if they spring from good intentions, actually hurt arms control. If Soviet leaders believe that Congress may cancel a program, they have less incentive to concede at the bargaining table. So legislators who try to constrain weapons systems make the president's job more difficult, and they may even block arms reduction.

Presidents often invoke the bargaining chip argument, sometimes in blunt fashion. In his 1987 State of the Union address, President Reagan warned that "enacting the Soviet negotiating position into American law would not be the way to win a good agreement. So I must tell this Congress I will veto any effort that undercuts our national security and our negotiating leverage."[30] Congressional hawks also preach the need to give the president negotiating leverage. Sens. Robert Dole (R-Kans.) and John Warner (R-Va.) introduced legislation in 1987 to declare that "the Congress should not seek to establish, in U.S. domestic law, positions on matters such as ASAT, nuclear testing, SALT II compliance, ABM Treaty interpretation . . . at the very moment that such sensitive arms control subjects are being negotiated. . . . Such action would inevitably disadvantage and undermine the United States Government in such negotiations."[31]

Even though proponents of the bargaining chip argument often claim that the president alone is empowered to conduct foreign affairs, the bargaining chip argument does not raise constitutional issues. The Constitution specifically authorizes Congress "to raise and support armies . . . to provide and maintain a navy; [and] to make rules for the government and regulation of the land and naval forces."[32] The meaning of these words is unambiguous. To quote Justice

Robert H. Jackson, "Congress alone controls the raising of the revenues and their appropriation and may determine in what manner and by what means they shall be spent for military and naval procurement."[33] Nowhere does the Constitution suggest that Congress will exercise its appropriations power only so long as the president's negotiating leverage is unaffected.

Arguments for bargaining chips, then, hinge on the question of effectiveness: Would the president be better able to negotiate agreements if Congress left acquisition decisions alone? Intuition suggests the answer is yes. Many observers doubt the United States can manage its foreign affairs with 535 Secretaries of State (to borrow a common refrain). Congress frequently resembles a rabble rather than an assembly, it cannot act in secret, and it often fails to act at all.[34] In comparison, the modern presidency is well suited to conduct foreign policy precisely because it can act decisively and in secret. Moreover, the Soviet Union would seem to have an incentive to bargain only when the United States possesses or is developing weapons that threaten key Soviet assets. After all, if the Soviet Union has nothing to fear, why should it negotiate?

Proponents of the bargaining chip argument contend that history supports their case. Safeguard is a frequently cited example. After the signing of the SALT I and ABM treaties, Secretary of State Henry Kissinger testified, "We could not have negotiated the limitations on offensive weapons if it had not been linked to limitations on defensive weapons and to their [the Soviets'] desire of stopping the deployment of [our] ABM System."[35] HASC claimed that "the evidence is persuasive that the Safeguard system has been an incentive to the SALT agreement and the hopeful beginning of limitations on strategic nuclear weapons."[36] The signing of the INF agreement was also taken by many to validate NATO's decision to pursue a dual-track policy on intermediate-range forces. "Without Pershing IIs . . . the Soviets almost certainly would not have agreed to dismantle their SS-20s."[37]

Not everyone, however, accepts the notion that successful negotiations depend upon accumulating weapons to trade. Gerard Smith, chief U.S. negotiator at the SALT I talks, concluded that President Nixon's bargaining chip strategy actually hampered negotiations. The lesson he drew was that "if restraining measures are not taken early in the development of new weapons systems, control becomes much more difficult."[38] Averell Harriman, former U.S. ambassador to Moscow, echoed these views. He argued that "the bargaining chip theory should be abandoned. It is utterly discredited."[39]

Skepticism toward bargaining chips has several roots. First, Soviet leaders may not accept the strategy. In 1987, for instance, the Soviet Union began to dismantle its medium-range SS-4 missiles well before an agreement was reached on INF forces.[40] Second, the theory assumes Soviet leaders will negotiate from a position of inferiority. Yet just the opposite may be true; they may counter their weaknesses with redoubled development efforts.[41] Third, the theory assumes the Soviets tailor their bargaining positions to political events in the United States. Yet Soviet leaders may be looking inward rather than outward. A study of the claim that SDI forced Moscow to reopen arms control negotiations in 1985 concluded that "internal dynamics and a more sophisticated analysis of political leverage rather than SDI are the driving factors behind increased Soviet interest in arms control."[42]

Fourth, history suggests that bargaining chips are not always bargained away.[43] The cruise missile provides the best example. Kissinger initially pushed the air force to develop cruise missiles because he believed the new technology would enhance U.S. negotiating leverage. When the air force later prevented him from cashing in the cruise missile chip, Kissinger could only lament, "How was I to know the military would come to love it?"[44] As a result, the bargaining chip strategy may "complicate negotiations by raising arms competition to higher levels, often levels more difficult to control."[45]

The possibility that weapons may not be traded away means that the bargaining chip strategy may force members of Congress to choose between funding a weapons system of dubious value or being accused of trying to sabotage the administration's arms control policy. This happened with the MX program. Given the missile's vulnerability to Soviet attack, many believed its deployment would not only fail to strengthen the U.S. nuclear force structure but also prove to be destabilizing in a crisis. On the other hand, President Reagan insisted that he needed MX to force Soviet concessions, although he could not guarantee that the missile would be bargained away. At a minimum, choosing between these conflicting options was not easy for many legislators.

Finally, the bargaining chip argument loses credence because it often appears simply to be a political ploy designed to force Congress to approve programs. DoD claimed that MIRVs would pressure the Soviets to accept constraints on its ABM system. Yet the United States did not push seriously for a MIRV ban after agreement was reached on defensive systems.[46] The Nixon and Ford administrations repeatedly argued that the Trident submarine was needed for bargaining leverage. Neither president, however, considered bargaining it away.[47] Hawkish members implore their dovish colleagues to respect the president's negotiating flexibility, but they do not obey their own strictures when they dislike the president's policies. Hawks paid little heed to President Carter's image when they blocked his proposal for a cruise missile carrier aircraft. Cases like these make bargaining chip arguments look like thinly disguised calls for congressional deference to the military.

History, then, does not firmly establish the effectiveness of bargaining chips. Yet whatever validity the theory may have, Congress is remarkably sensitive to the president's need for negotiating leverage. Criticism by hawks notwithstanding, Congress does not act irresponsibly on nuclear weapons matters. Members of Congress do not intentionally seek to complicate administration bargaining efforts. Indeed, Congress approves most weapons with little or no dissent. The GLCM and Pershing II missiles, for example, which formed the heart of NATO's dual-track policy and which ostensibly made an INF agreement possible, met only minor opposition in the House and Senate.

Even when Congress debates programs it respects the delicacy of the president's position. On the ABM and MX programs, Congress acceded to the arguments of Presidents Nixon and Reagan that the weapons were needed for bargaining leverage, despite considerable evidence that neither weapon would contribute much to U.S. national security. By the time Congress capped the deployment of MX, the missile had little, if any, potential as a bargaining chip. Congress banned ASAT testing, but stipulated that the moratorium would be lifted if the Soviet Union resumed testing of its satellite interceptor. In 1987 Sen. Sam Nunn (D-Ga.), chair of SASC, offered to postpone the debate on SDI test restrictions so that it would not coincide with Soviet Foreign Minister Edward Shevardnadze's visit to Washington.[48] Nunn made the offer (which the Republicans rejected) because he wanted to avoid any appearance that Democrats were undercutting the president's negotiating position.

The only instance where Congress flatly denied the president's request for negotiating leverage came in the dispute over the interpretation of the ABM Treaty. Yet unlike any other case, this episode raised a critical constitutional question, namely, does the president have the power to reinterpret a treaty after the Senate has given its advice and consent? The answer can only be no. As Senator Nunn argued at the time, if the "laws of the land can be changed by the President without coming back to Congress . . . then we are basically reversing 200 years of history. We are . . . beginning a monarchy because a monarchy can make those decisions without coming back to Congress."[49] No matter what kind of negotiating leverage a weapon (or research program) may give the executive branch, it should not come at the price of the Constitution.

Congress understands and respects the difficulties that presidents face in arms control negotiations far more than its critics acknowledge. Of course, some members of Congress would prefer to dictate foreign policy to the president, and others would like a coequal role with the White House in the formulation of foreign policy. Yet these legislators represent a minority view. Congress does *not* lead on nuclear weapons policy. It responds to presidential leadership and acts as a critic. Congress constrains weapons programs only after the executive branch fails repeatedly to make its case.

Conclusion

It is one thing to cast doubt on the criticisms leveled against Congress; it is another to argue that legislators should play an active role in the nuclear force acquisition process. Does an activist Congress serve the public interest? In the absence of an objective measure of the common good, the answer to this question all too often depends on one's views on the policies of the administration in office. Hawks who applauded the obstacles that Congress threw in the way of Jimmy Carter's nuclear weapons policies cried foul when Congress threw up obstacles to Ronald Reagan's policy proposals. Doves displayed much the same applause/boo attitude toward Congress but in reverse order.

Leaving aside partisan motives, there are three reasons why legislators should play an active role on nuclear weapons matters regardless of who occupies the Oval Office. One is that decentralizing authority often produces better public policy. "Good government as well as democracy demand fewer decisions by one representative alone, for war or in peace."[50] When Congress participates in the policy process it counters the narrowness of executive branch decision making.[51] Challenges from Capitol Hill, be they led by doves or hawks, force the executive branch to justify or revise its programs. While this does not guarantee better policies, it reduces the possibility that an administration will commit the country to an important policy without ample consideration of the potential ramifications.

An activist Congress also frustrates presidential initiatives that depart radically from the status quo. Participants typically berate Congress as obstructionist when their favored policy runs aground on Capitol Hill. But such complaints are fundamentally misplaced. In frustrating major policy changes Congress is only doing what it was designed to do. The Framers gave Congress the power to frustrate the president because they wanted to check executive power, to ensure that presidents built public support for their policies. Demanding that the president rally public support for his proposals is a reasonable requirement in a democracy. And the president is well situated to take his case to the public. As the single most important actor in the American political system the president commands access to the most important tool of policy persuasion, namely, the news media. Moreover, Congress is evenhanded in its activism. Republicans may protest that Congress blocked President Reagan's nuclear weapons proposals, but Jimmy Carter received as much if not more criticism from Congress.

A third strength of an activist Congress is that the American political system is based on the belief that the elected representatives of the people—the president *and* members of Congress—should decide national policy. Such a system of dual responsibility should not be abandoned without compelling reason. Despite much handwringing and lamenting to the contrary, no convincing evidence exists that congressional activism hurts the public interest. Moreover, even though the president is elected by all the people and members of Congress are not, this is no argument for congressional passivity on nuclear weapons matters. Legislators often bring views not held within the administration to the policy debate. The importance of airing diverse public views should not be dismissed, even if they are minority views, because the American democratic process is not based on the principle of majoritarianism.

Robust congressional debate over nuclear weapons policy was probably never more important than it is today. Dramatic changes in Soviet foreign policy, the collapse of communism in Eastern Europe, and the unification of Germany have rewritten the geopolitical map of Europe. America faces the task of constructing a nuclear weapons policy for the postcontainment era. Numerous questions must be answered. What should the United States arsenal look like in the year 2000? Does the United States need to build the B-2? the Midgetman SICBM? a rail garrison basing system for the MX? Has the need for strategic defense passed? Should the United States push vigorously to expand its lead in nuclear weapons technology at a time when the Soviet Union's economy is faltering? Given what is riding on the answers to these and other questions, it is critical that all views, majority and minority, be heard.

To argue for an activist Congress does not mean that Congress's role in nuclear weapons policy making is flawless. Legislators themselves readily admit that congressional decision making leaves much to be desired. Congress may wring its hands for several years over a controversial weapons system before making a final decision; it often devotes extensive time to trivial matters while ignoring important ones; and it typically questions the need for weapons programs only late in their development cycles if at all. Nevertheless, the failures of Congress should not obscure its successes. It does debate at least some critical issues—ABM, B-1, counterforce weapons, MX, Midgetman, ASAT, and SDI to name just the most prominent. These congressional debates ensure at a minimum that decisions about major nuclear weapons systems will not be made in ignorance.

Support for congressional activism also does not imply an endorsement of the role Congress staked out for itself in the 1930s. The experiences of those years (plus common sense) suggest that Congress is ill suited to lead the nation on defense and foreign affairs. But the events of the 1960s suggest that passivity on Capitol Hill also does not serve the public interest. Congress works best when it avoids both extremes. Given the complexity of nuclear weapons issues and their inevitable linkage to foreign policy, Congress maximizes its effectiveness when it acts as a critic, poking and prodding the executive branch to defend its acquisition decisions, rather than attempting to dictate policy.

Pessimists can argue, of course, that Congress is only a few short steps from usurping the president's authority. Over time, Congress may lose sight of its need to delegate authority to the executive branch and give in to an impulse to legislate. Even the services might not be able to use their power and expertise to prevent Congress from dictating nuclear weapons policy. As hawks fear, such extreme congressional activism *might* pose substantial costs to the American public, as it did in the 1930s. The likelihood that a domineering Congress will emerge in the future is slim. Yet the Constitution does not forbid Congress to err. The freedom to make mistakes is part and parcel of democratic government; "the test of a democracy is not that the right side wins the political battle but that there is a political battle."[52]

Congress not only has the right to participate in the nuclear force acquisition process but the obligation to do so. When Congress defers to the executive branch on defense and foreign policy matters it creates the functional equivalent of an autocracy, as the term *imperial presidency* implies. Whatever weaknesses democratic decision making may have, they are minor compared to those of autocratic decision making. Critics of Congress would do well to take this point to heart.

Notes

INTRODUCTION

1. Graham T. Allison and Frederic A. Morris, "Armaments and Arms Control: Exploring the Determinants of Military Weapons," *Daedalus* 104 (Summer 1975): 101.

2. Jonathan Eliot Medalia, "The U.S. Senate and Strategic Arms Limitation Policymaking, 1963–1972," Ph.D. diss., Stanford University, 1975, p. 10.

3. Nancy J. Bearg and Edwin A. Deagle, Jr., "Congress and the Defense Budget," in *American Defense Policy,* 4th ed., ed. John E. Endicott and Roy W. Stafford (Baltimore: Johns Hopkins University Press, 1977), p. 349.

4. See E. E. Schattschneider, *The Semisovereign People* (New York: Holt, Rinehart, 1961), pp. 1–3.

5. See David E. Price, *Who Makes the Laws? Creativity and Power in Senate Committees* (Cambridge, Mass.: Schenkman, 1972), pp. 2–9.

6. Alton Frye, "Congress: The Virtues of Its Vices," *Foreign Policy* 3 (Summer 1971): 125.

7. Among others see Barry M. Blechman, "The New Congressional Role in Arms Control," in *A Question of Balance: The President, the Congress, and Foreign Policy,* ed. Thomas E. Mann (Washington, D.C.: Brookings Institution, 1990).

8. See Edward J. Laurance, "The Changing Role of Congress in Defense Policy-Making," *Journal of Conflict Resolution* 20 (June 1976): 213–53, and Edward J. Laurance, "The Congressional Role in Defense Policy. The Evolution of the Literature," *Armed Forces and Society* 6 (Spring 1980): 431–54.

CHAPTER ONE   EXPLANATIONS

1. The term *conceptual lens* is from Graham Allison, *Essence of Decision: Explaining the Cuban Missile Crisis* (Boston: Little, Brown, 1971); v.

2. Quoted in Alton Frye, *A Responsible Congress: The Politics of National Security* (New York: McGraw-Hill, 1975), p. 5.

3. Quoted in John W. Kingdon, *Congressmen's Voting Decisions,* 3d ed. (Ann Arbor: University of Michigan Press, 1989), p. 98.

4. *Congressional Record,* 98th Cong., 1st sess., 1983, 129, pt. 10, 13553.

5. Position taking is "the public enunciation of a judgmental statement on anything likely to be of interest to political actors." David R. Mayhew, *Congress: The Electoral Connection* (New Haven: Yale University Press, 1974), p. 61.

6. See Les Aspin, "Games the Pentagon Plays," *Foreign Policy* 11 (Summer 1973): 80–92, and J. Ronald Fox, *Arming America: How the U.S. Buys Weapons* (Cambridge: Harvard University Press, 1974), pp. 136–40.

7. Adam Yarmolinsky and Gregory D. Foster, *Paradoxes of Power: The Military Establishment in the Eighties* (Bloomington: Indiana University Press, 1983), p. 99.

8. Anne Hessing Cahn, *Congress, Military Affairs and (a Bit of) Information* (Beverly Hills, Calif.: Sage, 1974), p. 8.

9. Quoted in Adam Yarmolinsky, *The Military Establishment: Its Impacts on American Society* (New York: Harper and Row, 1971), p. 53.

10. Quoted in Eugene Armand Dunne, Jr., "Variations in Committee Response to the House Reforms of the 1970s: A Study of the Armed Services and Banking Committees," Ph.D. diss., Harvard University, 1985, p. 49.

11. Fiscal oversight deals with adjusting line-item spending to reflect changes in the overall level of defense spending. Management oversight deals with whether DoD is spending funds efficiently and whether programs meet their performance specifications. Policy oversight deals with whether programs accomplish the missions they are designed to fulfill, whether the missions make sense, and whether programs have desirable foreign policy implications. See James M. Lindsay, "Congressional Oversight of the Department of Defense: Reconsidering the Conventional Wisdom," *Armed Forces and Society* 17 (Fall 1990): 7–33.

12. Michael A. West, "The Role of Congress in the Defense Budget Process—A Positive View," *Naval War College Review* 32 (May–June 1979): 92.

13. Quoted in Michael Ganley, "An Exclusive *AFJ* interview with: Representative Les Aspin, Chairman of the House Armed Services Committee," *Armed Forces Journal International,* April 1986, p. 43.

14. Thomas J. Downey, "On Congress and Security," *World Policy Journal* 1 (Winter 1984): 458.

15. Quoted in Louis Fisher, "Senate Procedures for Authorizing Military Research and Development," in U.S. Congress, Joint Economic Committee, *Priorities and Efficiency in Federal Research and Development,* 94th Cong., 2d sess., 1976, p. 26.

16. Fox, *Arming America,* p. 137.

17. See Edward J. Laurance, "The Changing Role of Congress in Defense Policy-Making," *Journal of Conflict Resolution* 20 (June 1976): 213–53.

18. The term *bile barreling* is derived from Gregg Easterbrook, "The Sky Isn't Falling: The Myth of the Airline 'Crisis,' " *New Republic,* 30 November 1987, p. 20.

19. The term *parochial imperative* is taken from Randall Fitzgerald and Gerald Lipson. *Pork Barrel: The Unexpurgated Grace Commission Story of Congressional Profligacy* (Washington, D.C.: Cato Institute, 1984), p. 1.

20. R. Douglas Arnold, *Congress and the Bureaucracy: A Theory of Influence* (New Haven: Yale University Press, 1979), pp. 32–33.

21. Quoted in Richard A. Stubbing with Richard A. Mendel, *The Defense Game: An Insider Explores the Astonishing Realities of America's Defense Establishment* (New York: Harper and Row, 1986), p. 91. (Emphasis added.)

22. Charles A. Vanik, "Congress is Deliberative: Compared to What?" in *The United States Congress,* ed. Dennis Hale (New Brunswick, N.J.: Transaction Books, 1983), pp. 16–18. (Emphasis added.)

23. Morris P. Fiorina, *Congress: Keystone of the Washington Establishment,* 2d ed. (New Haven: Yale University Press, 1989), p. 43. See also Mayhew, *Electoral Connection,* pp. 59–60.

24. Fiorina, *Keystone,* pp. 68–69.

25. Aspin, "Games the Pentagon Plays," p. 91.

26. Quoted in Andy Plattner, "House Freshmen Play a Minor Role . . . But Have Their Say on a Major Issue," *Congressional Quarterly Weekly Report,* 30 March 1985, p. 569.

27. "An Offer to Accept," *Daily Telegraph* (London), 9 April 1985.

28. For a bibliography of these works, see Bruce A. Ray, "Military Committee Membership in the House of Representatives and the Allocation of Defense Department Outlays," *Western Political Quarterly* 34 (June 1981): 222–34.

29. See Arnold, *Congress and the Bureaucracy,* pp. 80–91, 217–24. Arnold found that members of the House defense committees used their positions to deter DoD from closing bases in their districts. He did *not* examine whether the House defense committees influenced weapons contracts.

30. For a bibliography of these works, see James M. Lindsay, "Congress and the Defense Budget: Parochialism or Policy?" in *Arms, Politics, and the Economy: Historical and Contemporary Perspectives,* ed. Robert Higgs (New York: Holmes and Meier, 1990), p. 197.

31. See Lindsay, "Parochialism or Policy?" pp. 178–79, and James M. Lindsay, "Parochialism, Policy, and Constituency Constraints: Congressional Voting on Strategic Weapons Systems," *American Journal of Political Science* 34 (November 1990): 937.

32. William K. Muir, Jr., *Legislature: California's School for Politics* (Chicago: University of Chicago Press, 1982), p. 186.

33. *Congressional Record,* 97th Cong., 1st sess., 1981, 127, pt. 9:11946.

34. Jonathan E. Medalia, "Congress and the Political Guidance of Weapons Procurement," *Naval War College Review* 28 (Fall 1975): 20–21.

35. Mayhew, *Electoral Connection,* p. 115.

36. Elizabeth Drew, "A Political Journal," *New Yorker,* 20 June 1983, p. 56.

37. Arthur Bentley, *The Process of Government* (Bloomington, Ind.: Principia Press, 1935), p. 370.

38. See Lindsay, "Congressional Oversight," pp. 12–13, thur Maass, *Congress and the Common Good* (New York: Basic Books, 1983), p. 29.

39. Quoted in Deborah G. Adams and Benjamin F. Schemmer, "An Exclusive *AFJ* Interview with: Donald C. Latham, Assistant Secretary of Defense for Command, Control, Communications, and Intelligence," *Armed Forces Journal International,* February 1985, p. 58.

40. "An Interview with Congressman Phil Gramm," *Wall Street Journal,* 30 April 1981.

41. Quoted in Pat Towell with Steven Pressman, "House Gives President the Go-Ahead on MX," *Congressional Quarterly Weekly Report,* 30 March 1985, p. 566.

42. Frye, *A Responsible Congress,* p. 12.

43. John W. Kingdon, "Ideas, Politics, and Public Policies," Paper presented at the 1988 Annual Meeting of the American Political Science Association, Washington, D.C., p. 6.

44. Maass, *Congress and the Common Good,* p. 5.

45. Joseph M. Bessette, "Deliberation in Congress," Paper presented at the 1979 Annual Meeting of the American Political Science Association, Washington, D.C., p. 20.

46. Bernard Asbell, *The Senate Nobody Knows* (Baltimore: Johns Hopkins University Press, 1981), pp. 370–71.

47. Bernard K. Gordon, "The Military Budget: Congressional Phase," *Journal of Politics* 23 (November 1961): 694.

48. Raymond H. Dawson, "Congressional Innovation and Intervention in Defense Policy: Legislative Authorization of Weapons Systems," *American Political Science Review* 56 (March 1962): 57.

49. Edward A. Kolodziej, *The Uncommon Defense and Congress, 1945–1963* (Columbus: Ohio State University Press, 1966), p. 467.

50. Robert L. Bledsoe and Roger Handberg, "Changing Times: Congress and Defense," *Armed Forces and Society* 3 (Spring 1980): 415–29; Arnold Kanter, "Congress and the Defense Budget: 1960–1970," *American Political Science Review* 66 (March 1972): 129–43; and Arnold Kanter, *Defense Politics* (Chicago: University of Chicago Press, 1979).

51. See Richard P. Cronin, "An Analysis of Congressional Reductions in the Defense Budget: Fiscal Years 1971–1976," Congressional Research Service, Report No. 76-205 F, 16 September 1976; Richard P. Cronin, "Memorandum to Rep. Les Aspin: Analysis of Congressional Changes to the FY 1978 Defense Budget," inserted in *Congressional Record*, 96th Cong., 1st sess., 1979, 125, pt. 6:7844–46; Lawrence J. Korb, "Congressional Impact on Defense Spending, 1962–1973: The Programmatic and Fiscal Hypotheses," *Naval War College Review* 4 (December 1973): 49–61; and Alice C. Maroni, "Analysis of Congressional Changes to the FY 1984 Defense Budget," Congressional Research Service, Report No. 84-763 F, 2 October 1984.

52. See Fiorina, *Keystone,* p. 39, and Mayhew, *Electoral Connection,* p. 121.

53. George Berkeley, "Three Dialogues between Hylas and Philonius, In Opposition to Sceptics and Atheists," in *The Empiricists* (Garden City, N.Y.: Anchor, 1974), p. 221.

CHAPTER TWO   THE DEFENSE COMMITTEES

1. Bernard K. Gordon, "The Military Budget: Congressional Phase," *Journal of Politics* 23 (November 1961): 695.

2. Quoted in Raymond H. Dawson, "Congressional Innovation and Intervention in Defense Policy: Legislative Authorization of Weapons Systems," *American Political Science Review* 56 (March 1962): 52.

3. Quoted in "Armed Services Committees: Advocates or Overseers?" *Congressional Quarterly Weekly Report,* 25 March 1972, p. 676.

4. For a bibliography and a dissent, see Keith Krehbiel, "Are Congressional Committees Composed of Preference Outliers?" *American Political Science Review* 84 (March 1990): 149–63.

5. For discussion of the American Security Council ratings, see Bruce A. Ray, "The Responsiveness of the U.S. Congressional Armed Services Committees to Their Parent Bodies," *Legislative Studies Quarterly* 5 (November 1980): 504–5.

6. For discussion of why the ideological gap between HASC and the full House increased, see Ray, "Responsiveness," pp. 505–13.

7. See R. Douglas Arnold, *Congress and the Bureaucracy: A Theory of Influence* (New Haven: Yale University Press, 1979), pp. 95–128; Carol F. Goss, "Military Com-

mittee Membership and Defense-Related Benefits in the House of Representatives," *Western Political Quarterly* 25 (June 1972): 215–33; Bruce A. Ray, "Military Committee Membership in the House of Representatives and the Allocation of Defense Department Outlays," *Western Political Quarterly* 34 (June 1981): 222–34; Bruce A. Ray, "Federal Spending and the Selection of Committee Assignments in the U.S. House of Representatives," *American Journal of Political Science* 24 (August 1980): 494–510; and Leonard G. Ritt, "Committee Position, Seniority, and the Distribution of Government Expenditures," *Public Policy* 24 (Fall 1976): 463–89.

8. Kenneth A. Shepsle, *The Giant Jigsaw Puzzle: Democratic Committee Assignments in the Modern House* (Chicago: University of Chicago Press, 1978), pp. 63–93.

9. Richard F. Fenno, Jr., *Congressmen in Committees* (Boston: Little, Brown, 1973), p. 97, and Richard F. Fenno, Jr., *The Power of the Purse* (Boston: Little, Brown, 1966), pp. 141–43.

10. Interviews.

11. See Charles S. Bullock III, "Motivations for U.S. Congressional Committee Preferences: Freshmen of the 92d Congress," *Legislative Studies Quarterly* 1 (May 1976): 201–12, and Steven S. Smith and Christopher J. Deering, *Committees in Congress* (Washington, D.C.: CQ Press, 1984), pp. 83–119.

12. Smith and Deering, *Committees in Congress*, p. 106.

13. Charles S. Bullock III, "U.S. Senate Committee Assignments: Preferences, Motivations, and Success," *American Journal of Political Science* 29 (November 1985): 797.

14. Eugene Armand Dunne, Jr., "Variations in Committee Response to the House Reforms of the 1970s: A Study of the Armed Services and Banking Committees," Ph.D. diss., Harvard University, 1985, p. 65.

15. *Congressional Record,* 91st Cong., 1st sess., 1969, 115, pt. 21:28156.

16. Michael Barone, Grant Ujifusa, and Douglas Matthews, *The Almanac of American Politics 1972* (Boston: Gambit, 1972), p. 50.

17. Clayton Fritchey, "Who Belongs to the Senate's Inner Club?" *Harper's Magazine,* May 1967, pp. 104–10.

18. Quoted in Robert V. O'Brien, Jr., "The Senate and the B-1 Bomber: A Case Study in Congressional Decision-Making," Baccalaureate thesis, Harvard University, 1975, p. 42.

19. The literature on the congressional reforms of the 1970s is large. For discussions of reforms and the defense committees specifically, see Dunne, "Variations in Committee Response," pp. 218–379, and James M. Lindsay, "Congress and Defense Policy: 1961 to 1986," *Armed Forces and Society* 13 (Spring 1987): 371–401.

20. Craig Liske and Barry Rundquist, "The Politics of Weapons Procurement: The Role of Congress," *Monograph Series in World Affairs,* vol. 12, no. 1 (Denver: Social Science Foundation and Graduate School of International Studies, University of Denver, 1974), p. 55.

21. O'Brien, "Senate and the B-1 Bomber," pp. 43–44.

22. Dunne, "Variations in Committee Response," p. 569.

23. Alton Frye, *A Responsible Congress: The Politics of National Security* (New York: McGraw-Hill, 1975), pp. 101–4.

24. Smith and Deering, *Committees in Congress,* pp. 203–27.

25. Interviews.

26. See U.S. Congress, Senate Committee on Appropriations, *Department of Defense Appropriations for Fiscal Year 1969: Part 2*, 90th Cong., 2d sess., 1968, pp. 859–92.

27. See U.S. Congress, Senate Committee on Appropriations, *Department of Defense Appropriations for Fiscal Year 1986: Part 3*, 99th Cong., 1st sess., 1985, pp. 827–61.

28. J. Ronald Fox, *Arming America: How the U.S. Buys Weapons* (Cambridge: Harvard University Press, 1974), p. 148. See also Anne Hessing Cahn, *Congress, Military Affairs and (a Bit of) Information*, (Beverly Hills, Calif.: Sage, 1975), pp. 19–29, and Edward J. Laurance, "The Changing Role of Congress in Defense Policy-Making," *Journal of Conflict Resolution* 20 (June 1976): 223–29.

29. See *Congressional Record*, 90th Cong., 2d sess., 1968, 114, pt. 22:29178.

30. Fox, *Arming America*, pp. 131–32.

31. See Cahn, *Military Affairs*, pp. 24–29; Laurance, "Changing Role of Congress," pp. 223–29; Smith and Deering, *Committees in Congress*, p. 278.

32. See Louis Fisher, "Senate Procedures for Authorizing Military Research and Development," in U.S. Congress, Joint Economic Committee, *Priorities and Efficiency in Federal Research and Development*, 94th Cong., 2d sess., 1976, pp. 38–39.

33. U.S. Congress, Senate Committee on Armed Services, *Department of Defense Authorization for Appropriations for Fiscal Year 1987: Part 4*, 99th Cong., 2d sess., 1986, p. 1590.

34. William S. Cohen, "The U.S. Senate and the Presidency," in *National Security Policy: The Decision-Making Process*, ed. Robert L. Pfaltzgraff, Jr., and Uri Ra'anan (Hamden, Conn.: Archon Books, 1984), p. 232.

35. See Cahn, *Military Affairs*, p. 19, and Michael A. West, "The Role of Congress in the Defense Budget Process—A Positive View," *Naval War College Review* 32 (May–June 1979): 92.

36. U.S. Congress, House Committee on Armed Services, *Department of Defense Authorization for Appropriations for Fiscal Year 1975*, 93d Cong., 2d sess., 1974, p. 3583. See also Fox, *Arming America*, p. 138.

37. U.S. Congress, House Committee on Appropriations, *Department of Defense Appropriations for 1987: Part 6*, 99th Cong., 2d sess., 1986, p. 86.

38. Quoted in Pat Towell, "House Members Criticize Troubled B-1 Bomber," *Congressional Quarterly Weekly Report*, 7 March 1987, p. 431.

39. See Robert J. Art, "Congress and the Defense Budget: Enhancing Policy Oversight," *Political Science Quarterly* 100 (Summer 1985): 232–33.

40. U.S. Congress, Senate Committee on Armed Services, *National Defense Authorization Act for Fiscal Year 1986*, 99th Cong., 1st sess., S. Rept. 41, 1985, p. 159.

41. Quoted in "Counting Calls for Military Witnesses," *New York Times*, 4 March 1986. See also U.S. Congress, House Committee on Foreign Affairs, *Fundamentals of Nuclear Arms Control: Part 9—The Congressional Role in Nuclear Arms Control*, 99th Cong., 2d sess., 1986, p. 21.

42. Quoted in Michael R. Gordon, "Bomber Cost to Stay Secret Despite Congress's Requests," *New York Times*, 15 March 1986.

43. Quoted in O'Brien, "Senate and the B-1 Bomber," p. 28.

44. U.S. Congress, House Committee on Armed Services, *Authorizing Appropriations, Fiscal Year 1972, for Military Procurement, Research and Development, and Reserve Strength, and for Other Purposes,* 92d Cong., 1st sess., H. Rept. 232, 1971, p. 92.

45. *Congressional Record,* 4 August 1986, p. S10233.

46. See Art, "Congress and the Defense Budget," p. 229, and Lindsay, "Congress and Defense Policy," pp. 375–76.

47. Quoted in "Advocates or Overseers?" p. 673.

48. Frye, *A Responsible Congress,* p. 105.

49. U.S. Congress, Joint Committee on Atomic Energy, *Military Applications of Nuclear Technology, Part 1,* 93d Cong., 1st sess., 1973, p. 20. (Emphasis added.) See also U.S. Congress, Joint Committee on Atomic Energy, *Military Applications of Nuclear Technology, Part 2,* 93d Cong., 1st sess., 1973, p. 32.

50. See *Military Applications of Nuclear Technology, Part 1,* p. 1, and *Military Applications of Nuclear Technology, Part 2,* p. 54.

51. See Smith and Deering, *Committees in Congress,* pp. 112–13.

52. Fred Kaiser, "Oversight of Foreign Policy: The U.S. House Committee on International Relations," *Legislative Studies Quarterly* 2 (August 1977): 261. See also Fenno, *Congressmen in Committees,* pp. 71–73, and Francis O. Wilcox, *Congress, the Executive Branch, and Foreign Policy* (New York: Harper and Row, 1971), p. 6.

53. U.S. Congress, Joint Economic Committee, *The MX Missile and Strategic Programs,* 97th Cong., 1st sess., 1981, p. 1.

54. See Robert Lyle Butterworth, "The Arms Control Impact Statement: A Programmatic Assessment," *Policy Studies Journal* 8 (Autumn 1979): 76–84; U.S. Congress, House Committee on International Relations, *Evaluation of Fiscal Year 1979 Arms Control Impact Statements: Toward More Informed Congressional Participation in National Security Policymaking,* 95th Cong., 2d sess., 1979; and *Fundamentals of Nuclear Arms Control,* pp. 21–23.

55. Alan Platt, *The U.S. Senate and Strategic Arms Policy, 1969–1977* (Boulder, Colo.: Westview Press, 1978), p. 103.

56. *Congressional Record,* 13 April 1983, p. H2005.

CHAPTER THREE   THE FLOOR

1. See Pat Towell, "House Sustains Carter Defense Program," *Congressional Quarterly Weekly Report,* 30 April 1977, pp. 797–98.

2. See Stanley Bach, "Parliamentary Strategy and the Amendment Process: Rules and Case Studies of Congressional Action," *Polity* 15 (Spring 1983): 574–92, and Walter J. Oleszek, *Congressional Procedures and the Policy Process,* 2d ed. (Washington, D.C.: CQ Press, 1984), pp. 125–99.

3. On the rise in amendment activity on the defense bill, see James M. Lindsay, "Congress and Defense Policy: 1961 to 1986," *Armed Forces and Society* 13 (Spring 1987): 373–74. On the rise of amending activity more generally, see Steven S. Smith, *Call to Order: Floor Politics in the House and Senate* (Washington, D.C.: Brookings Institution, 1989).

4. See Samuel P. Huntington, *The Common Defense: Strategic Programs in National Politics* (New York: Columbia University Press, 1961), p. 131.

5. George H. Gallup, *The Gallup Poll: Public Opinion 1937–1971*, vol. 3 (New York: Random House, 1972), and *Gallup Opinion Index*, nos. 79–184 (January 1973–January 1981). See also Robert Dahl, *Controlling Nuclear Weapons: Democracy Versus Guardianship* (Syracuse, N.Y.: Syracuse University Press, 1985), pp. 91–92.

6. *Gallup Report*, nos. 185–225 (February 1981–June 1984). See also Dahl, *Controlling Nuclear Weapons*, p. 91, and Howard Schuman, Jacob Ludwig, and Jon A. Krosnick, "The Perceived Threat of Nuclear War, Salience, and Open Questions," *Public Opinion Quarterly* 50 (Winter 1986): 519–36.

7. See Michael T. Hayes, "Incrementalism as Dramaturgy: The Case of the Nuclear Freeze," *Polity* 19 (Spring 1987): 443–63; Pam Solo, *From Protest to Policy: The Origins and Future of the Freeze Movement* (Cambridge, Mass.: Ballinger, 1988); and Douglas C. Waller, *Congress and the Nuclear Freeze: An Inside Look at the Politics of a Mass Movement* (Amherst: University of Massachusetts Press, 1987).

8. Waller, *Congress and the Nuclear Freeze*, pp. 13–14.

9. Robert Scheer, *With Enough Shovels: Reagan, Bush and Nuclear War* (New York: Random House, 1982), p. 38.

10. David R. Mayhew, *Congress: The Electoral Connection* (New Haven: Yale University Press, 1974), p. 62.

11. Lindsay, "Congress and Defense Policy," p. 374.

12. *Congressional Record*, 91st Cong., 1st sess., 1969, 115, pt. 19:25320.

13. "House Votes $21.3-Billion Defense Procurement Bill," *Congressional Quarterly Weekly Report*, 10 October 1969, p. 1950.

14. Mayhew, *Electoral Connection*, p. 73.

15. See Carl J. Friedrich, *Constitutional Government and Democracy: Theory and Practice in Europe and America*, rev. ed. (Boston: Little, Brown, 1941), pp. 589–91.

16. Michael A. West, "The Role of Congress in the Defense Budget Process—A Positive View," *Naval War College Review* 32 (May–June 1979): 89.

17. Alton Frye, *A Responsible Congress: The Politics of National Security* (New York: McGraw-Hill, 1975), pp. 40–41.

18. *Congressional Record*, 1 October 1985, p. S12341.

19. The most complete discussion of congressional involvement in the MIRV program is Frye, *A Responsible Congress*, pp. 47–66. See also Stephen Joseph Flanagan, "Congress and the Evolution of U.S. Strategic Arms Limitation Policy: A Study of the Legislature's Role in National Security Affairs, 1955–1979," Ph.D. diss., Tufts University, 1979, pp. 136–62; Ted Greenwood, *Making the MIRV: A Study of Defense Decision Making* (Cambridge, Mass.: Ballinger, 1975), pp. 121–35; Seymour M. Hersh, *The Price of Power: Kissinger in the Nixon White House* (New York: Summit Books, 1983), pp. 147–67; Jonathan Eliot Medalia, "The U.S. Senate and Strategic Arms Limitation Policymaking, 1963–1972," Ph.D. diss., Stanford University, 1975, pp. 140–56; and Ronald L. Tammen, *MIRV and the Arms Race: An Interpretation of Defense Strategy* (New York: Praeger, 1973), pp. 115–26.

20. Quoted in Chalmers Roberts, "Democrats Back Arms Freeze," *Washington Post*, 8 April 1970.

21. See Lynn Davis, *Limited Nuclear Options: Deterrence and the New American Doctrine*, Adelphi Paper, no. 121 (London: International Institute for Strategic Studies, 1975).

22. Quoted in Alan Platt, *The U.S. Senate and Strategic Arms Policy, 1969–1977* (Boulder, Colo.: Westview Press, 1978), p. 75.

23. Ibid., p. 85.

24. See U.S. Congress, House Committee on Foreign Affairs, *Congress and Foreign Policy 1983,* 98th Cong., 2d sess., 1984, p. 86.

25. See Barbara Sinclair, *Majority Leadership in the House* (Baltimore: Johns Hopkins University Press, 1983), pp. 93–97.

26. Lauren H. Holland and Robert A. Hoover, *The MX Decision: A New Direction in U.S. Weapons Procurement Policy?* (Boulder, Colo.: Westview Press, 1985), p. 239, and interviews.

27. See Pat Towell, "MX Gains Narrow House OK, but Further Battles Expected," *Congressional Quarterly Weekly Report,* 23 July 1983, p. 1483; Pat Towell, "The Switchers: In the End, a Near Draw," *Congressional Quarterly Weekly Report,* 19 May 1984, p. 1159; Pat Towell, "House Toughens Restrictions on Production of MX Missile After Prodding by Leadership," *Congressional Quarterly Weekly Report,* 2 June 1984, pp. 1291–93; and Pat Towell with Steven Pressman, "House Gives President Go-Ahead on MX," *Congressional Quarterly Weekly Report,* 30 March 1985, p. 565.

28. See Fred Kaplan, "How Aspin Piloted Defense Bill," *Boston Globe,* 17 August 1986; Mary McGrory, "Showdown with Aspin," *Boston Globe,* 13 September 1985; and Andy Plattner, "To Les Aspin, MX Victory Brings Some Pain," *Congressional Quarterly Weekly Report,* 30 March 1985, p. 564.

29. Oleszek, *Congressional Procedures,* p. 207.

30. See Barry M. Blechman, "The New Congressional Role in Arms Control," in *A Question of Balance: The President, the Congress, and Foreign Policy,* ed. Thomas E. Mann (Washington, D.C.: Brookings Institution, 1990), p. 130, and Joseph White, "The Functions and Power of the House Appropriations Committee," Ph.D. diss., University of California, Berkeley, 1989, pp. 349–51.

31. Interviews.

32. For a discussion of the growing use of CRs, see Joseph White, "The Continuing Resolution: A Crazy Way to Govern?" *Brookings Review* 6 (Summer 1988): 28–35.

33. Interview.

34. Alan Ehrenhalt, "In the Senate of the '80s, Team Spirit Has Given Way to the Rule of Individuals," *Congressional Quarterly Weekly Report,* 4 September 1982, pp. 2175–82.

CHAPTER FOUR   SELECTED CASES

1. U.S. Congress, House Committee of Conference, *Authorizing Appropriations for Fiscal Year 1977 for Military Procurement, Research and Development, Active Duty Reserve and Civilian Personnel Strength Levels, Military Training Student Loads, and for Other Purposes,* 94th Cong., 2d sess., H. Rept. 1305, 1976, p. 40.

2. Thomas Powers, "Choosing a Strategy for World War III," *Atlantic Monthly,* November 1982, p. 83.

3. John Edwards, *Super Weapon: The Making of MX* (New York: W. W. Norton, 1982), pp. 136–38.

4. Lauren H. Holland and Robert A. Hoover, *The MX Decision: A New Direction in*

U.S. Weapons Procurement Policy? (Boulder, Colo.: Westview Press, 1985), p. 142.

5. U.S. Congress, House Committee on Armed Services, *Department of Defense Supplemental Appropriation Authorization Act, 1979,* 96th Cong., 1st sess., H. Rept. 90, 1979, p. 2.

6. See Lauren Holland, "The Use of NEPA in Defense Policy Politics: Public and State Involvement in the MX Missile Project," *Social Science Journal* 21 (July 1984): 53–71; Holland and Hoover, *MX Decision,* pp. 95–120, 159–80; and Jonathan Medalia, "Domestic Considerations Affecting Deployment of a Multiple Protective Shelter Structure Basing System for the MX Missile," Congressional Research Service, 11 March 1980.

7. U.S. Congress, Senate Committee on Armed Services, *Department of Defense Authorization for Appropriations for Fiscal Year 1983 and Supplemental Authorization for Appropriations for Fiscal Year 1982,* 97th Cong., 2d sess., S. Rept. 330, 1982, p. 59.

8. Quoted in Holland and Hoover, *MX Decision,* p. 226.

9. Ibid., p. 230.

10. See Elizabeth Drew, "A Political Journal," *New Yorker,* 20 June 1983, and Strobe Talbott, *Deadly Gambits* (New York: Alfred A. Knopf, 1984), pp. 300–340.

11. U.S. President's Commission on Strategic Forces, *Report of the President's Commission on Strategic Forces,* 6 April 1983, p. 16.

12. Ibid., p. 15.

13. See Michael Pertschuk, *Giant Killers* (New York: W. W. Norton, 1986), pp. 188, 199.

14. *Congressional Record,* 98th Cong., 2d sess., 1984, 130, pt. 12: 16526.

15. See John Steinbruner and Barry Carter, "Organizational and Political Dimensions of the Strategic Posture: The Problems of Reform," *Daedalus* 104 (Summer 1975): 131–54.

16. U.S. Congress, House Committee on Armed Services, *Authorizing Appropriations, Fiscal Year 1971, for Military Procurement, Research and Development, and Reserve Strength, and for Other Purposes.* 91st Cong., 2d sess., H. Rept. 1022, 1970, p. 42.

17. John Newhouse, *Cold Dawn: The Story of SALT* (New York: Holt, Rinehart, and Winston, 1973), p. 239.

18. U.S. Congress, House Committee on Armed Services, *Hearings on Military Posture and H.R. 12604: Part 2,* 92d Cong., 2d sess., 1972, p. 10241.

19. U.S. Congress, House Committee on Armed Services, *Authorizing Appropriations, Fiscal Year 1973, for Military Procurement, Research and Development, Certain Construction for the Safeguard Antiballistic Missile System, Active Duty and Reserve Strength, and for Other Purposes,* 92d Cong., 2d sess., H. Rept. 1149, 1972, p. 21.

20. U.S. Congress, Senate Committee on Armed Services, *Authorizing Appropriations for Fiscal Year 1973 for Military Procurement, Research and Development, Construction Authorization for the Safeguard ABM, and Active Duty and Selected Reserve Strength, and for Other Purposes,* 92d Cong., 2d sess., S. Rept. 962, 1972, p. 29.

21. U.S. Congress, House Committee on Appropriations, *Department of Defense Appropriations Bill, 1973,* 92d Cong., 2d sess., H. Rept. 1389, 1972, p. 217.

22. Stephen Joseph Flanagan, "Congress and the Formulation of Defense Policy: The Trident Case," Master's thesis, Tufts University, 1975, p. 147.

23. U.S. Congress, House Committee on Appropriations, *Department of Defense Appropriations Bill, 1974,* 93d Cong., 1st sess., H. Rept. 662, 1973, p. 171.

24. Flanagan, "Trident Case," p. 19.

25. U.S. Congress, Senate Committee on Armed Services, *Authorizing Appropriations for Fiscal Year 1975 for Military Procurement, Research and Development, and Active Duty, Selected Reserve and Civilian Personnel Strengths, and for Other Purposes,* 93d Cong., 2d sess., S. Rept. 884, 1974, p. 102.

26. U.S. Congress, Senate Committee on Appropriations, *Department of Defense Appropriation Bill, 1975,* 93d Cong., 2d sess., S. Rept. 1104, 1974, p. 167.

27. U.S. Congress, House Committee of Conference, *Department of Defense Supplemental Appropriation Act, 1979,* 96th Cong., 1st sess., H. Rept. 282, 1979, p. 8.

28. David N. Schwartz, *NATO's Nuclear Dilemmas* (Washington, D.C.: Brookings Institution, 1983), p. 226.

29. U.S. Congress, House Committee on Appropriations, *Department of Defense Appropriation Bill, 1980,* 96th Cong., 1st sess., H. Rept. 450, 1979, p. 388.

30. U.S. Congress, Senate Committee on Appropriations, *Department of Defense Appropriation Bill, 1980,* 96th Cong., 1st sess., S. Rept. 393, 1979, p. 179.

31. The literature on NATO's "dual-track" policy is immense. Among others see Leon V. Sigal, *Nuclear Forces in Europe: Enduring Dilemmas, Present Prospects* (Washington, D.C.: Brookings Institution, 1984).

32. *Congressional Record,* 97th Cong., 1st sess., 1981, 127, pt. 21:28024–25.

33. Schwartz, *NATO's Nuclear Dilemmas,* p. 241.

34. U.S. Congress, House Committee on Appropriations, *Department of Defense Appropriation Bill, 1983,* 97th Cong., 2d sess., H. Rept. 943, 1982, p. 107.

35. Ibid.

36. See Paul B. Stares, *The Militarization of Space: U.S. Policy, 1945–1984* (Ithaca, N.Y.: Cornell University Press), pp. 120–28.

37. Ibid., p. 207.

38. U.S. Congress, Senate Committee on Appropriations, *Department of Defense Appropriation Bill, 1982,* 97th Cong., 1st sess., S. Rept. 273, 1981, p. 114.

39. See Larry Pressler, *Star Wars: The Strategic Defense Initiative Debates in Congress* (New York: Praeger, 1986), pp. 8–12.

40. See Barry M. Blechman, "The New Congressional Role in Arms Control," in *A Question of Balance: The President, the Congress, and Foreign Policy,* ed. Thomas E. Mann (Washington, D.C.: Brookings Institution, 1990), p. 127.

41. U.S. Congress, House Committee of Conference, *Making Appropriations for the Department of Defense for the Fiscal Year Ending September 30, 1984,* 98th Cong., 1st sess., H. Rept. 567, 1983, p. 55.

42. Cover letter from Ronald Reagan to Speaker of the House of Representatives, *Report to Congress on U.S. Policy on ASAT Arms Control,* The White House, March 31, 1984, *Weekly Compilation of Presidential Documents,* 9 April 1984, vol. 20, no. 14, pp. 462–63.

43. U.S. Congress, House Committee on Appropriations, *U.S. Policy on ASAT Arms Control: A Communication from the President of the United States,* 98th Cong., 2d sess., H. Doc. 197, 1984.

44. *Congressional Record,* 98th Cong., 2d sess., 1984, 130, pt. 12:1582.

45. U.S. Congress, House Committee of Conference, *Department of Defense Authorization Act, 1985,* 98th Cong., 2d sess., H. Rept. 1080, 1984, p. 267.

46. *Congressional Quarterly Almanac 1984* (Washington, D.C.: Congressional Quarterly, 1985), pp. 62–64.

47. U.S. Congress, House Committee of Conference, *Department of Defense Authorization Act, 1986,* 99th Cong., 1st sess., H. Rept. 235, 1985, p. 322.

48. U.S. Congress, House Committee on Appropriations, *Department of Defense Appropriations for 1985: Part 2,* 98th Cong., 2d sess., 1984, p. 190. (Emphasis added.) See also David C. Morrison, "Antisatellite Debate Reignited," *National Journal,* 28 January 1989, p. 239.

49. See *Congressional Record,* 26 June 1985, pp. H4961–H4968.

50. See Robert J. Art and Stephen E. Ockenden, "The Domestic Politics of Cruise Missile Development, 1970–1980," in *Cruise Missiles,* ed. Richard K. Betts (Washington, D.C.: Brookings Institution, 1981), pp. 361–62, and Nick Kotz, *Wild Blue Yonder: Money, Politics, and the B-1 Bomber* (New York: Pantheon Books, 1988), pp. 180–99.

51. Quoted in "Two Views on What's 'Wrong' with Carter's Fiscal 1979 Budget Request for the Navy," *Congressional Quarterly Weekly Report,* 20 May 1978, p. 1258.

52. On Congress and counterforce programs in the 1970s, see Alan Platt, *The U.S. Senate and Strategic Arms Policy, 1969–1977* (Boulder, Colo.: Westview Press, 1978), pp. 71–96. On congressional interest in cruise missiles, see Henry D. Levine, "Some Things to All Men: The Politics of Cruise Missile Development," *Public Policy* 25 (Winter 1977): 131–40.

53. See David C. Morrison, "The Navy's Vanishing Nuclear Arsenal," *National Journal,* 13 September 1986, pp. 2184–85.

54. Les Aspin, "Congress versus the Defense Department," in *The Tethered Presidency: Congressional Restraints on Executive Power,* ed. Thomas M. Franck (New York: New York University Press, 1981), p. 246.

55. John W. Finney, "Halt of Sentinel is Traced to a Ten-Month-Old Memo," *New York Times,* 9 February 1969.

56. Levine, "Some Things to All Men," p. 126.

57. See Alton Frye, *A Responsible Congress: The Politics of National Security* (New York: McGraw-Hill, 1975), pp. 111–16, and Platt, *Strategic Arms Policy,* p. 107.

58. *Congressional Record,* 93d Cong., 2d sess., 1974, 120, pt. 6: 9490–91.

59. Harvey Brooks, "The Military Innovation System and the Qualitative Arms Race," *Daedalus* 104 (Summer 1975): 91–92.

60. See ibid., pp. 90–91, and Thomas A. Dine, "Military R&D: Congress' Next Area of Policy Penetration," *Bulletin of the Atomic Scientists* 34 (February 1978): 34.

CHAPTER FIVE   AGENDAS

1. See Stanley J. Heginbotham, "Congress and Defense Policymaking: Toward Realistic Expectations in a System of Countervailing Parochialisms," in *National Security Policy: The Decision-Making Process,* ed. Robert L. Pfaltzgraff, Jr., and Uri Ra'anan (Hamden, Conn.: Archon Books, 1984); James M. Lindsay, "Congressional Oversight of the Department of Defense: Reconsidering the Conventional Wisdom," *Armed Forces*

and Society 17 (Fall 1990): 7–33; and Warner Schilling, "The Politics of National Defense: Fiscal 1950," in *Strategy, Politics, and Defense Budgets,* ed. Warner Schilling, Paul Y. Hammond, and Glenn Snyder (New York: Columbia University Press, 1962), pp. 54–94.

2. See Les Aspin, "Games the Pentagon Plays," *Foreign Policy* 11 (Summer 1973): 80–92, and J. Ronald Fox, *Arming America: How the U.S. Buys Weapons* (Cambridge: Harvard University Press, 1974), pp. 136–40.

3. Randall B. Ripley, *Congress: Process and Policy,* 2d ed. (New York: W. W. Norton, 1978), p. 15.

4. Quoted by Rep. Robert Dornan (R-Calif.) in *Congressional Record,* 95th Cong., 2d sess., 1978, 124, pt. 4:4066, and confirmed in a telephone conversation with Jerry Gideon of Representative Dornan's office, 11 May 1988.

5. See Roger Morris, "Eight Days in April: The Press Flattens Carter with the Neutron Bomb," *Columbia Journalism Review,* November–December 1978, pp. 25–30; Barry Rubin, "The Media and the Neutron Warhead," *Washington Review of Strategic and International Studies* 1 (July 1978): 90–94; Deborah Shapely, "The Media and National Security," *Daedalus* 111 (Fall 1982): 199–209.

6. Interview.

7. Joseph White, "The Functions and Power of the House Appropriations Committee," Ph.D. diss., University of California, Berkeley, 1989, p. 359.

8. *Congressional Record,* 95th Cong., 2d sess., 1978, 124, pt. 4:4066.

9. Nick Kotz, *Wild Blue Yonder: Money, Politics, and the B-1 Bomber* (New York: Pantheon Books, 1988), pp. 168–70, 182–84, and U.S. Congress, House Committee on Armed Services, *Hearings on H.R. 8390, Supplemental Authorization for Appropriations for FY78,* 95th Cong., 1st sess., 1977, p. 82.

10. For examples see G. William Whitehurst, *Diary of a Congressman* (Norfolk, Va.: Donning, 1983), p. 43, and U.S. Congress, House Committee on Armed Services, "HASC Cuts $6 Billion, Adds $6 Billion," *HASC Tasks* (April 1988).

11. "Where Does the SDI Money Go?" *Space and Security News* 4 (December 1987): 19.

12. Jacques Gansler, *The Defense Industry* (Cambridge: MIT Press, 1980), p. 43.

13. George C. Wilson, "Bombs Away: It's the Battle for Pork-Barrel Hill," *Washington Post National Edition,* 3 March 1986, p. 27.

14. David R. Mayhew, *Congress: The Electoral Connection* (New Haven: Yale University Press, 1974), p. 118.

15. On the "negativity bias" of voters, see Daniel Kahneman and Amos Tversky, "Choices, Values, and Frames," *American Psychologist* 39 (April 1984): 341–50.

16. For discussions on local opposition to Sentinel, see "Major Lobby Effort Surrounds Sentinel ABM System," *Congressional Quarterly Weekly Report,* 21 March 1969, pp. 409–11, and Ernest J. Yanarella, *The Missile Defense Controversy: Strategy, Technology, and Politics, 1955–1972* (Lexington: University of Kentucky Press, 1977), pp. 146–52. On local opposition to ELF, see Lowell L. Klessig and Victor L. Strite, *The ELF Odyssey: National Security Versus Environmental Protection* (Boulder, Colo.: Westview Press, 1980). On local opposition to MPS basing, see Robert Herschman, "The Great Basin: First Casualty of the MX?" *Atlantic Monthly,* April 1980, pp. 4–10; Lauren Holland, "The Use of NEPA in Defense Policy Politics: Public and State Involve-

ment in the MX Missile Project," *Social Science Journal* 21 (July 1984): 53–71; and Lauren Holland and Robert A. Hoover, *The MX Decision: A New Direction in U.S. Weapons Procurement Policy?* (Boulder, Colo.: Westview Press, 1985), pp. 95–108.

17. Terry Jay Miller, "The Interaction Between the Private, Public, and Third Sector in the Defense Contract Award Process: Lobbying for Defense Contracts for Los Angeles County, 1952–1972," Ph.D. diss., University of Southern California, 1974, p. 105.

18. Quoted in Craig Liske and Barry Rundquist, "The Politics of Weapons Procurement: The Role of Congress," *Monograph Series in World Affairs,* vol. 12, no. 1 (Denver: Social Science Foundation and Graduate School of International Studies, University of Denver, 1974), p. 85.

19. Ibid., p. 82.

20. John Pike and David G. Bourns, *SDI Top Twenty Contractors* (Washington, D.C.: Federation of American Scientists, n.d.), p. 2.

21. On ALCM see Kenneth P. Werrell, *The Evolution of the Cruise Missile* (Maxwell Air Force Base, Ala.: Air University Press, 1985). On ATACMS see Jesse James, "Tactical Nuclear Modernization—The NATO Decision That Won't Go Away," *Arms Control Today* 18 (December 1988): 21.

22. For various reasons declaratory policy differs from how the United States would actually use its nuclear forces in war. See Desmond Ball, "U.S. Strategic Forces: How Would They Be Used?" *International Security* 7 (Winter 1982–83): 32–33.

23. See Alan Platt, *The U.S. Senate and Strategic Arms Policy* (Boulder, Colo.: Westview Press, 1979), pp. 71–96.

24. *Congressional Record,* 91st Cong., 2d sess., 1970, 116, pt. 19:26386.

25. U.S. Congress, Senate Committee on Armed Services, *The Nomination of James Schlesinger to be Secretary of Defense,* 93d Cong., 1st sess., 1973, pp. 61–62.

26. Holland and Hoover, *MX Decision,* p. 70.

27. David M. Maxfield, "$90.7-Billion Defense Bill Sent to Conference," *Congressional Quarterly Weekly Report,* 22 November 1975, p. 2555.

28. "Text of Reagan Address on Defense Policy," *Congressional Quarterly Weekly Report,* 26 March 1983, p. 632. (Emphasis added.)

29. Quoted in Larry Pressler, *Star Wars: The Strategic Defense Initiative Debates in Congress* (New York: Praeger, 1986), p. 66.

30. Quoted in Paul N. Stockton, "Arms Development and Arms Control: The Strange Case of the MX Missile," in *American Politics and Public Policy,* ed. Allan P. Sindler (Washington, D.C.: CQ Press, 1982), p. 244.

31. See, for example, the testimony in *Hearings on H.R. 8390,* pp. 60, 77, 172–73.

32. See Whitehurst, *Diary of a Congressman,* pp. 194–206.

33. Quoted in Paul B. Stares, *The Militarization of Space: U.S. Policy, 1945–1984* (Ithaca, N.Y.: Cornell University Press, 1985), p. 127.

34. Quoted in Pat Towell, "House Rebuffs Reagan on Anti-Satellite Tests," *Congressional Quarterly Weekly Report,* 26 May 1984, p. 1219.

35. Harvey Brooks, "The Military Innovation System and the Qualitative Arms Race," *Daedalus* 104 (Summer 1975): 91, and Alton Frye, *A Responsible Congress: The Politics of National Security* (New York: McGraw-Hill, 1975), p. 22.

36. Frye, *A Responsible Congress,* p. 43.

37. Interview.

38. Quoted in Elizabeth Drew, "A Political Journal," *New Yorker,* 20 June 1983, p. 55.

39. Albert G. Gore, "A Fork in the Road," *New Republic,* 5 May 1982, pp. 13–16.

40. Quoted in Michael Ganley, "An Exclusive *AFJ* Interview with Representative Les Aspin, Chairman of the House Armed Services Committee," *Armed Forces Journal International,* April 1986, p. 40.

41. Frye, *A Responsible Congress,* pp. 52–53.

42. Les Aspin, "Congress versus the Defense Department," in *The Tethered Presidency: Congressional Restraints on Executive Power,* ed. Thomas M. Franck (New York: New York University Press, 1981), p. 262.

CHAPTER SIX   DECISIONS

1. Frank Whelon Wayman, "Arms Control and Strategic Arms Voting in the U.S. Senate: Patterns of Change, 1967–1983," *Journal of Conflict Resolution* 29 (June 1985): 234. (Emphasis in the original.)

2. Robert A. Bernstein and William W. Anthony, "The ABM Issue in the Senate, 1968–1970: The Importance of Ideology," *American Political Science Review* 68 (September 1974): 1198–1206.

3. Richard Fleisher, "Economic Benefit, Ideology, and Senate Voting on the B-1 Bomber," *American Politics Quarterly* 13 (April 1985): 200–211.

4. Craig Liske and Barry Rundquist, "The Politics of Weapons Procurement: The Role of Congress," *Monograph Series in World Affairs,* vol. 12, no. 1 (Denver: Social Science Foundation and Graduate School of International Studies, University of Denver, 1974), p. 82.

5. J. Ronald Fox with James L. Field, *The Defense Management Challenge: Weapons Acquisition* (Boston: Harvard Business School Press, 1988), p. 92.

6. *Congressional Record,* 94th Cong., 2d sess., 1976, 122, pt. 12:14142.

7. See Nick Kotz, *Wild Blue Yonder: Money, Politics, and the B-1 Bomber* (New York: Pantheon Books, 1988), pp. 123–57, and Norman J. Ornstein and Shirley Elder, *Interest Groups, Lobbying and Policymaking* (Washington, D.C.: CQ Press, 1978), pp. 187–220.

8. On the battle between Carter and Congress over national water policy, see Randall Fitzgerald and Gerald Lipson, *Pork Barrel: The Unexpurgated Grace Commission Story of Congressional Profligacy* (Washington, D.C.: Cato Institute, 1984), pp. 1–12.

9. As a general rule district-level data are not publicly available. DoD publishes data on prime contracts but only for individual counties and cities. Converting these into district-level data is problematic. See James M. Lindsay, "Congress and the Defense Budget: Parochialism or Policy?" in *Arms, Politics, and the Economy: Historical and Contemporary Perspectives,* ed. Robert Higgs (New York: Holmes and Meier, 1990), p. 178.

10. James M. Lindsay, "Parochialism, Policy, and Constituency Constraints: Congressional Voting on Strategic Weapons Systems," *American Journal of Political Science* 34 (November 1990): 936–60.

11. For a discussion of the rise of partisan voting on defense and foreign policy is-

sues in the Senate, see Peter Trubowitz, "Ideology, Party, and U.S. Foreign and Defense Policy: An Analysis of Senate Voting, 1947–1984," Ph.D. diss., Massachusetts Institute of Technology, 1986. On the rise of party voting in Congress more generally, see Samuel C. Patterson and Gregory A. Caldeira, "Party Voting in the United States Congress," *British Journal of Political Science* 18 (January 1988): 111–31.

12. Lawrence S. Rothenberg, "Do Interest Groups Make a Difference? Lobbying, Constituency Influence, and Public Policy," Paper presented at the annual meeting of the Midwest Political Science Association, Chicago, April 1989.

13. James M. Lindsay, "Testing the Parochial Hypothesis: Congress and the Strategic Defense Initiative," *Journal of Politics,* 53 (August 1991).

14. Mike Barnicle, "A Primary Tout Sheet," *Boston Globe,* 14 February 1988.

15. John W. Kingdon, *Congressmen's Voting Decisions,* 3d ed. (Ann Arbor: University of Michigan Press, 1989), pp. 43–45, and Warren E. Miller and Donald E. Stokes, "Constituency Influence in Congress," *American Political Science Review* 57 (March 1963): 45–56.

16. Morris P. Fiorina, *Representatives, Roll Calls, and Constituencies* (Lexington, Mass.: D.C. Heath, 1974); pp. 89–119; Thomas Flinn and Harold Wolman, "Constituency and Roll Call Voting: The Case of Southern Democratic Congressmen," *Midwest Journal of Political Science* 10 (May 1966): 192–99; John Jackson, *Constituencies and Leaders in Congress: Their Effects on Senate Voting Behavior* (Cambridge: Harvard University Press, 1974); Duncan MacRae, *Dimensions of Congressional Voting* (Berkeley and Los Angeles: University of California Press, 1958); and Miller and Stokes, "Constituency Influence," pp. 45–56.

17. Fred Barnes, "The Man to Beat," *New Republic,* 7 March 1988, p. 13.

18. See Robert Weissberg, "Assessing Legislator-Constituency Policy Agreement," *Legislative Studies Quarterly* 4 (November 1979): 610–16.

19. See Joseph P. Kalt, *The Economics and Politics of Oil Price Regulation: Federal Policy in the Post-Embargo Era* (Cambridge: MIT Press, 1981), pp. 259–78; Joseph P. Kalt and Mark A. Zupan, "Capture and Ideology in the Economic Theory of Politics," *American Economics Review* 74 (June 1984): 279–300; James B. Kau and Paul H. Rubin, *Congressmen, Constituents, and Contributors: Determinants of Roll Call Voting in the House of Representatives* (Boston: Martinus Nijhoff, 1982), pp. 63–81; and Lindsay, "Testing the Parochial Hypothesis." Sam Peltzman claims to show that the public views of members are surrogates for constituency interests but inferential problems cast doubt on the validity of his conclusion. See Sam Peltzman, "Constituent Interest and Congressional Voting," *Journal of Law and Economics* 27 (April 1984): 181–210, and the critique of Peltzman's argument by Robert A. Bernstein, *Elections, Representation, and Congressional Voting Behavior: The Myth of Constituency Control* (Englewood Cliffs, N.J.: Prentice Hall, 1989), p. 96.

20. Kingdon, *Congressmen's Voting Decisions,* p. 265.

21. Ibid., p. 46.

22. Interview. See also ibid.; John W. Kingdon, "Ideas, Politics, and Public Policies," Paper presented at the annual meeting of the American Political Science Association, Washington, D.C., September 1988, p. 15; Norman Luttbeg, ed., *Public Opinion and Public Policy: Models of Political Linkage,* 3d ed. (Itasca, Ill.: Peacock, 1981); Donald J. McCrone and Walter J. Stone, "The Structure of Constituency Representation: On

Theory and Method," *Journal of Politics* 48 (November 1986): 956–75; and L. Harmon Zeigler and Harvey Tucker, *The Quest for Responsive Government* (North Scituate, Mass.: Duxbury, 1978).

23. Keith T. Poole, "Recent Developments in Analytical Models of Voting in the U.S. Congress," *Legislative Studies Quarterly* 13 (February 1988): 127.

24. See Raymond A. Bauer, Ithiel de Sola Pool, and Lewis Anthony Dexter, *American Business and Public Policy,* 2d ed. (Chicago: Aldine, Atherton, 1972), pp. 414–24; Lewis Anthony Dexter, "The Representative and His District," *Human Organization* 16 (Spring 1957): 2–13; and Richard F. Fenno, Jr., *Home Style: House Members in Their Districts* (Boston: Little, Brown, 1978), pp. 1–30.

25. Poole, "Recent Developments," p. 129.

26. Wayman, "Strategic Arms Voting," p. 239.

27. See Bernstein, *Myth of Constituency Control,* pp. 15–18; Patricia Hurley and Kim Hill, "The Prospects for Issue-Voting in Contemporary American Elections: An Assessment of Citizen Awareness and Representation," *American Politics Quarterly* 8 (October 1980): 425–48; and Donald E. Stokes and Warren E. Miller, "Party Government and the Saliency of Congress," *Public Opinion Quarterly* 26 (Winter 1962): 531–46.

28. Interview.

29. Interview.

30. See Kingdon, *Congressmen's Voting Decisions,* p. 41.

31. Quoted in Hedrick Smith, *The Power Game: How Washington Works* (New York: Random House, 1988), p. 152.

32. [Rep.] Dave Nagle, *Congressional Update,* July 1988, p. 3. [A mailing to the residents of the Third Congressional District of Iowa.]

33. Interview.

34. Interview.

35. See Mayhew, *Electoral Connection,* p. 118.

36. Kotz, *Wild Blue Yonder,* p. 138.

37. Interview.

38. John MacDougal, "Congress and the Campaign to Stop the M-X Missile," Photocopy, Department of Sociology, Lowell University, Lowell, Mass., 1988, pp. 16–17.

39. Quoted in Elizabeth Drew, "A Political Journal," *New Yorker,* 20 June 1983, p. 75. (Emphasis added.)

40. Pat Towell with Steven Pressman, "House Gives President the Go-Ahead on MX," *Congressional Quarterly Weekly Report,* 30 March 1985, p. 565.

41. Quoted in Andy Plattner, "House Freshmen Play a Minor Role . . . But Have Their Say on a Major Issue," *Congressional Quarterly Weekly Report,* 30 March 1985, p. 568.

42. Towell, "Go-Ahead on MX," p. 563.

43. Smith, *Power Game,* p. 152.

44. Quoted in Pat Towell with Nadine Cohodas and Steven Pressman, "Senate Hands Reagan Victory on MX Missiles," *Congressional Quarterly Weekly Report,* 23 March 1985, p. 518.

45. Stephen Joseph Flanagan, "Congress and the Evolution of U.S. Strategic Arms Limitation Policy: A Study of the Legislature's Role in National Security Affairs, 1955–1979," Ph.D. diss., Tufts University, 1979, p. 176.

46. *Congressional Record,* 92d Cong., 1st sess., 1971, 117, pt. 26:34018.

47. Quoted in Hedrick Smith, "Reagan's MX Victory: Eye on Audience Overseas," *New York Times,* 20 March 1985.

48. See Lindsay, "Parochialism, Policy, and Constituency Constraints," p. 943, and Lindsay, "Testing the Parochial Hypothesis."

49. Les Aspin, "The Defense Budget and Foreign Policy: The Role of Congress," *Daedalus* 104 (Summer 1975): 155.

50. James M. McCormick and Michael Black, "Ideology and Senate Voting on the Panama Canal Treaty," *Legislative Studies Quarterly* 8 (February 1983): 45–64.

51. *Gallup Report* 220–221 (January–February 1984): 14; Louis Harris, "Doubts Arise over U.S. Military Involvement in Lebanon," *The Harris Survey,* no. 76, 22 September 1983; and Philip J. Powlick, "Foreign Policy Decisions and Public Opinion: The Case of the Lebanon Intervention," Paper presented at the annual meeting of the American Political Science Association, Washington, D.C., September 1988.

52. See *Gallup Report,* no. 220–221, p. 15, and *Gallup Report* 264 (September 1987): 24.

53. Flanagan, "Congress," p. 98.

54. Ernest J. Yanarella, *The Missile Defense Controversy: Strategy, Technology, and Politics, 1955–1972* (Lexington: University of Kentucky, 1977), p. 160.

55. Henry A. Kissinger, *White House Years* (Boston: Little, Brown, 1979), p. 551.

56. John W. Finney, "Expansion of ABM Backed by Senate by 52-to-47 Vote," *New York Times,* 13 August 1970.

CHAPTER SEVEN   CONGRESS AND DEFENSE POLICY

1. Nick Kotz, *Wild Blue Yonder: Money, Politics, and the B-1 Bomber* (New York: Pantheon Books, 1988), p. 213.

2. Barry M. Blechman, "The New Congressional Role in Arms Control," in *A Question of Balance: The President, the Congress, and Foreign Policy,* ed. Thomas E. Mann (Washington, D.C.: Brookings Institution, 1990), pp. 109–10.

3. See Kenneth Robert Mayer, "The Politics and Economics of Defense Contracting," Ph.D. diss., Yale University, 1988, pp. 249–69.

4. Craig Liske and Barry Rundquist, "The Politics of Weapons Procurement: The Role of Congress," *Monograph Series in World Affairs,* vol. 12, no. 1 (Denver: Social Science Foundation and Graduate School of International Studies, University of Denver, 1974), p. 82.

5. Kotz, *Wild Blue Yonder,* p. 129.

6. See Edward J. Laurance, "The Changing Role of Congress in Defense Policy-Making," *Journal of Conflict Resolution* 20 (June 1976): 214–21, and Edward J. Laurance, "The Congressional Role in Defense Policy Making: The Evolution of the Literature," *Armed Forces and Society* 6 (Spring 1980): 432–33.

7. Samuel P. Huntington, *The Common Defense: Strategic Programs in National Politics* (New York: Columbia University Press, 1961), pp. 123–35.

8. Douglas Nelson and Eugene Silberberg, "Ideology and Legislator Shirking," *Economic Inquiry* 25 (January 1987): 15–25.

9. Mayer, "Defense Contracting," pp. 160–99.

10. Ibid., p. 197.

11. Ibid., p. 198.

12. *Congressional Record,* 24 September 1987, p. S12676.

13. Liske and Rundquist, "Politics of Weapons Procurement," p. 63. (Emphasis in the original.)

14. Richard L. Berke, "Lobbying Steps Up on Military Buying as Budget Shrinks," *New York Times,* 9 April 1990.

15. Richard C. White, "Congressional Limitations and Oversight of Executive Decision-Making Power: The Influence of Members and of the Staff," in *National Security Policy: The Decision-Making Process,* ed. Robert L. Pfaltzgraff, Jr., and Uri Ra'anan (Hamden, Conn.: Archon Books, 1984), p. 243.

16. Quoted in Gregg Easterbrook, "When Is a Nuclear Weapon Not a Nuclear Weapon?" *New England Monthly,* July 1987, p. 40.

17. Michael Barone and Grant Ujifusa, *The Almanac of American Politics 1988* (Washington, D.C.: National Journal, 1988), p. 798.

18. *Television News Index and Abstracts: October 1986* (Nashville, Tenn.: Vanderbilt Television News Archive, 1986), pp. 1841–45.

19. See Robert Coram, "The Case Against the Air Force," *Washington Monthly,* July–August 1987, pp. 17–24; Morton H. Halperin and David Halperin, "The Key West Key," *Foreign Policy* 53 (Winter 1983–84): 114–30; and David C. Morrison, "Pentagon Dogfighting," *National Journal,* 8 October 1988, pp. 2524–28.

20. Richard Stubbing with Richard A. Mendel, *The Defense Game: An Insider Explores the Astonishing Realities of America's Defense Establishment* (New York: Harper and Row, 1986), p. 142, and "The Best Weapons," *U.S. News and World Report,* 10 July 1987, p. 27.

21. See White, "Congressional Limitations and Oversight," pp. 244–47.

22. See Kenneth R. Mayer, "Patterns of Congressional Influence in Defense Contracting," in *Arms, Politics, and the Economy: Historical and Contemporary Perspectives,* ed. Robert Higgs (New York: Holmes and Meier, 1990).

23. David R. Mayhew, *Congress: The Electoral Connection* (New Haven: Yale University Press, 1974), pp. 52–61.

24. Mayer, "Defense Contracting," p. 220. (Emphasis in the original.)

25. See Tim Carrington, "Stingy Les Aspin Has This Penchant for Oshkosh Trucks: They Are Made in His State, So What if the U.S. Army Doesn't Want Any More?" *Wall Street Journal,* 9 June 1988; Ralph G. Carter, "Senate Defense Budgeting, 1981–1988: The Impacts of Ideology, Party, and Constituency Benefit on the Decision to Support the President," *American Politics Quarterly* 17 (July 1989): 332–47; and Robert Higgs, "Hard Coals Make Bad Law: Congressional Parochialism versus National Defense," *Cato Journal* 8 (Spring–Summer 1988): 79–106.

26. For an exception see Hedrick Smith, *The Power Game: How Washington Works* (New York: Random House, 1988), pp. 182–84.

27. Herbert W. Stephens, "The Role of the Legislative Committees in the Appropriations Process: A Study Focused on the Armed Services Committees," *Western Political Quarterly* 24 (March 1971): 147.

28. Randall Fitzgerald and Gerald Lipson, *Porkbarrel: The Unexpurgated Grace Commission Story of Congressional Profligacy* (Washington, D.C.: Cato Institute, 1984), p. 13.

29. U.S. Congress, House Committee on Conference, *Increasing the Statutory Limit on the Public Debt,* 99th Cong., 1st sess., H. Rept. 433, 1985, p. 39.

30. Dick Armey and Barry Goldwater, "Close the Obsolete Military Bases," *Washington Post,* 7 May 1987.

31. See Charlotte Twight, "Institutional Underpinnings of Parochialism: The Case of Military Base Closures," *Cato Journal* 9 (Spring–Summer 1989): 73–105, and Charlotte Twight, "DoD Attempts to Close Military Bases: The Political Economy of Congressional Resistance," in *Arms, Politics, and the Economy: Historical and Contemporary Perspectives,* ed. Robert Higgs (New York: Holmes and Meier, 1990).

32. R. Douglas Arnold, *Congress and the Bureaucracy: A Theory of Influence* (New Haven: Yale University Press, 1979), pp. 95–128.

33. Ibid., pp. 107, 116.

34. "To Mop Up Military Gravy," *New York Times,* 29 April 1988.

35. U.S. Congress, Senate Committee on Armed Services, *Organization, Structure and Decisionmaking Procedures of the Department of Defense, Part 1,* 98th Cong., 1st sess., 1983, p. 9.

36. G. William Whitehurst, *Diary of a Congressman* (Norfolk, Va.: Donning, 1983), p. 43.

37. Quoted by Howard Kurtz, "On Hill, Legislators Erect Home-District Defenses," *Washington Post,* 7 April 1985.

38. Quoted in "Empire State Bacon," *National Journal,* 21 February 1987, p. 407.

39. U.S. Congress, House Committee on Armed Services, *Base Closures and Realignments,* 99th Cong., 1st sess., 1985, p. 8. (Emphasis added.)

40. Fitzgerald and Lipson, *Porkbarrel,* pp. 25–26.

41. Kotz, *Wild Blue Yonder,* pp. 17–18.

42. See Charles Peters, "Tilting at Windmills," *Washington Monthly,* May 1987, p. 6.

43. Interview.

44. See Mike Mills, "Base Closings: The Political Pain Is Limited," *Congressional Quarterly Weekly Report,* 31 December 1988, pp. 3625–29.

45. See John Felton, "While Senate Blunts Most Arms Challenges," *Congressional Quarterly Weekly Report,* 9 August 1986, pp. 1789–90; Smith, *Power Game,* p. 191; and Pat Towell, "House Balks at Navy's 'Homeporting' Plan," *Congressional Quarterly Weekly Report,* 28 June 1986, pp. 1493–95.

46. Frank E. Smith, *Congressman from Mississippi* (New York: Random House, 1964), p. 127.

47. This same point is made in John W. Kingdon, *Congressmen's Voting Decisions,* 3d ed. (Ann Arbor: University of Michigan Press, 1989), pp. 67–68; John W. Kingdon, "Ideas, Politics, and Public Policies," Paper presented at the annual meeting of the American Political Science Association, Washington, D.C., September 1988, p. 21; Nelson and Silberberg, "Ideology and Legislator Shirking," pp. 15–25; and Douglass C. North, "Ideology and Political-Economic Institutions," *Cato Journal* 8 (Spring–Summer 1988): 26–27.

48. Kingdon, "Ideas, Politics, and Public Policies," p. 21. (Emphasis in the original.)

49. Interview.

50. For example, see *Congressional Record*, 92d Cong., 1st sess., 1971, 117, pt. 25:33296–315.

51. John D. Isaacs, "The Lobbyist and the MX," *Bulletin of the Atomic Scientists* 39 (February 1983): 56. See also Michael Pertschuk, *Giant Killers* (New York: W. W. Norton, 1986), pp. 181–228.

52. David C. Morrison, "'Star Wars': A Thriving Cottage Industry," *National Journal,* 23 May 1987, pp. 1368–69.

53. See Richard F. Fenno, Jr., *Home Style: House Members in Their Districts* (Boston: Little, Brown, 1978), pp. 1–30.

54. Ibid., p. 201.

55. See Richard Fleisher, "Economic Benefit, Ideology, and Senate Voting on the B-1 Bomber," *American Politics Quarterly* 13 (April 1985): 207.

56. Fitzgerald and Lipson, *Porkbarrel,* p. 13.

57. Kotz, *Wild Blue Yonder,* p. 11.

58. Interviews.

59. Mayhew, *Electoral Connection,* pp. 15–16.

60. Carol F. Goss, "Military Committee Membership and Defense-Related Benefits in the House of Representatives," *Western Political Quarterly* 25 (June 1972): 232. (Emphasis in the original.)

61. *Congressional Record,* 99th Cong., 1st sess., 1985, 131, pt. 4:5031.

62. Kotz, *Wild Blue Yonder,* p. 218.

63. U.S. Congress, House Committee on Appropriations, *Base Closures and Realignments Proposed by Department of Defense, Fiscal Year 1979,* 96th Cong., 1st sess., 1979, p. 109.

64. U.S. Congress, House Committee of Conference, *Military Construction Authorization Act, 1980,* 96th Cong., 1st sess., H. Rept. 595, 1979, p. 22.

65. Quoted in Hedrick Smith, "MX and the New Guns-and-Butter Argument," *New York Times,* 19 March 1985.

66. For a bibliography see Robert A. Bernstein, *Elections, Representation, and Congressional Voting Behavior: The Myth of Constituency Control* (Englewood Cliffs, N.J.: Prentice-Hall, 1989), pp. 77–93.

67. See Martha Derthick and Paul J. Quirk, *The Politics of Deregulation* (Washington, D.C.: Brookings Institution, 1985), and Paul J. Quirk, "Ideas, Interests, and Deregulation: The Politics of Ideas in Congress," Paper presented at the annual meeting of the American Political Science Association, Washington, D.C., September 1988.

68. Morris P. Fiorina, *Congress: Keystone of the Washington Establishment,* 2d ed. (New Haven: Yale University Press, 1989), p. 45.

CHAPTER EIGHT   INFLUENCE

1. U.S. Congress, House Committee on Armed Services, *Authorizing Appropriations for Aircraft, Missiles, and Naval Vessels,* 87th Cong., 2d sess., H. Rept. 1406, 1962, p. 7.

2. See Milton Leitenberg, "The Neutron Bomb—Enhanced Radiation Warheads," *Journal of Strategic Studies* 5 (September 1982): 341–69, and Barry Rubin, "The Media and the Neutron Warhead," *Washington Review of Strategic and International Studies* 1 (July 1978): 90–94.

3. John W. Finney, "Halt of Sentinel is Traced to a Ten-Month-Old Memo," *New York Times*, 9 February 1969. See also Alton Frye, *A Responsible Congress: The Politics of National Security* (New York: McGraw-Hill, 1975), p. 44, and Ernest J. Yanarella, *The Missile Defense Controversy: Strategy, Technology, and Politics, 1955–1972* (Lexington: University of Kentucky Press, 1977), pp. 146–55.

4. Jimmy Carter, *Keeping Faith: Memoirs of a President* (New York: Bantam Books, 1982), p. 81.

5. See Lauren H. Holland and Robert A. Hoover, *The MX Decision: A New Direction in U.S. Weapons Procurement?* (Boulder, Colo.: Westview Press, 1985), p. 226.

6. See David C. Morrison, "The Navy's Vanishing Nuclear Arsenal," *National Journal*, 13 September 1986, pp. 2184–85, and Jesse James, "Tactical Nuclear Modernization—The NATO Decision That Won't Go Away," *Arms Control Today* 18 (December 1988): 21.

7. Frye, *A Responsible Congress*, p. 45. See also Stephen Joseph Flanagan, "Congress and the Evolution of U.S. Strategic Arms Limitation Policy: A Study of the Legislature's Role in National Security Affairs, 1955–1979," Ph.D. diss., Tufts University, 1979, p. 178, and Jonathan Eliot Medalia, "The U.S. Senate and Strategic Arms Limitation Policymaking, 1963–1972," Ph.D. diss., Stanford University, 1975, p. 137.

8. Frye, *A Responsible Congress*, p. 45. See also Flanagan, "Congress," p. 178.

9. David Halberstam, *The Best and the Brightest* (New York: Random House, 1969), p. 72.

10. Morton Halperin, *Bureaucratic Politics and Foreign Policy* (Washington, D.C.: Brookings Institution, 1974), p. 298, and Yanarella, *Missile Defense Controversy*, p. 125.

11. Kenneth P. Werrell, *The Evolution of the Cruise Missile* (Maxwell Air Force Base, Ala.: Air University Press, 1985), p. 156.

12. Bernard K. Gordon, "The Military Budget: Congressional Phase," *Journal of Politics* 23 (November 1961): 694–95.

13. See Nick Kotz, *Wild Blue Yonder: Money, Politics, and the B-1 Bomber* (New York: Pantheon Books, 1988), pp. 207–15.

14. See U.S. Congress, House Committee of Conference, *Department of Defense Authorization Act 1984*, 98th Cong., 1st sess., H. Rept. 352, 1983, pp. 84–85.

15. Interview.

16. See Tom Harkin, "Star Wars: A Trojan Horse for ASAT Weapons," *Arms Control Today* 19 (March 1989): 3–9, and David C. Morrison, "Antisatellite Debate Reignited," *National Journal*, 28 January 1989, pp. 238–39.

17. See Louis Henkin, *Foreign Affairs and the Constitution* (New York: W. W. Norton, 1975), p. 123.

18. See Carter, *Keeping Faith*, p. 80.

19. Duncan Clarke, "The Role (and Nonrole) of the Arms Control and Disarmament Agency in the Coordination and Integration of National Security Policy," in *Public Policy and Political Institutions: United States Defense and Foreign Policy—Policy Coordination and Integration*, ed. Duncan Clarke (Greenwich, Conn.: JAI Press, 1985), p. 215.

20. James Schlesinger, "The Role of the Secretary of State," in *Reorganizing the Pentagon: Leadership in War and Peace*, ed. Robert J. Art, Vincent Davis, and Samuel P. Huntington (New York: Pergamon-Brassey's, 1985), p. 261.

21. Henry A. Kissinger, *The White House Years* (Boston: Little, Brown, 1979), p. 396.

22. R. Jeffrey Smith, "Trucks, Trenches, Trains and Blimps," *Science,* 9 April 1982, p. 153.

23. *Congressional Record,* 92d Cong., 1st sess., 1971, 117, pt. 25:33305.

24. Tim Weiner, "The Dark Secret of the Black Budget," *Washington Monthly,* May 1987, p. 33.

25. George C. Wilson, "Bombs Away: It's the Battle for Pork-Barrel Hill," *Washington Post National Weekly Edition,* 3 March 1987, p. 27.

26. See David C. Morrison, "Dancing in the Dark," *National Journal,* 11 April 1987, pp. 867–73, and Weiner, "Black Budget," pp. 31–35.

27. Weiner, "Black Budget," p. 33.

28. Quoted in Morrison, "Dancing in the Dark," p. 868.

29. Joseph White, "The Functions and Power of the House Appropriations Committee," Ph.D. diss., University of California, Berkeley, 1989, p. 360.

30. Quoted in Weiner, "Black Budget," p. 31.

31. Interview.

32. Interviews.

33. Hedrick Smith, *The Power Game: How Washington Works* (New York: Random House, 1988), p. 185.

34. Kotz, *Wild Blue Yonder,* pp. 20–21.

35. Interview.

36. Les Aspin, "The Defense Budget and Foreign Policy: The Role of Congress," *Daedalus* 104 (Summer 1975): 157.

37. See John J. Hamre, "Potential New Patterns of Congressional Review of Defense Budget Requests," in *Toward a More Effective Defense: Report of the Defense Organization Project,* ed. Barry M. Blechman and William J. Lynn (Cambridge, Mass.: Ballinger, 1985), pp. 174–75, and U.S. Congress, Senate Committee on Armed Services, *Defense Organization: The Need for Change,* 99th Cong., 1st sess., S. Prt. 86, 1985, pp. 594–610.

38. The joint national security committee proposal dates back to Harold D. Lasswell, *National Security and Individual Freedom* (New York: McGraw-Hill, 1950), pp. 106–8. On policy subcommittees, see Robert J. Art, "Congress and the Defense Budget: Enhancing Policy Oversight," *Political Science Quarterly* 100 (Summer 1985): 247–48.

39. This argument is developed at length in James M. Lindsay, "Congress and the Defense Budget," *Washington Quarterly* 11 (Winter 1988) 57–74.

40. Quoted in Charles W. Whalen, Jr., *The House and Foreign Policy: The Irony of Congressional Reform* (Chapel Hill: University of North Carolina Press, 1982), p. 154.

41. See Aspin, "Defense Budget and Foreign Policy," pp. 170–72.

42. Robert Pastor, *Congress and the Politics of U.S. Foreign Economic Policy, 1929–1976* (Berkeley and Los Angeles: University of California Press, 1980), p. 112.

43. Sen. William S. Cohen (R-Maine) as quoted in Steven Emerson, "Stymied Warriors," *New York Times Magazine,* 13 November 1988, p. 112.

44. Michael Ganley, "How's That Again? You're Opposed to What?" *Armed Forces Journal International,* March 1986, p. 18.

45. Duncan Clarke, *Politics of Arms Control: The Role and Effectiveness of the U.S. Arms Control and Disarmament Agency* (New York: Free Press, 1979), p. 97. See also Clarke, "Arms Control and Disarmament Agency," pp. 215–16.

46. U.S. Congress, General Accounting Office, "Weapons Testing: Quality of DoD Operational Testing and Reporting," Report No. PEMD-88-32BR, July 1988, p. 3.

47. Quoted in Sarah Helm, "'Resistance,' Not Reform, At Pentagon," *Washington Post,* 23 September 1987.

48. See Barry R. Weingast and Mark J. Moran, "Bureaucratic Discretion or Congressional Control? Regulatory Policymaking by the Federal Trade Commission," *Journal of Political Economy* 91 (October 1983): 765–800.

49. Interviews.

CHAPTER NINE   CONGRESS AND ITS CRITICS

1. For a bibliography see James M. Lindsay, "Congress and the Defense Budget," *Washington Quarterly* 11 (Winter 1988): 74.

2. Gregg Easterbrook, "What's Wrong with Congress?" *Atlantic Monthly,* December 1984, p. 61.

3. Stanley J. Heginbotham, "Congress and Defense Policymaking: Toward Realistic Expectations in a System of Countervailing Parochialisms," in *National Security Policy: The Decision-Making Process,* ed. Robert L. Pfaltzgraff, Jr., and Uri Ra'anan (Hamden, Conn.: Archon Books, 1984), p. 251.

4. *Myers v. United States,* 272 U.S. 52 (1926), p. 293.

5. Gerard Smith, *Doubletalk: The Story of the First Strategic Arms Limitation Talks* (New York: Doubleday, 1980), p. 472.

6. Randall B. Ripley, *Congress: Process and Policy,* 2d ed. (New York: W. W. Norton, 1978), pp. 17–18.

7. See Lindsay, "Congress and the Defense Budget," pp. 57–74.

8. See the testimony in U.S. Congress, Senate Temporary Select Committee to Study the Senate Committee System, *Senate Resolution 127, To Study the Senate Committee System, Parts 1 and 2,* 98th Cong., 2d sess., 1984.

9. Jacqueline Calmes, "'Trivialized' Filibuster Is Still a Potent Tool," *Congressional Quarterly Weekly Report,* 5 September 1987, p. 2118, and Alan Ehrenhalt, "In the Senate of the '80s, Team Spirit Has Given Way to the Rule of Individuals," *Congressional Quarterly Weekly Report,* 4 September 1982, pp. 2179–80.

10. Interview.

11. Robert Dahl, *Controlling Nuclear Weapons: Democracy Versus Guardianship* (Syracuse, N.Y.: Syracuse University Press, 1985).

12. Walter Millis, "Our Defense Program: Master Plan or Makeshift?" *Yale Review* 39 (Spring 1950): 391.

13. See John Steinbruner and Barry Carter, "Organizational and Political Dimensions of the Strategic Posture: The Problems of Reform," *Daedalus* 104 (Summer 1975): 137–38.

14. U.S. Congress, Senate Committee on Armed Services, *Authorizing Appropriations for Fiscal Year 1974 for Military Procurement, Research and Development, Construction Authorization for the Safeguard ABM, and Active Duty and Selected Reserve*

Strength, and for Other Purposes, 93d Cong., 1st sess., S. Rept. 385, 1973, p. 28.

15. R. Jeffrey Smith, "Air Force Takes Aim at a Big Bird," *Science,* 16 April 1982, p. 273.

16. H. A. Feiveson, "Thinking About Nuclear Weapons," *Dissent* 29 (Spring 1982): 187.

17. Steven E. Miller, "Politics over Promise: Domestic Impediments to Arms Control," *International Security* 8 (Spring 1984): 82.

18. Lauren H. Holland and Robert A. Hoover, *The MX Decision: A New Direction in U.S. Weapons Procurement Policy?* (Boulder, Colo.: Westview Press, 1985), p. 144.

19. Pat Towell, "Tower Criticizes Reagan Strategic Arms Plan," *Congressional Quarterly Weekly Report,* 3 October 1981, p. 1890.

20. Dahl, *Controlling Nuclear Weapons,* p. 44.

21. Samuel P. Huntington, *The Common Defense: Strategic Programs in National Politics* (New York: Columbia University Press, 1961), pp. 130–31.

22. Carl Sagan, "Nuclear War and Climatic Catastrophe: Some Policy Implications," *Foreign Affairs* 62 (Winter 1983–84): 292.

23. U.S. Congress, House Committee on Science and Technology, *The Climatic, Biological, and Strategic Effects of Nuclear Winter,* 98th Cong., 2d sess., 1984, p. 115.

24. Alton Frye, *A Responsible Congress: The Politics of National Security* (New York: McGraw-Hill, 1975), p. 22.

25. Harvey Brooks, "The Military Innovation System and the Qualitative Arms Race," *Daedalus* 104 (Summer 1975): 91.

26. Frye, *A Responsible Congress,* p. 34.

27. Dahl, *Controlling Nuclear Weapons,* p. 98.

28. See ibid., pp. 43–47.

29. Frye, *A Responsible Congress,* p. 27.

30. "Text of Reagan's State of the Union Address," *Congressional Quarterly Weekly Report,* 31 January 1987, p. 199.

31. *Congressional Record,* 11 September 1987, p. S12012.

32. *Constitution of the United States of America,* Article I, Section 8.

33. *Youngstown Co. v. Sawyer,* 343 U.S. 579 (1952), p. 643.

34. The classic critique is Alexis De Tocqueville, *Democracy in America* (Garden City, N.Y.: Anchor Books, 1969), p. 229.

35. U.S. Congress, Senate Committee on Foreign Relations, *Strategic Arms Limitation Agreements,* 92d Cong., 2d sess., 1972, p. 410.

36. U.S. Congress, House Committee on Armed Services, *Authorizing Appropriations, Fiscal Year 1973, for Military Procurement, Research and Development, Certain Construction for the Safeguard Antiballistic Missile System, Active Duty and Reserve Strength, and for Other Purposes,* 92d Cong., 2d sess., H. Rept. 1149, 1972, p. 24.

37. Morton H. Kondracke, "The Reagan Method," *New Republic,* 30 November 1987, p. 12.

38. Smith, *Doubletalk,* p. 472.

39. U.S. Congress, Senate Committee on Foreign Relations, *Detente,* 93d Cong., 2d sess., 1974, p. 8.

40. Michael R. Gordon, "New Data Reduce Russian Missile Force," *New York Times,* 12 December 1987.

41. Samuel B. Payne, Jr., "The Soviet Debate on Strategic Arms Limitations: 1969–72," *Soviet Studies* 27 (January 1975): 27–45.

42. Jack Mendelsohn and James P. Rubin, "SDI as Negotiating Leverage," *Arms Control Today* 16 (December 1986): 9.

43. See Robert J. Bresler and Robert C. Gray, "The Bargaining Chip and SALT," *Political Science Quarterly* 92 (Spring 1977): 65–88.

44. Quoted in Leslie H. Gelb, "Another U.S. Compromise Position is Reported Reached on Strategic Arms," *New York Times,* 17 February 1976.

45. Bresler and Gray, "Bargaining Chip," p. 85.

46. See Graham T. Allison and Frederic A. Morris, "Armaments and Arms Control: Exploring the Determinants of Military Weapons," *Daedalus* 104 (Summer 1975): 121; Bresler and Gray, "Bargaining Chip," pp. 68–69; and Seymour M. Hersh, *The Price of Power: Kissinger in the Nixon White House* (New York: Summit Books, 1983), pp. 163–65.

47. Bresler and Gray, "Bargaining Chip," pp. 73–74.

48. *Congressional Record,* 15 September 1987, p. S12095.

49. *Congressional Record,* 15 September 1987, p. 12078.

50. Louis Henkin, "Foreign Affairs and the Constitution," *Foreign Affairs* 66 (Winter 1987–88): 310.

51. See Heginbotham, "Congress and Defense Policymaking," pp. 250–61.

52. Michael Walzer, "Deterrence and Democracy," *New Republic,* 2 July 1984, p. 19.

Index

Designed by David C. denBoer
Composed by Brushwood Graphics, Inc.
in Times Roman text and Melior display.
Printed on 50-lb., Glatfelter, B-16
and bound in Holliston Roxite B
by Thomson-Shore, Inc.